Satisfaction
Guaranteed

Satisfaction Guaranteed

an *Unconventional Report to Today's Consumers*

BOOTON HERNDON

New York
St. Louis
San Francisco
Düsseldorf
Johannesburg
Kuala Lumpur
London
Mexico
Montreal
New Delhi

McGRAW-HILL BOOK COMPANY

Panama
Rio de Janeiro
Singapore
Sydney
Toronto

Herndon, Booton.
  Satisfaction guaranteed.

  1. Ward (Montgomery) and Company.   I. Title.
HF5467.W3H47   381′.45′000973   72-6159
ISBN 0-07-028350-8

1234567890 HABP 765432

*The editors for this book were Dale Dutton, W. Hodson Mogan,
Ross Kepler, and Lydia Maiorca, the designer was Naomi Auerbach, and
its production was supervised by Teresa F. Leaden. It was set in Caledo
by University Graphics, Inc.*

*It was printed by Halliday Lithograph Corporation and bound by The
Book Press.*

Contents

Preface

S*atisfaction Guaranteed* presents in two words an obvious solution to most of the problems of consumerism. They are, unfortunately, easier to say than do. The man who first put the principle into effect on a national basis nearly a hundred years ago did not handle color TV, highly styled garments made of synthetic fabrics or self-cleaning ovens. At that time, a stove was something that burned as long as you put coal or wood in it, and a dishwasher was a pair of hands in a basin of soapy water.

To maintain the guarantee of satisfaction in this age of labor-saving devices has required the evolution of a concept of frightening complexity. It's hard enough, as any consumer knows, to get one item that always works; to guarantee satisfaction on more than 100,000 separate items, each accurately described in a big, colorful, free catalog, is a challenge that seems super-human. Only three organizations in the entire world even attempt it; this book is based on the efforts of the first, Montgomery Ward and Company.

As I personally find people a lot more exciting than companies, I've tried to describe this merchandising concept through the individual men and women involved in it. I don't think of Montgomery Ward as an institution designed to grind out a profit as much as a group of interesting people doing an absorbing job.

Understanding them, you will also understand merchandising and be better informed in consumerism. You may even be able to beat the boys at their own game. This book will help you determine quality merchandise, buy it at the lowest price, get it serviced properly and use your credit wisely.

Nor will all this constitute a big hassle. Believe it or not, these people love to work with well-informed consumers. They're just cocky enough to think that the more you know, the more you'll appreciate their products and the way they do business.

Nobody claims that this concept of merchandising is perfect. It's so new that a lot of people actually engaged in it don't really understand it. There are no reference works on it; it doesn't even have a name. It needs improving, modifying, polishing. But as a consumer, if not a consumerist, I'm convinced that no other method comes close to it.

A broader potential is its capacity for the improvement of socio-economic conditions through the efforts of its leaders. It's a popular belief that a normal human being undergoes some monstrous change when he becomes a corporate executive. But leaders of the mass-merchandising industry simply cannot afford to be pro-company to the extent of being anti-people. They recognize the simple pragmatic fact that in dealing directly with the public, selling billions of dollars worth of merchandise to tens of millions of people, they're a lot better off working with those people than against them.

Working with people encompasses not only responsiveness to social responsibility, but direct participation. Those who have risen to the top in this competitive business have had to develop and demonstrate management skill and efficiency.

They are exceptionally well-fitted for voluntary community activities.

With encouragement from leaders at the top and realization that their industry is dependent upon its relationship with its customers and the very nature of its community, its managers can be, should be and most often are, men of conscience who put social responsibility into action.

1

Ethology of the Consumer

It was a Big Day in Grand Rapids—the new shopping mall was opening up. The high school band played good and loud. City and county officials, and the local Congressman up for re-election, made their speeches. Members of the Run For Your Life Club, led by a barrel-chested man in his late seventies, jogged seven miles from the downtown YMCA, carrying a flaming torch in the rain. Miss Michigan, shivering in an evening gown, cut the ribbon.

That snip ended five years' work in developing the North Kent Mall —a local department store at one end, sixty shops including six shoe stores in the middle and the key to the whole operation, the big Montgomery Ward store, at the other.

But with the end of the ceremonies the real show began. The thousands of shoppers, consumers like you and me, charged in like defensive tackles trying to get the quarterback. Men taking a day off, teenagers cutting school and, most of all, housewives with and without small children, swarmed in and scattered throughout the store —bigger than two football fields.

They whipped fishing rods in air, opened and closed the new third door on the refrigerators, mentally compared the screens of the color TVs with those at home, stared incredulously at the microwave oven which would roast the Thanksgiving turkey in an hour, felt the material and examined the workmanship of the garments on the racks, whistled at the boys' way-out flares and the girls' body shirts, leafed through the catalogs and grabbed credit applications. To hell with the problems of home, country and the world.

As a young woman accomplishing the impossible feat of clutching a shopping bag, the hands of two small children and two balloons, put it, "I wouldn't miss this for anything. It gets me out of the house and it's fun!"

Opening day, whether of a big shopping center or an individual store, probably takes place somewhere in America every day. But it doesn't have to be opening day for the great majority of the American people to engage in our most popular pastime, shopping. Our big stores provide what is truly the greatest show on earth. Women tired of being cooped up with the kids on a rainy morning go shopping. Whole families looking for something to do Saturday or bored on a hot summer night go to browse in the air-conditioned shopping center. When husbands work late, or play golf late, what do the wives do? Go to the store.

Today's consumers still spend time and money in the smaller establishments —specialty shops, boutiques, furniture stores —

downtown or in the shopping centers, but you find yourself and your neighbors today going back more and more to the big department stores and the chains. They put themselves where you can get to them, and they try to carry just about everything you want.

Three of them, Sears, J. C. Penney and Montgomery Ward, go the limit. If you can't find it in their stores, check their catalogs. Even the biggest stores can't squeeze in everything in every size and color. The catalog houses list an overwhelming variety of merchandise, with meticulous descriptions and exact illustrations. With the catalog you can pick out what you want, compare specifications and prices, or just spend some time looking and drooling.

In the 100 years since Aaron Montgomery Ward mailed out a one-page list of 30 items, the catalog has become a way of life in

Easy to look at, but the catalog is much more than pretty girls. Actual illustrations of goods offered, meticulous descriptions of style, material, color, price — all this makes the catalog a consumer guide for most lines of merchandise.

America. It's so much a part of our lives we just accept it. Recently a friend of mine returned from an assignment in the Philippines. His wife said that in the days before they left dozens of people, from European diplomats to their domestic servants, tried to buy their catalogs. Some of the books were three years old, and exchange rates and import duty made it difficult to actually order anything, but they were still offered $5 apiece for them.

"Women can show pictures of dresses to their seamstresses and have duplicates made," she said. "Same with furniture. There are a lot of cheap imports in the Philippines — washing machines, sewing machines, refrigerators — and people buy the ones closest to those in the catalog. They're damn good reading and wonderful propaganda. Foreigners can't believe that in America we can just haul off and buy all these things."

I told this to my wife and she said you don't have to go abroad to appreciate The Catalog. "Of all my friends I don't know a single one who doesn't check the catalog before buying a major appliance," she said. "And you can tell by the little hopeful squiggles what the children really want for Christmas."

With the catalog, a telephone or order blank, and oh yes, money, you can do your Christmas shopping, furnish a house or buy all your family's clothes without leaving home. In order for the catalog chains to do this, you make the people in their buying departments work like dogs. They have to anticipate what you want, order it and guarantee payment for it, all in time to have the photographers take pictures of it, the copywriters describe it and the publishers print it. And if you don't like it, they're stuck with it.

I was visiting with L. O. Reynolds, manager of Montgomery Ward's shoe department, one day, and we got to talking about our teenaged kids. He leaned forward conspiratorially.

"How would you like to make your daughter think you're a hero?" he said. I said I'd like it a lot. "Okay," he said, "What's her shoe size?"

I told him and a week or so later a box came in the mail. In it was a pair of the ugliest shoes I'd ever seen. They were ankle height, of rough leather with a sloppy fringed flap all around. Sue, my daughter, loved them. She wore them to school and all the kids raved about them. She gave me a great big kiss. A few months later squaw boots were in all the stores and everybody was wearing them, but by that time Sue's were worn out. She'd gotten one of the first pairs made; L. O. had anticipated what a teenaged girl would want, and made me a hero.

It doesn't always work out this way; sometimes it's just the opposite. Sometimes the product you and I buy falls to pieces, or just won't work. Sometimes we can't get it fixed. Sometimes we find ourselves being billed for something we've already paid for—plus service charge. Our problems with the things we buy make up a national conversation piece.

Two of the questions that perplex us today, as human beings as well as consumers, are:

Who are we and where are we going?

Why can't we get things that work, or have them fixed if they don't?

These two questions are interwoven and both involve the nature of man. Our intellectual friends are turning out books and articles on the origin and destiny of the human race. Anthropologists study and make observations on where or what we came from, amd how it applies to us today. Ethologists go out into the natural habitat of our fellow residents on the planet, the birds and beasts, and find striking similarities which may help us understand ourselves better. Sociologists wrap the whole thing up, and offer advice, some of it conflicting, on how the human race can avoid blowing ourselves out of existence, polluting ourselves out of clean land, water and air, overpopulating ourselves out of sustenance or rioting ourselves into another dark age.

But although many of us are concerned about the future of humanity, our worry is softened by the fact that, after all, we won't be here then. What we're directly involved in is what humanity produces and consumes today. If you need proof, just tell a friend about the troubles you're having with your automobile, dishwasher, clothes, air conditioner or what have you, and I'll bet you 100 to one he or she comes right back at you with an equally harrowing account. We're all consumers; using up things — ham and eggs, shoes, typewriters, ourselves — is a fundamental fact of life.

This is the way it has always been, but today people are making a study of it. It has a name: consumerism. Someday some university will give a degree in it, and we'll have graduate consumerists.

One intellectual I know maintains seriously that consumerism is becoming our national religion. Its major social function is to maintain public order: in order to pay for the things you've already charged and buy more to maintain the life-style you've come to worship, you've got to obey the rules of society. You can't pay for your new color TV if you're in jail. As more people join the affluent society, fewer are left to cause trouble. Self-policing may not be just around the corner, but if you stroll through any shopping center on Saturday you'll see people there you wouldn't have seen ten years ago. And they're buying. With credit cards yet.

Shopping, the great national pastime, is a game almost everyone can play; indeed, if the country is to continue to grow and prosper, you've got to play. Just as all living organisms, from algae to humans, must consume to exist, so does our whole concept of civilization depend upon consumption. The most learned economists may turn out treatises by the ton, but all that really matters to most of us is the simple law that large-scale consumption.means prosperity. Many of us have the notion that when we're prosperous we buy things. It's the other way around: when we buy things, we're prosperous. If your spouse fusses at you for buying something, just say it's your patriotic duty.

We learned in school that nature abhors a vacuum. Prosperity abhors an empty hanger on the dress rack, an empty space in the row of refrigerators. In the retail business all items are reduced to the same common denominator: stock keeping unit, or SKU. An SKU can be a pair of panty hose, a tire, or a range with over and under ovens. Once you take an SKU off the shelf, the store has to make like a vacuum and pull another one in to take its place. The suction may extend over tens of thousands of miles, through distribution centers and transportation systems, through the machinery, labor and executives of factories, all the way back to the cotton plant, oil well or iron mine. Somewhere in there it may well pass through the inventiveness of the human mind, because somebody is working on a better SKU than the one you just bought, or one that does not exist today but which you won't be able to do without tomorrow.

The question follows naturally: If consumption is vital to our personal, national and terrestrial life, then why can't the people who produce what we consume make things right? Why should garments shrink, appliances quit, machinery stop and things break?

Well, most of them don't, but those aren't the ones we talk

We consumers love to go shopping. Above, a big store drags us in even at night—in the rain. Below, the new trend—an enclosed all-weather mall. This one has three large stores, 75 smaller shops and professional offices. There's even room to exhibit full lines of campers.

about. I have a small refrigerator that has been running steadily and unnoticed for 30 years. I don't even know what brand it is but I sure as hell know the name of the big one in the utility room, the one with the busted shelf that we can't get fixed.

Most of us have so many appliances around the house that it's simply a matter of odds that some are bound to cause trouble, sometime.

We also overlook the fact that many of the pieces of equipment in the engine room we used to call a kitchen are more complicated than they used to be. A stove was once something that burned as long as you put wood or coal in it; the circuitry in a self-cleaning oven today is as complicated as that in a color television set.

Another factor is carelessness on the part of the people who make what you buy, just as you may be careless sometime in making something for somebody else. The only way to guarantee the perfection of anything complex is to have experts inspect and test it every step of the way, the way they do the equipment in which men fly to the moon. But that costs billions, a little more than you'd want to pay for an electric can opener. And even then things go wrong.

Finally, of course, some people turn out junk. Schlock, they call it in the retail industry. There are fellow humans, maybe the guy next door, who manufacture inferior merchandise, and there are people who sell it—usually to the people who can least afford it.

But we aren't prisoners of our technology, or of the schlock houses. There are many ways in which we can defend ourselves. We'll discuss them in this book, which is a kind of atlas of the world of consumerism.

I entered this world about two years ago. Going into new areas and reporting on them is my business. In the past five years I've stuck my nose into the automotive world of Henry Ford II, and explored our last frontier, the exciting state of Alaska. Then I was offered the opportunity to wander around in the consumer-oriented industry with no restrictions. I thought that, after swirling through unexplored passes in the remote Brooks Range in single-engine planes and encountering oilfield roughnecks and North Slope grizzlies, I'd have a kind of vacation. Well, there may not have been the same element of danger, but I found equal parts of absorbing interest, conflict, excitement and enthusiasm.

I was particularly fortunate in the choice of a company: Montgomery Ward. It's more fun to start from scratch, and I knew practically nothing about it. In my hometown Wards is a dingy little catalog store a block from the railroad tracks. I'd never been in it.

Montgomery Ward to me was a series of memories. When I was a boy my family got both Wards and Sears catalogs, and I remember looking at both, and wishing. My first high top boots, with rawhide laces, came from Monkey Ward — the package was hanging on the mailbox when I came home from school — and I smeared them with neat's-foot oil, put them on and went out in the snow to see if they were waterproof. I don't remember if they were, but I sure do remember, after I came back in and warmed my feet over the hot air register, the smell of oil-treated leather filling the house.

I remember the famous photograph of Sewell Avery, chairman of the board of Montgomery Ward, being carried out of his office by soldiers during World War II. Then there was something about a man named Louis Wolfson trying unsuccessfully to gain control of the company in 1955.

That added up to just about all I knew of Montgomery Ward. Surely a most unusual choice for a man to write a book about the company, but then the man who made the choice, Robert V. Guelich, vice president of public relations, is a rather unusual man himself. A Phi Beta Kappa and Harvard MBA, Bob is surely the calmest public relations man in the business. But he is most effective in unusual situations. As the senior Air Force officer on a special projects plane during World War II, he managed to have the plane flown from its base in California to its destination in the Pacific by way of Paris; Bob had never been to Paris. For a journalistic exploration into a Chicago-based national retail organization, he came to Charlottesville, Virginia, to sign up a man who had practically never heard of the company. I guess he'd practically never heard of me, either.

Aside from its role in consumerism, Wards furnishes a dramatic story; it's an Arthur Hailey novel in fact. Though a century old, and the creator of the mail-order business, in 1961 Montgomery Ward was just about down the drain. Serious suggestions had been made to wipe the whole thing out, sell its properties and split the take among the stockholders. Today the company is prosperous in every respect, run by tigers with a social conscience, and contributing to the nation. The story of how its leaders turned it around is both exciting and informative.

While I was running around the country looking Wards over I was of course keeping up with my own bag, the field of communications. Writers are just like anybody else—we want to know what the competition is doing—and I followed the trends in what people were reading. Most of the nonfiction best sellers were either dollars-and-cents exposés written by members of the Ralph Nader school or think stuff dealing with man's past, present and future. Alvin Toffler's "Future Shock" said that things are moving so fast we just won't be able to take it. Charles Reich's "The Greening of America" said that we'll all be happily stoned in bell-bottomed blue jeans and won't care. Robert Ardrey's trilogy—"African Genesis," "Territorial Imperative" and "Social Contract"—drew heavily upon reports of anthropologists and ethologists to make the case that homo sapiens, contrary to the tenets of the man-is-sweet-and-pure-school, is an aggressive animal with several built-in driving forces.

I knew I was studying consumerism. What I hadn't realized was that in doing so I had become an ethologist. I hadn't been studying only a segment of industry, but man himself in his most natural environment —trade.

A million or so years ago we were probably all hunters. We began sharpening sticks and chipping rocks to make the job easier, and toolmakers developed. Then some smart fellow swapped a piece of flint for a chunk of fresh-killed meat and trade began. A wandering trader settled on a camel route and started a tribe of people whose religious guidelines, the Ten Commandments, are still used by most of us in the western world. A sea captain looking for an ocean trading route between Europe and the Orient discovered the New World.

Today the retailing industry in just one part of the New World, the United States, is the largest business in the entire world. It is the one that deals most frequently with all the people of our country —rich or poor, white, black or oriental, Catholic, Protestant or Jew, young or old. It connects the producer with the consumer; the gross national product rests upon it.

And if you're looking for someone to head up a civic project, try the retail industry. It contains the greatest number of proven leaders —more than one million managers.

To the student of human behavior this is a group that's fascinating to observe. In them the motivating forces that make us tick are displayed like merchandise on the table. As for consumerism, if there is an answer to the problem here are the people who are looking for it hardest. (They're consumers, too, and bitch as loud as anybody —about the other fellow's product.)

From my observations as an ethologist in this important area of homo sapiens, late Twentieth Century model, I hope to make a positive, constructive statement in this book. Sure, I know we may be on the verge of blowing ourselves up. We've got polluted air and water, and we're messing up the countryside. You can pay too much for something that won't work and too much to have it fixed or not fixed, get mugged on Main Street by junkies and know damned well that not every child growing up in bountiful America has the same opportunity to be President. But plenty of other people are exposing the shortcomings of civilization. My bag is optimism.

In the realm of material possessions, more of us are better off than ever before. We are healthier, wealthier and wiser. Man the competitor, man the toolmaker and man the social animal have combined to produce mass manufacturing and mass distribution. The combination turns natural resources into consumer products and thus into wealth—money for education, communication, protection, all our institutions. It influences the very nature of mankind. It gives us more time to enjoy the good things of life and to preserve them through activities of social responsibility, more time to learn and think and wonder, and to write nasty letters about things that don't work. It has forced us to have more concern for our fellow man than ever before, and more opportunity to do something about it.

The people involved in this book are doing what comes naturally, only most of them do it better. If they prove nothing else, together or separately, they demonstrate the value of the individual—in some cases the indispensable individual. Whenever I hear young persons complain that they don't want to be corporate cogs, holes punched in a card, I remember that it took just one man to found not only a giant corporation but an entire new method of merchandising, just one man to almost ruin the same company, and just one man to save it. And when I read that man is really not motivated by aggression, and desire for possessions and territory, and that corporate executives are men without social conscience, I remember that the man who saved Montgomery Ward was motivated by those very instincts, and that his own example of social responsibility has made the company a working model of practical do-goodism which even a knee-jerk liberal like me can appreciate.

Only a couple of hours after I wrote that sentence, the very same day, I happened to pick up a copy of *The Saturday Review*. Here's what I saw:

"When I grow up? Well, I want to assume responsibility of a gigantic corporation, taking the helm at a time when the company has been suffering severe reverses and turn it around, making it a model of efficiency and a leader in its field. But first of all I want to be a human being responding to the needs of my fellow man."

(Cartoon by Henry Martin. Copyright 1971, Saturday Review, Inc.)

I had to laugh, a little self-consciously, at the coincidence. I stand on my description, but the cartoon doesn't apply. When the man who saved Montgomery Ward was that age his primary ambition was to stop stuttering.

2

Men and Challenge

The main banking floor of the Continental Illinois National Bank and Trust Company of Chicago takes up an entire city block. On a clear day you can see some four hundred people in it, deciding whether or not to lend other people the bank's money. One day in the fall of 1961 two visitors bypassed the arena and were ushered into the cozy, paneled den-like office, complete with wood-burning fireplace, of the vice chairman, Donald M. Graham. He came around from behind his desk to shake hands warmly and to sit down with them in the comfortable leather chairs.

One of the men was John Barr. Graham, like most of the financial and industrial leaders in Chicago, liked Barr and sympathized with him. Six years before, because he was loyal, acceptable and available, Barr had suddenly been called upon to fill the immediate and unexpected vacancy as chairman and chief executive officer of the sick giant, Montgomery Ward and Company.

A lawyer with little retailing experience, Barr himself was the first to admit that he didn't know how to run the extremely complex national retail organization. There are only three such companies in the world: Wards, Sears and Penney. Barr had

brought in one executive after another, but they had not alleviated the giant's symptoms. Now the dividends had been cut in
half, the hoard of cash was gone and there was a possibility that
the 90-year old company, a household word in the nation and
pride of its headquarters city, might cease to exist.

To many of its 60,000 stockholders, mostly people of moderate means, the collapse of the company would be a severe blow,
but to leaders of Chicagoland like Don Graham, it would be a
calamity. Chicago is the biggest small town in the world. Most
of its big wheels don't even live within the city limits, commut-
ing instead from its quietly affluent suburbs, but they are
loyal in a super-Rotary way to both Chicago and their bedroom
communities. They *care.* If Chicago lost Montgomery Ward it
would be like the Chicago Bears, Cubs, White Sox, Black
Hawks and Bulls all finishing at the bottom of their leagues in
the same year. And it could happen.

In the face of such a possible disaster, Graham's pleasure that
day was in John Barr's companion, a tall, athletic-looking man in
his fifties named Robert E. Brooker whose friends, and Graham
knew he had a lot of them, called him Tom. Brooker was Barr's
latest candidate for the role of Moses to the children of Wards.
Graham had seen others aspire to the challenge, and not even
find the right road, much less part the waters, but this one was
different.

Tom Brooker was the first with the background for the job.
Barr had tried, but he had never been able to pry an executive
out of the only training grounds in existence, the retail colossus
of Chicago, the USA, the world, and probably the galaxy, Sears,
Roebuck and Company. Tom Brooker, however, had been both
a vice president and director of Sears, and president of one of
of Sears' major suppliers, Whirlpool Corporation. Barr had
made a pass at Brooker before, but only for a vice presidency,
and Brooker hadn't even considered it. Now he was coming in
as president, and with authority; the deal included the replacement of several retiring members of the board of directors with
men who would back him up. It was not mentioned at the time,

but Graham himself would, in less than a year, be one of those directors.

Another reason why the heart of Don Graham, Chicago banker, filled with joyful optimism was the purpose of the visit. Brooker wanted to borrow a million dollars. He wanted to borrow a million dollars in order to buy stock in Montgomery Ward. *A million dollars worth!* A million dollars for a stock that was steadily going down. Such a purchase in this company of small and scattered stockholders would make Tom Brooker far and away the largest owner. Graham could foresee the impact of the purchase on the 72,000 demoralized employees of Montgomery Ward. Here was a man who was betting a million bucks on his confidence that he could both cure the company and collect the bill.

Of course it would be the Continental Illinois National Bank and Trust Company's million bucks, but that was all the better. "There was no question as to giving him the money," Graham told me years later. "He had plenty of security."

This in itself was also pleasing to the bank president. As has often been observed, it is easy to borrow money from a bank if you already have so much you don't need it. But that is simplistic. Put another way, Brooker was using his own money as leverage to get Graham's. As a banker, considering the going rate of interest, Graham loved being levered. On a broader scale, he appreciated Brooker's financial sagacity in using someone else's money.

Brooker didn't go into detail at the time—he didn't have to— but years later he explained to me exactly what he intended to gain out of the transaction.

"I was offered a liberal compensation to join Montgomery Ward," he said, "but it wasn't all that much more than what I was receiving at Whirlpool. I looked upon the purchase of stock as a means to increase that compensation. You see, I was confident that I could double the value of Montgomery Ward stock in five years. With a million dollars invested, that would mean a capital gains income of $200,000 a year. I had a stock option which would do about the same. I didn't realize just how bad off Montgomery Ward was, and it took me eight years to double the million. So it wasn't $200,000 extra a year, but, let me see, $125,000. But that was still a reasonable return."

Within ten years the total value of Brooker's holdings in the company — purchase and option — had grown to about three and a half million, and Brooker figured that it would double again in five years.

Tom Brooker is an all-around man, the perfect image of the champion of capitalism, the King Arthur of a commercial Camelot. His shining sword, which he wields with patient skill, has a hilt of mass manufacturing, a blade of mass distribution. In his concept, the two synergize to make more good things available to more people at less cost. The key is the integration of production with sales, and it's easier to say it than do it. At Montgomery Ward he has done both. We will discuss how he did it throughout the book.

Brooker has a sincere concern for his fellow man, which he expresses as just good business. He backs up his concern with money, time and a gentle pressure, like a polite tidal wave, exerted on any Chicago executive silly enough not to pledge one per cent of his salary to the Chicago Community Fund. (He gives *two*.) He is patient with his assistants and kind to his wife, children and dog. If he hadn't paid $100 to attend a Spiro Agnew dinner I'd call him a perfect Consciousness II; give him 1⅞.

Tom Brooker is a man of many facets, but of all the great driving forces of mankind the one he most typifies is the acquisition of wealth and property. He is money-oriented. He likes it himself, and he uses it as a carrot to get people to work for him. A half dozen or so of his top executives wound up their sincere encomiums of him with the final clincher: "And besides, he's making me rich."

Brooker is honestly pleased that they are happy with their wealth, but as the corporate leader of a group of executives he has a more pertinent interest in their welfare. Both stockholders and customers of Montgomery Ward, he believes, benefit from the fact that members of his top echelon are all millionaires. They can afford to make wise decisions.

Brooker also demonstrates the territorial imperative. One of his first actions on assuming the presidency of Montgomery Ward was to redesign his office and install his own bathroom. It was in the middle of winter and an outside wall had to be broken through. "With all I had to do, I didn't have time to walk a hundred yards around the corner to go to the toilet," he told me, but I think much more was involved. With architectural aid he both designed and supervised the construction of his home in Winnetka; it's handsome and in good taste.

To build his lodge in the Bahamas he designed it in Chicago, then had it fabricated in sections in Massachusetts, trucked it to Florida, barged it to Deep Water Key and assembled it there. "I even picked out all the sheets and towels," he said.

Brooker's home is not only his castle, but a gracious extension of his office. He and his wife, the former Sally Smith of Los Angeles, like to entertain at dinner parties; after the small talk at dinner the men usually retire to the study for more serious discussions in informal comfort. Tom Brooker's study is his ear to the ground; he hears not only what has happened, but what is going to happen.

Tom knew that he was going to have to bring some talent in from outside the company. A patient and optimistic man, at the beginning he underestimated the number of people he would need. He was confident in his own knowledge of procuring merchandise, but to implement his grand design for Wards he would have to have someone thoroughly familiar with operating big stores in metropolitan areas. One man met those specifications exceptionally well. Tom knew him personally; he had brought him into Sears 15 years before and had seen him grow. In a funny little coincidence both men, though college graduates, had changed many a customer's tires during the appropriate stage in their careers.

Brooker's Number One pick was, he knew, happy in his position as manager of the Los Angeles district for Sears. But he was enthusiastic and ambitious. He had to have his eye on the next step up the ladder: vice president of the western region. Brooker did not tell me this—it's an educated guess—but I think he had advance knowledge that the job was going to open up before his man was ready for it. It was going to be filled for three years by the future president of Sears, a lawyer named Arthur M. Wood, in order to give him executive seasoning.

Ambitious men do not want to wait three years. Brooker planned a trip to Los Angeles. . . .

The tall candle on the corner table in the Grand Hotel overlooking Taipei flickered gently, and was reflected a thousand times in the twinkling lights of the Oriental city below. The meal was sumptuous and the service impeccable but the vintage wine was missing; to the handsome couple talking earnestly the additional stimulation of alcohol would be a waste. They were Edward S. Donnell and his wife Rose, and for several months now they had been struggling with the greatest decision of their life together. Though they shared the deep emotion of the moment, both knew that the final answer could come only from within Ed himself. Rose had determined that years before, when a Phi Beta Kappa planning to go into medicine, she had chosen instead to be a wife in the full pre-women's-liberation sense.

For two weeks now they had been traveling through the Orient, hoping that so far from the distractions of home—Rose's mother was taking care of the four kids and Ed's staff was running the district—they could make an intelligent decision.

A tall, thin blond man with a high forehead and a boyish expression of interest and enthusiasm, Ed had had some project or other going practically all of his life. At the age of 7, the youngest kid on the block with only a widowed mother to defend him, Ed had set up a lemonade stand, then a bottle collection agency. The other kids found it was more profitable to work for him than to pick on him. Ed was 50 years old when I first met him in 1970, but it was easy for me to picture him as a baseball pitcher in high school and then at Duke, bearing down in the clutches, grinning all over his face in victory. It's less easy to picture him changing tires in the Goodrich tire center in Cambridge, Maryland, but if a customer wanted a tire at lunch hour, it was the manager who put it on.

After a couple of years Ed saw a greater opportunity with Sears. Tom Brooker, then head of Sears' tire department went down to Washington to look him over, and Ed was hired at double his previous salary. Working out of a small office, he assembled and directed a staff of four salesmen, and put Sears into the commercial tire business in the Washington area.

Thorough and tireless, when he was sent to Mexico City as Sears general sales manager, he first took a total-immersion course in Spanish, had a lesson before going to work each morning, and within a year was able to carry on his office duties in the language of the country. Those were happy years in Mexico. He became manager of the largest store in Mexico City. It came complete with a luxurious penthouse. Ed says he's the only man who fathered two children under a Sears roof and got away with it.

As he developed Sears in Mexico, he kept up his interest in competitive sport by helping to organize the Little League, building it to the point that thousands of kids were involved. Learning, working, organizing, directing, calling on an unlimited supply of physical and mental energy, Ed became president of Sears in Mexico. By the time he was 41, he was the top man in Sears' top area, greater Los Angeles, with sales of $300 million a year.

Ed loves merchandise, the feel of it, the looks of it. He likes to display it properly, get it out of the store and into the hands of the people. He made regular visits to all the stores in his area, leading the store manager and staff from department to department, suggesting, criticizing, complimenting. He'd forget time, food and even the restroom. One of his store managers, who smoked heavily and started out the day with several cups of coffee, followed him around in misery with both a craving for a cigarette and a bursting bladder. "The long tall bastard must eat dry oatmeal for breakfast," he said.

This was about the worst thing you could say about Ed Donnell. The popular stereotype of the hard-driving, whip-cracking, ass-chewing, fire-happy businessman falls all to pieces when applied to him. Ed is such a decent, thoughtful, consider-ate man that if you told me you disliked him I'd think there was something the matter with you. And yet, underneath the veneer of a few million years of human development, Ed is the perfect example of the huntsman of the tribe. The friendly smile and interest in his fellow man do not contradict his fierce competi-tiveness; they are part of it. You don't have to make people hate you to accomplish. Just as his primitive ancestors—and people like the gregarious, hardworking Eskimos today—loved the preparations for the hunt, the plans, the stalking, and finally the kill with its payoff in fresh meat and covering for the tribe, so was Ed at his happiest in planning a campaign to sell an extra gross of panty hose. His life is based on competition, accomplish-ment, projects.

Rose, who had regularly put in almost a full day working with the blind in Mexico City, continued with community affairs in Los Angeles. She was one of the pioneers among corporate executives' wives in working with voluntary services. "Rose paved the way," a man who was then a Sears vice president told me. As for Ed, he had confidence that in due course he would reach even greater heights in the company, but southern Cali-fornia was a pleasant place to wait in line.

Into this executive paradise came a tiny hint of impending worry: a letter from Tom Brooker saying he was coming to Los Angeles and would like Ed to have breakfast with him. Ed had an inkling of what he wanted to talk about. A few months be-fore, in the fall of '61, Ed had been surprised to hear that Tom had left aggressive Whirlpool to become president of pokey old Wards. They were good friends, but he hoped Tom wouldn't ask him to follow him. At that time the entire after-tax profits at Montgomery Ward were about the same as the pre-tax profit of Ed's group of stores in Los Angeles.

At breakfast Tom scribbled some figures on a piece of paper and passed it to Ed over the eggs. It proposed a salary of about the same that Ed was getting at Sears—next to the officer level, he probably had the highest income in the company. It proposed a stock option of 25,000 shares at $32. It spelled out the job: vice president of the eastern region, from Maine to Florida, with headquarters in Baltimore. Two years later, Tom implied, Ed would take over the responsibility of all Ward's field operations, and ultimately the presidency. Ed knew Tom so well that he took the offer as a full commitment. His first impulse was to refuse it, then and there. He was happy where he was, and he had a future with the company. He had moved Rose around a lot, and he had learned that, after several years, women like to stick their toe in the sand and stay put. He suffers from hay fever and he was physically comfortable in southern California; he knew he wouldn't be in Baltimore or Chicago.

Sears was the unquestioned leader in the field; Ward's recovery, in spite of Ed's respect for Tom Brooker, was by no means assured. But where lies the greater opportunity, with a corporate giant rich in manpower or with a company barren in personnel with nowhere to go but up?

Ed said he would discuss the matter with Rose, and let Tom know. They did discuss it, but didn't make a decision. Then another factor entered the discussion. Arthur Wood was sent from Chicago to be west coast vice president, a job Ed could not help but covet. General Robert E. Wood, the man who made Sears what it is today, wrote Ed a personal letter saying that if he continued to make progress he would succeed Art Wood in about three years. Now it boiled down to whether Ed wanted to be vice president of Wards immediately or wait three years for Sears.

He and Rose decided to get away from it all and think it over. They traveled through Japan, then on to Taiwan, but it wasn't

Ed and Rose Donnell

much of a sightseeing trip. They carried their dilemma with them, right into the dining room of the Grand Hotel in Taipei.

As they looked at each other in the candlelight, and repeated the same old arguments, something President Eisenhower had said in a recent speech popped into Ed's mind. Young people should live dangerously, was the way Ed remembered it; when a new and tempting challenge presented itself, take a shot at it.

"I guess what he meant," Ed told Rose, "was that we ought to accept this challenge. Damn it, let's go."

"Okay," Rose said. Her mate was off on another hunt.

And Tom Brooker had his man.

3

Your Purchasing Agent

In homes all over America today, perhaps at this moment, a happy wife is greeting her husband at the door and pulling him into the bedroom. If he's getting any ideas en route he's in for disillusionment: The purpose of the trip is to show him the new matching bedspreads and draperies.

Unless sales figures lie it's happening in hundreds of homes. The fabric may be a traditional floral pattern, or bold modern stripes. The price may run from $15 or so up into three figures. The handsome new acquisition may have come from a Ward retail store, or have been ordered out of the catalog, or even perhaps, at a much higher price for the most expensive fabric, from the swankiest store in town.

To the lady of the house they represent hours of shopping resulting in a joy to the owners' eyes and the envy of the neighbors. To the husbands they mean peace for a time, and a bill. To all of us—consumers, stockholders, taxpayers, those who benefit from the ultimate application of the principles of the affluent society, they represent a new concept expressed in a magic phrase: integration of production and sales.

Maybe at this moment you could care less about such merchandising gobbledy gook, *integration of production and sales.*

What you want is merchandise, good quality at a good price, and to hell with the mumbo-jumbo. But if you are really interested in what you buy, how much you pay for it and how long it will last, stick with me a little longer.

For whether you are interested in sewing machines or fishing tackle, hot pants or business suits, dolls or 10-speed racers, vacuum cleaners or lawn mowers, the more you know about the principle of integration of production and sales the better off you'll be in the daily skirmishes between shopper and merchant.

On this concept the ultimate in consumerism is based. It is the modern response of the consumer-oriented industry to the challenge of the consumer.

Let's go on with those bedspreads. They're pretty, after all, and they make the ladies happy. Those I have in mind are manufactured by a Chicago-based firm owned by Gene Edson, a friendly man with a slightly harassed look, a messy desk and a French secretary named Jacqueline. He took over the family business several years ago. One of his customers was Montgomery Ward. They had an established procedure. He and a buyer from the Ward's domestics department would get together periodically and haggle.

"It was a typical buyer-seller relationship," Edson said, "dog eat dog. Even when we got the order, we'd sometimes get stung. I'd buy the fabrics and manufacture the goods, but if Wards couldn't sell all they'd ordered, they'd refuse to accept the responsibility for what I was holding for them. Sometimes they'd miss out, too. They'd get more orders than they could fill. Their customers would get mad and go somewhere else. Tough."

As a Chicagoan, Gene Edson heard that Tom Brooker had become president of Wards, but he saw no reason to go out and dance in the street. Wards had been having new presidents for years. This one seemed to be pushing something called a known-cost contract. The way the buyer explained it, it sounded like a stupid deal for both of them. Edson would be expected to open up his books so that the buyer would know how much profit he was making; the buyer would be committed to take Edson's products even if he could get them cheaper somewhere else. In a rare moment of agreement both agreed the whole thing was crazy, and continued to do business the normal way, dog eat dog.

A couple of years went by and then, instead of the buyer, the head of the department came around. He was a new man with Wards, named James Lutz. "I liked that guy the minute he walked in the door," Gene Edson told me later.

At the time Edson had no idea that the new manager of the home furnishings department had, not long before, been getting $80,000 a year for doing absolutely nothing. Nor would he have known that during that period Jim Lutz was miserable. I think I could make do under such conditions—46 years old, $80,000 a year and some nice investments—but not Jim Lutz. He was lonely. A few months before he had been president of McCrory's, $135,000 a year plus a chauffeured limousine. It had been a matter of prestige in the New York garment district to be seen having lunch with Jim Lutz; now the same people wouldn't even return his phone calls.

"I saw men I thought were friends cross the street so they wouldn't have to speak to me," Jim told me. "Why? I'll tell you in the language of the district. I didn't have an order book, that's why."

James Lutz had come to the United States from Germany in '39, when he was 21. His father saw trouble coming and advised his son to go to America. Jim arrived in Chicago with $1.75 in his pocket and got a job with Sears cutting carpets. Educated in merchandising and textiles, he progressed rapidly, even with four years of military service—infantry lieutenant in the South Pacific. He was Sears' youngest buyer, youngest department manager. One year when his salary was $15,000 his bonus was $30,000.

Then McCrory, the big low-priced retail chain, wooed him away. Lutz was secure and happy at Sears; it took a 65-page contract providing for every contingency to get him. The McCrory honeymoon lasted only three years.

"I had a disagreement with the board of directors and I got fired," Jim told me bluntly. He still didn't like to talk about it. Actually he had questioned some of the policies of the company and tendered his resignation. For not working, his annual compensation was reduced to $80,000.

A man can have a good income, a summer home and a sailboat, and still be frustrated. One of the great driving forces in nature, from the pecking order in the chicken yard to the publish-or-perish in academia, is the desire for status. It is particularly galling for a man who has had it, who has been president of a big company, to have it no longer. It tears at his soul.

Jim Lutz was offered two jobs. One was the presidency of a large, low-end discount operation. The other was manager of the piece goods and notions department of Montgomery Ward—the same job he had left four years before, only this time instead of with the prestigious Sears, it was with a company still struggling for existence. It would seem to be a simple choice, only now there was another factor in the equation: integrity.

The desire for integrity seems to be unique to man; it's certainly more complex than one chicken pecking another. Ethical behavior is the ultimate level in man's development from his earliest grouping. For homo sapiens to develop, mores had to be established. A member of a hunting party on whose success the tribe depended would do a better job if he had some assurance that nobody back at the settlement was messing around with his mate or stealing his possessions. A fighter defending his tribal territory against attack should have no fear of getting clobbered from behind by one of his own people. From such basic laws founded on survival grew more sophisticated protections, including the voluntary desire on the part of some members of society to play fair with their fellow man.

As Jim Lutz put it, he didn't want to go into a cat-eat-dog

type of business, he didn't want to go into the jungle. He wanted to become a part of a benevolent environment in which management is more cognizant of people, of human values and sensitivities. He had known Tom Brooker and Ed Donnell at Sears, and knew that they were men of integrity. He believed in their philosophy of business, and felt that he could help them implement it.

But from president to department manager was still a big step down, in income as well as status, for in going with a competing business he would forfeit his compensation from McCrory. Brooker could not offer him anywhere near as much for working as he was already getting for not working. Nor could Brooker offer him a better position or even explain why not. The reason was that he had already brought in several men from Sears to fill high positions. Most had blended in well, but there was still some resentment; Ward old-timers even today occasionally speak of the Sears mafia. Brooker believed that Lutz would prove himself and move up on merit, but he could promise him nothing.

Lutz discussed his dilemma with Edward Gudeman, a former vice president of Sears with whom he had worked closely; it was Gudeman who had given him that 200 per cent bonus. Gudeman was now with Lehman Brothers and a member of the board of Montgomery Ward. A cultured, understanding man who knew Jim well, Gudeman advised him to take the job.

"But I've been president of a big company!" Jim said. "Now I'll just be a department manager."

"You shouldn't have that attitude," Gudeman said. "If you don't become an officer in the company within a reasonable time, you're not as good as I think you are."

Brooker, in the meantime, suggested that his previous employer would probably be quite happy to renegotiate the termination settlement. Lutz accepted a lower figure, and Brooker made up the difference. Jim Lutz, former president, became a department manager.

And that's all he was to Gene Edson when he walked in

Edson's office that day, yet Edson knew he was a man he could work with in complete trust. Thanks to Lutz's knowledgeability, enthusiasm and sincerity, Edson found himself accepting the concept he'd previously rejected. The way Lutz explained it, the Edson-Wards relationship would be a two-way street. Under the new leadership of Tom Brooker the new Wards was going to grow, grow, grow. And with that growth, it would need suppliers it could count on to grow along with it. As Jim talked, Gene saw the line on the Ward sales graph going up, up, up, and Edson, Inc., going right up with it. Each would be completely open with the other. Edson, Inc., would open its books to Wards, Wards would open its books to Edson. (Gene had never known what volume the department he was dealing with at Wards was doing, or his percentage of it.) Gene would have the security of knowing that the Montgomery Ward order would be firm — provided, of course, he met the specifications. He could schedule production far in advance. As for Jim Lutz, instead of dissipating his time and that of his personnel scurrying around trying to buy merchandise at a nickel less, his department could devote full attention to getting the best quality from a loyal supplier, and going all out merchandising it.

When the Lutz cyclone finally blew itself out the door, Edson was convinced. But he was not hypnotized. Negotiations went on for some time. He had to realize that his aim was no longer simply to maximize his profit, Wards simply to minimize its cost. This was a new ball game. Lutz started right out with the premise that Edson was entitled to a return on its investment, one which would enable the company to knock itself out for good old Wards. He also offered less risk and the opportunity for growth. But he wanted the agreement to extend into the future, with built-in provisions for increased or decreased cost of capital improvements, labor and materials. The only way to accomplish this was for Wards to know as much about Edson as Edson.

"In this kind of contract," Jim said, "the best one is the one you stick in the drawer and forget about."

Even after he and Lutz had agreed on most of the issues, Gene Edson had one strong reservation. He didn't want to give Wards more than 50 per cent of his production.

"I didn't want to be a captive of Wards or anybody else," he told me. "I believed that there was a lot to be done in the world and I was still young enough to try to do it."

But he couldn't even get an argument with Lutz on that point. Jim couldn't have agreed with him more. He didn't want Edson, or any other supplier, to be totally dependent on Wards. To avoid getting fat and complacent, any company needs the stimulation of competition in the open market. Wards didn't know it all, not by a long shot. By continuing to supply other outlets, Edson could get an additional feedback on trends and changing styles. Everybody would benefit.

Over the years the rapport between the two companies has grown even stronger. "Our books are open to each other," Gene told me, "but it's pretty rare that either of us checks the other. Jim Lutz promised growth and Wards delivered it. I have had to expand existing plants and build new ones. We've prospered."

Edson politely declined to show me his books—I'm not Montgomery Ward—and so did the current manager of the department—I'm not Gene Edson, either. But in the five years after the contract was signed the department's sales went up 38%, and Edson's share went up 75%. Both are doing all right.

In the meantime Lutz had become executive vice president, merchandise. Ward's procurement division with its staff of technical experts had also grown; Brooker had brought in one of his assistants from his days at Sears, John A. Marchese, to head it. Marchese is one of several vice presidents reporting to Lutz. Lutz himself can walk into a factory room and, just by listening, tell whether the work is going well. Marchese's slipstick boys can make detailed analyses. They all wanted to help Edson with its expansion program.

At first Gene Edson said he didn't need any advice—"I fought those guys from the first day they walked in the door," he said.

"But I'm grateful now. They showed me a lot about my business — that's for sure, for absolute sure. Traditionally in the needle trades, quality control means looking at the finished product and that's it. Now we inspect from the day the fabric comes in the door. We follow every product every step of the way. We inspect the inspectors. Not just Wards, but all of our customers benefit from this quality control program. Even if we wanted to operate on two levels of workmanship, it wouldn't be practical. You can't train good people to accept one standard of inspection for one item, a lower standard for another. Whatever goes out of our plants, no matter who it's for, is sewn with the same number of stitches, inspected with the same care. You can go from Wards to Marshall Field and pay a lot more for one of our bedspreads, but it's the fabric that's more expensive. The quality of workmanship is the same, and it's the best."

So that's how Gene Edson's bedspreads and draperies comprise one application of the concept Tom Brooker brought to Montgomery Ward: integration of production and sales. Under the open book system of procurement, manufacturer and retailer can work together in a mercantile buddy system to provide quality at a reasonable cost. I won't say inexpensive, because you can pay $60 for a king-sized bedspread at Wards, and much more than that in swankier stores. But without the steady year-round operation which the Ward volume assures, uninterrupted by costly shutdowns, layoffs and start ups, the cost would certainly be higher. Without the technical assistance of Ward's experts, welcomed by Edson, the quality might be lower. Whichever way you look at it, you, the consumer, benefit by it.

It's a happy situation enjoyed by many of the 7,000 firms which supply Montgomery Ward with merchandise, and certainly all of the 300 major suppliers. Later on we'll take a look at the other and more obvious integer of the equation, selling the product. Without Ward's mass merchandising system keeping his plants humming, Edson would have to get more for his bedspreads, or give less quality. You'd pay more, no matter where you bought them. But before going into the area of merchandising, and how you can get the best bargains, let's go on with how the merchant acquires the merchandise for you in the first place.

Shortly after Aaron Montgomery Ward revolutionized the retail business by sending out a list of items available to anybody anywhere at the same price—*1 Gent's Cassimere coat (send size) $3.50*—he offered an additional service to his customers. For a 5 per cent service fee, he'd shop around for items not on the list and send them out. To people in rural America—at that time the majority—this was a valuable service. He became their purchasing agent.

On a far more sophisticated scale, the national catalog-retail chain provides this service today. One day I was moaning to Curt Ward, manager of Montgomery Ward's sporting goods department, about my tennis racket problems. The racket I'd been using had been discontinued, and I had to start all over again and find one I liked out of a dozen or more brands.

Well, I hit Curt at just the right time. He and one of his buyers, Edward J. Burke, had just made the decision that, what with tennis booming, Wards could compete with the pro shops and sporting goods stores in marketing a quality racket. That brought them to my problem: *which* racket? They couldn't stock all the brands, and wouldn't if they could. For many reasons Wards sells goods under its own label.

Curt and Ed's choice of a racket to bear that label was many thousand times more difficult than mine. If I'm unhappy with a racket, well, I'm out forty bucks. But under Montgomery Ward's simple, straightforward policy, satisfaction guaranteed or your money back, if they picked a lemon they would have to refund the purchase price to maybe thousands of dissatisfied tennis buffs.

Ed and his assistants purchased and studied 14 separate

Need a new tennis racket? Need anything? *Here is one way in which Wards acts as your purchasing agent. Ed Burke looked at every major brand and had them tested in the lab. Tony Roche checked them out on the court. Curt Ward, department manager, bet a large chunk of Montgomery Ward's money that their selection was right. Because if it wasn't, and the racket proved unsatisfactory, thousands of customers would demand—and get—their money back.*

brands of tennis rackets. Technicians in the research laboratory made exhaustive tests on construction and materials, including tensile strength of extruded aluminum. Tony Roche, the Australian star on Ward's sports advisory staff, tested the rackets on the court. On the basis of all the facts at hand, Curt chose the racket manufactured by Chemold.

After all this research, I'd be foolish not to take advantage of it, and of Curt Ward's personal recommendation. I'm in company not only with other Ward customers, but Roche, Rod Laver, Margaret Court and several other pros; we all use the same racket. Ward's merchandise usually comes in three different grades, *good,* *better* and *best,* with corresponding prices. My wife and I play a lot of tennis and we're both happy with the *better* rackets at about $29. So are our friends, who borrow them frequently. I have to admit, however, that I also have a couple of *best* rackets, with gold finish, specially treated leather grips and better strings. Whichever I use, I think it was very nice of Curt, Ed and Tony to make the decision for me.

Wards and the other catalog chains, act as our purchasing agents on a much large scale, for many of the staple commodities we use in American life today. Take automobile tires, for example. With all the multiplicity of brand names, grades within brands, advertising claims and price differences, a man can go crazy trying to decide which tire to buy at which price. Making the decision for the tire customer was one of the many major problems that Tom Brooker faced when he became president of Wards.

For 30 years the company had been procuring its famous Riverside tires from the United States Rubber Company. When Sewell Avery had become president of the company back in 1931, the Ward private label for automobile tires, Riverside, had long been accepted by American motorists as a fine product. He determined to keep it that way. The problem was how. We have seen, in bedspreads, two methods by which a large chain may procure merchandise for its customers: buying in the open market and negotiating known-cost contracts. Avery saw the weakness of the former as it pertained to a commodity with the volume and profit of tires, but he did not have the purchasing expertise necessary to go the known-cost route. Instead, he chose a third method. He arranged with U.S. Rubber to buy tires at cost plus 6 per cent. The system worked well for a quarter of a century, but then it boomeranged—on Montgomery Ward, on its customers and on Tom Brooker.

Brooker had acquired a much bigger can of worms in Montgomery Ward than he had anticipated. For one thing, he had actually been sold a bill of goods as far as inventory was concerned. Some $50 million worth of merchandise turned out to be outmoded stuff that storekeepers had been stashing away in basements all over the country. An even more important stock in trade, personnel, was also overvalued. For years hundreds of the best brains in Montgomery Ward had been departing the company. Many had been fired in the reign of terror that began around 1950 as a by-product of Avery's senility; others had simply given up on Avery's status quo policy and gotten out.

Some good executives were left, but Brooker had to ferret them out and rebuild their confidence. After I got to know Brooker I found myself wondering why a man of his caliber was not better known in the national business community (*Fortune's* first piece on him was May, 1970). James J. Nance, a prominent industrialist who'd wound up his career as chairman and chief executive officer of the Central National Bank of Cleveland and was a friend and consultant to Tom Brooker, gave me the obvious expanation. "For a long period there Tom was the most overworked executive in America. He was putting in 18 hours a day on that one company."

One of his most time-consuming and frustrating duties was meeting with the many departments of Montgomery Ward in an effort both to inspire the people and to get them to speak up. He first introduced himself and then held periodic meetings with members of the 40 merchandise departments, located not only in Chicago but in New York and Oakland as well. Departmental reviews were new to the company and it took him some time to gain confidence and get any feedback. One of the departments in which he at least got answers was tires. John Sebastian, the manager, had been with Wards since 1937, and his department produced the greatest volume and profit in Wards. Sebastian knew his business and he had a common bond with Brooker in that both had worked for Firestone Tire and Rubber Company. Brooker had done so well as head of the western region of Firestone stores that Sears had made the unprecedented move of going outside the company for a man to head up one of its most important departments, automotive accessories. In his first meeting with Sebastian and a dozen of the top men in the Ward tire department, Brooker could talk tire language with tire people. What was wrong?

In the ensuing dialogue it turned out that practically nothing was right. The problem began with the tire supplier. U.S. Rubber was running, in effect, three separate operations. It manufactured original-equipment tires, the kind that come on new cars, to one set of specifications. It manufactured tires for its own dealers under another set of specifications. Finally, it manufactured tires for two private labels, Riverside and Atlas. Wards demanded exacting specifications for Riverside.

Another difficulty was inherent in the cost-plus type of contract. Under such an arrangement, a company can grow fat and lazy. Wards had no provision in its contract by which it could do anything about controlling costs. U.S. Rubber's major customer was paying its share of the overhead without question, why should its executives knock themselves out keeping it down? One of the results of this corporate indolence was reflected in U.S. Rubber's labor contracts; work rules amounted to featherbedding. (Before the current management of U.S. Rubber gets mad at me for bringing up past history, I'd better say that everything comes out happily in the end.)

The increasing cost to Wards brought about by these deteriorating conditions forced the company to price its tires higher than Sears, which had a known-cost contract with its supplier. Volume decreased, and with it profit. Then, in the period just before Brooker came to Wards, the roof fell in. Wards customers, as well as other users of U.S. Rubber tires, began having frightening and upsetting experiences. They'd be driving along when the tread of the tire would suddenly come loose from the body. It might just flap against the fender, or it might wrap itself around the axle. When such a thing happens, if you live through it, first you're scared and then you're mad. And you take it out on the guy who sold you the tire.

The cause of the trouble proved to be a sophisticated new compound developed by U.S. Rubber. It had performed excellently in tests made by the company's research laboratory on tires taken right off the line. But the customer doesn't get his tire right off the line. By the time it goes through the distribution system, it could be a year old before it's mounted on your rim. In the case of the new compound, an unforeseen phenomenon occurred during the aging process: the oxygen molecules became detached from the polymer and oxidized the cement which bonded the rubber tread to the cord fabric.

From Brooker's experience with tires he estimated that Montgomery Ward was due an adjustment from U.S. Rubber, and suggested to Sebastian that he ask for $2 million. Somewhat to his surprise, Sebastian got a substantial part of it. In the meantime, of course, the defect had been remedied.

In Sebastian's opinion, the other problems with U.S. Rubber could also be remedied within the company. Brooker did not embarrass John by disagreeing, but suggested that he investigate other suppliers, and Sebastian accepted the suggestion. He considered several sources, but almost automatically eliminated the smaller rubber companies. In his conversations with Brooker, and from his knowledge of Brooker's successful tenure as vice president of factories with Sears, Sebastian was familiar with Brooker's strong belief in the advantages of mass manufacturing. To Brooker mass manufacturing can be plotted by a line extending into the galaxy. Greater production provides more and better research and engineering, savings effected by larger purchases of raw materials, and increased efficiency of labor. All these add up to reduced prices for superior goods which brings in incremental volume—which starts the whole thing all over again.

Incremental volume is the key, whether the product is refrigerators, brassieres or tires. If a company is already turning out 10,000 whatchamacallums at a profit, the manufacturing cost of each additional whatchamacallum, or increment, is less and the profit more. The additional income can be spread out over the entire production to lower the cost, improve the product, or both. Everybody—manufacturer, retailer, consumer— benefits.

To Brooker this is not merely a philosophy, but a hard fact. In the 25 years between 1945 and 1970, he once pointed out to me, the gross sales of Whirlpool, with which he had a relationship for 10 of those years, grew from $8 million to $1.2 billion. Incremental volume provided by Sears was a major factor. You can't argue with a growth of 15,000 per cent.

There wasn't any point, in short, in John Sebastian's considering any company which could not supply the demand for Riverside tires, present and future. Of the big companies, Armstrong, of course, was eliminated; it manufactures tires for Sears. Goodyear was on the verge of signing a contract to supply Penneys through its subsidiary, Kelly Springfield, and probably couldn't have handled both outlets. General was a possibility, but Sebastian considered its operations too centralized; transportation of the finished product is an important factor in distribution efficiency.

The logical choice, therefore, was B. F. Goodrich. It was a good company with a good product; according to Brooker's Law of Incremental Volume, Montgomery Ward's business would have a whopping impact. To prove it, Brooker called in his super auditor, Kermit Pickett, whom he'd hired his second day as president. He asked Pickett to examine Goodrich's annual statements and work up some figures on the effect of incremental volume, courtesy of Montgomery Ward.

Pickett's findings impressed Brooker, and shocked the daylights out of Goodrich. Somebody had been figuring out a way to dump forty million dollars in their lap and they didn't even know about it.

In the meantime Sebastian had been thinking about the deliberate oversight of Firestone Tire and Rubber Company. He knew that Firestone had never been interested in private labels, but he thought it should at least be considered. "Why don't we go to Firestone, too?" he asked Brooker.

Brooker's expression gave no hint of what he thought of the suggestion. At that time he was glad to get any suggestion from anybody at Wards, even one as crazy as that. He well knew the attitude of Harvey S. Firestone, the founder of the company, toward mail order houses, and though Firestone was no longer alive, his influence was. Brooker's mind went back to the early days of the depression, when he was making his mark at Southern California Edison Company. An executive who wanted to see the young man—he was 29—get ahead and knew that the road would be slow in the depression-hit utilities field, told him of an opening in the comparatively new chain of Firestone stores. In looking into the potential of the job, Brooker learned the reason Harvey Firestone had founded the stores in the first place. He didn't like either mail order houses or the competition they were giving him, and set up the store network in retaliation. Even if he only made a nickel a store, he said, they would help maintain production at the factory.

In Brooker's 10 years with the company he had come to know the second generation Firestones well, and kept up the friendship when he left. He knew the company, and he knew that Firestone wasn't about to go into cahoots with the mail order business.

"John," he told Sebastian, "I'm afraid they'll turn us down. But I don't have any objection to trying, and if you really think they're interested, call them up and see if they'd like us to make a presentation."

So Sebastian, not knowing that he was attempting the impossible, called Firestone and was told that they would listen to the Ward offer. Surprised but still not too optimistic, Brooker authorized Kermit Pickett to draw up some figures for Firestone. The presentation was made to the board of directors.

Now U.S. Rubber was fighting to hold the Ward account, Goodrich was fighting to get it, and Firestone was getting interested. About that time Brooker attended a meeting of the board of trustees of his alma mater, the University of Southern California. Leonard Firestone, one of the patriarch's sons, was chairman of the board of trustees. He was also an owner of the California Angels, and after the meeting he and Brooker went to a night game.

Between innings Firestone suddenly asked, "What do you think Father would think about us taking on a mail order company?"

"Well, Leonard," Brooker said, "your father always moved when it was time to move. He put us in the retreading business when everybody thought that was crazy. I think that maybe his view on mail order might change during this period."

"I think so, too," Firestone said, "I'm going back to the board meeting next week and we're going to push to get this business."

From then on the Firestone executives pursued Wards aggressively. Brooker himself felt that the incremental volume would be of greater value to Goodrich, and would rub off on the Goodrich-Wards relationship. Brooker believes in strong and loyal ties between supplier and merchandiser. "If Goodrich had been more aggressive, they would have had that business," he told me later. "They wanted it. But Firestone understood the proposition thoroughly, and they really started to compete."

One of the factors involved was geographical distribution. Goodrich insisted that it was more economical to ship tires than to build regional plants; Pickett, after long discussions, decided in favor of the Firestone network of plants which would reduce shipping costs.

Sebastian was impressed by the way in which Firestone executives studied the problem and came up with operational techniques superior to those he had accepted at U.S. Rubber. He also determined that the Firestone specifications would meet the Riverside specifications; it would not be necessary to manufacture to different standards. He checked with several owners of large fleets of vehicles and found they were pleased with Firestone mileage and performance.

The decision was made to go with Firestone. Then came four months of head-knocking. Firestone had no experience with known-cost contracts and was reluctant to open up its books to Wards. But Wards insisted. It wants to know the cost structure of every department of every company with which it does business. It doesn't want its customers to pay for some other company's frills like labor featherbedding or the president's yacht.

With Firestone the hassle finally came down to the company's participation in the Indianapolis Speedway. Sebastian could see how Wards would gain from the research and development end of it, but he saw no point in paying for the promotional aspects. The name on those tires whizzing around the speedway is Firestone, not Riverside. Each side compromised; Wards agreed to a percentage of the Firestone's overall Speedway operations, without checking the books to see how much which driver gets.

The final contract covered just about everything else— escalating and de-escalating clauses on Firestone's labor and materials, Ward's volume. Those increments again. The first order was for $40 million worth of tires.

By 1971 the amount had more than doubled; Firestone built another plant in northern California to take care of additional demand. Including tires supplied by the Gates Tire and Rubber Company for customers in the Denver area, Ward's tire department went over $150 million in 1971. The relationship has not only been profitable, but happy. Firestone likes Wards, and Wards likes Firestone. And customers obviously like both. Wards tries to keep its advertised sales prices 10 to 20 per cent below that of the major brands. The specifications spelled out in the catalog tell you exactly what you're getting, which is more than you can say for a TV advertisement.

As for me, I figure John Sebastian knows more about tires than I do so I let him do the work. Later on I'll pass on to you his advice on what grade of tire to buy, and the advice of Ward's marketing experts on when to buy it.

The happy ending includes U.S. Rubber. It had offered to meet any price Firestone or Goodrich could make. The decision was up to Brooker; his position was that to accept would put U.S. Rubber in a deficit position. That's no favor. The financial trauma of losing the Ward account forced the company to take drastic action. After the tumult and the shouting, U.S. Rubber came back to a strong position in the industry.

From the managerial side, the Wards-Firestone story has a double moral: Listen to your executives even when they are making a suggestion you know is ridiculous, and go to baseball games with the right people.

The Rag Game . . .

I was walking down a corridor of Ward headquarters in Chicago one morning when I heard an outburst of shrill cries coming from the company auditorium. It sounded like a crowd of teenaged girls at a rock concert. I pushed open one of the double doors of the auditorium and squeezed in.

On the stage, at mid-morning on a working day, a fashion show was going on. It was the seasonal showing of the new Ward line, presented with a theme, imaginative lighting and narration by the stylish little bundle of energy who coordinates Ward's fashions, Rita Perna. The show was designed for the fashion press, but somebody had gotten the idea that maybe Ward employees might like to see it too and they were attending in shifts, every hour on the hour. As the models came out, in styles so new they wouldn't be on sale for another month or so, the audience, mostly female, gasped and giggled and pointed and cheered.

The show presented the newest in male fashions, too. A young man with longish hair and rippling muscles barely covered by a skintight jump suit came out and slowly turned, showing the cut of the garment and, incidentally, his bulging muscles and handsome profile. He got a chorus of delighted squeals. As he left the stage a plaintive voice called out, "Don't let him go!"

Some stunning girls in mod clothes came out and it was my turn to enjoy the show. I wasn't alone, either. A tall, slender man had sneaked in and was standing in the darkened rear of the room. He was Tom Brooker, grinning all over his face.

"Man, you're really getting a kick out of this," I observed.

"Who doesn't like to look at pretty girls in pretty clothes?" he answered. He stood there, obviously enjoying the show himself and delighted that the employees could see it, until it ended.

Well, if anybody had a right to enjoy a Wards fashion show it was Tom Brooker. There sure hadn't been anything like that when he first came to Wards. Rita Perna, internationally known in the fashion world and, as assistant vice president, Ward's first woman officer, told me what it was like back then. Rita had been hired by Sewell Avery in his last year with the company. She was impressed with the quality of the coats and suits; oh, they were full of quality. The materials included Forstmann and Strook woolens, and the stitching was strong and secure. A mid-western farm wife in the time of the depression, who made her own clothes and made them to last, would really have appreciated the materials and workmanship. But Wards would have to turn the clock back a quarter of a century in order to find people who'd buy those frumpy styles. As for the cheaper dresses, ugh. Glop and gloop.

As a fashion-oriented, sophisticated New Yorker, Rita would seem to be miscast as fashion coordinator for the Monkey Ward of the fifties. But, like a lot of older Ward employees who had stuck it out during the worst of times, she began to see the potential of the tired giant. She was impressed with its immensity. In the New York garment district, even on Fifth Avenue, the atmosphere is frantic and unstable. Fashion people change their minds every minute on the minute; dealing in comparatively small quantities, they can afford to. But, to jump forward in time and show Wards as it is today, the contrast is awesome. Any idea, any decision, affects thousands of people and hundreds of thousands of dollars. Not only sweeping new style changes, but little things like a new hanger to better display the dress on the rack, or a new color, have to be considered in terms of a program which will cost millions and have lasting effects all across the country.

After a couple of years Rita managed to get authorization to attend the couturier showings in Paris. As a representative of staid old Montgomery Ward she attended the showings of such designers as Balenciaga, Givenchy, and Dior. She brought back a couple of designs and had them made up, but Ward's customers weren't buying Givenchy that year.

Rita realized that the customary procedure—go to Paris showings, buy a design for a dress or a suit or coat, bring it back and have it made up for whatever you think the traffic will bear—wouldn't work for Wards. Paris designers didn't have its customers in mind. Instead of buying designs, Rita gradually began going directly to internationally known designers, telling them about the customers, seeking their advice. Out of this grew the Ward Designer Advisory Council. Rita had it going in a small way when Tom Brooker became president of Wards.

"He's my hero," she told me. "He's the epitome of great taste in everything, his home, the way he lives . . ."

"Don't lay it on too thick," I interrupted the lady. "Let's . . ."

"No, no, no, but that's true," she interrupted me right back. "That is very true. He has created an atmosphere that has rubbed off on all the other people around him so that we can really discuss fashion and design in relation to Wards. One night he gave a dinner party in his home—oh, this was terribly exciting—for about 20 of Chicago's top industrialists, their wives and our designers, and he said he wanted to have a happening. We weren't going to talk about details like skirt lengths, but about mood. We had slides and everything. It was an art evening, art and fashion. Not many hard-headed businessmen who run giant multimillion dollar corporations have this kind of sensitivity."

With this kind of support Rita was able to get the biggest names in fashion from both America and abroad to work with Wards. Would you believe Rudi Gernreich, Jacques Heim, St. Laurent? I attended one of her fashion shows at the Waldorf, along with a hundred fashion editors. Designers so famous they only have one name, like Simonetta of France and Clodagh of Dublin, gave expert and newsworthy answers to questions on major fashion issues. The editors also saw the fashion show, and were impressed. "This is big news," a fashion editor who

When Simonetta gives advice on shoes, buyers listen.

Rita and friends discuss fashion trends.

had flown in from the west coast told me, scribbling away on her pad. "They've had the guts to design whole lines in enormous quantities, and show them to us when they're not even on sale yet."

For all her clout in the fashion world, Rita Perna can't accomplish a thing without the administrative and buying expertise of hundreds of people in the New York and Los Angeles offices. In 1961, at the beginning of the new Wards, the entire "A" line of merchandise, which includes all wearing apparel from underwear to scarves, was, like the company itself, in trouble. The New York buying office was on the fringe of the downtown business district—"You couldn't even find a place to have lunch in down there," Rita said.

Brooker moved it up to Seventh Avenue at 31st Street, and it now occupies several floors of what is officially known as the Montgomery Ward building. It's perhaps fitting that the vice president in charge of this entire operation, so heavily dependent upon women's buying whims, reached that eminence as a result of a telephone conversation between two women. . . .

It was a difficult call for one woman to make to another. Sally Brooker was in San Francisco with her husband, and she telephoned a friend in town, Dorel Abbott. They knew each other through church work—both are Christian Scientists. Though Dorel's husband, Richard L. Abbott, is 17 years younger than Tom Brooker, the two men had had a long and pleasant business relationship at Sears.

"Dorel," Sally said, "I don't usually conduct my husband's business for him, but Tom wants to know if Dick would like to come back to Chicago."

"Oh, Sally," Dorel cried, "you've ruined my day!"

Sally knew exactly how she felt. Less than a year before she and Tom had finally finished their luxurious home in Benton Harbor, Michigan, headquarters of Whirlpool. It was a magnificent piece of architecture and she looked at it with pride and happiness. On the day the last tree was planted on the elaborately landscaped grounds, Tom came home to announce that he had decided to take the presidency of Montgomery Ward. She had left her new home without protest and she knew that Dorel would not let her happiness in San Francisco be a factor in the decision Dick Abbott would now have to make.

Corporate wives are frequently pictured in New York-oriented fiction and TV shows as frustrated and neglected women, relieving their anxieties with pills, alcohol and extramarital affairs. That's hogwash. Though I wouldn't want to classify exquisitely groomed and well-traveled Sally Brooker and stylish, athletic Dorel Abbott as stereotypes, for each is an individual in her own right, still they typify a much truer picture of the corporate wives I have met at Wards.

Both women accepted their husbands' business lives. When Tom Brooker went out on the road for three weeks at a time, running the western states for Firestone, he always suggested on his weekends home that they go out to dinner; he knew she'd been cooped up in the house while he was away. But she, knowing that he had been eating in restaurants, insisted on doing the cooking.

Dick Abbott, a rising young manager in the Sears organization, and Dorel were transferred so many times that the legs of their grand piano looked ready to fall off.

Dick was working in the corporate office of Sears when the chain of California music stores Dorel had inherited got into difficulty. On six hours' notice he made the decision to leave Chicago, took over the business and salvaged it to the point that they could sell out for a substantial sum. The Abbotts liked San Francisco and stayed on. Dick acquired a small manufacturing company, and was active in his church, the United Fund and the YMCA. "I was actively retired," he said.

Then came the telephone call. It took three months to decide but the opportunity to become part of the turn around of Montgomery Ward was too much of a challenge for a man like Dick Abbott to refuse. He gave the sick old company only a 50-50 chance of surviving, but if it did he'd be part of the team responsible.

So he and Dorel left their happy home in San Francisco and went back to Chicago.

His contribution to the reorganization of the company over the next few years was obviously just what Tom Brooker had expected. "We have very few people in the corporation, in any corporation, who can think way out in front, what are we going to do in 10 years," Brooker told me, "and Dick Abbott is one of those people."

After Dick had established a rapport with the Ward people in the Chicago headquarters, Brooker offered him one of the four regional vice presidencies. Dick said that he'd prefer to be in the buying end. Tom is a quiet-spoken man with a poker face but his eyes twinkle when he hears what he wants to hear. Dick saw the twinkle and recognized immediately the Sears managerial characteristic of testing an executive by proposing the opposite. He had given the right answer.

"How'd you like to take over the New York buying office then?" Tom asked.

Dick knew very well that Dorel hated New York. It was almost a phobia with her. When he got home that night she was in the kitchen, cooking dinner.

"Sit down for a minute," he said. "I've got something to discuss with you. . . . Tom Brooker wants me to go to New York. What do you think about it?"

"What did you tell him?"

"Well, I said I'd go."

"Then why are you asking me?" she said, but then she forced a smile. She knew she was on the way to New York.

Years later, happy in her Park Avenue apartment that's so large the grand piano with the battered legs is almost lost in one corner, she explained what might be the credo of the corporate wife: "He has enough to battle at the office. He doesn't need any more of it at home."

When I went to New York to look over Abbott's empire my wife, Bonnie, went along with me. She'd helped research my book on Alaska, where women wear pants with baggy bottoms, and I thought this would be more in her line. Bonnie has a good figure and she likes to be well-dressed; she often makes her own clothes.

Though she's from New York, a visit to the Montgomery Ward building was not her idea of a big homecoming. She hadn't spent her childhood with a catalog the way I had; I guess big-city girls aren't as interested in high-top boots and .22 rifles. As for buying clothes from Montgomery Ward or any other mass merchandiser, forget it.

But any woman, from big city or small town, loves to shop, and to become involved with Dick Abbott's operation is to go on a vicarious shopping binge. The 19 departments spend $400 million, buying from sources from all over the world. We talked with dozens of people, all excited and enthusiastic about buying things for Wards.

Like Ward's merchandise, Ward's people come in all varieties, from petite Rita Perna to big Jim Love. A former tackle for the University of Maryland, Jim had deliberately chosen to go with Wards in 1949 because of the company's reputation for turmoil. Under such conditions he was confident he could get ahead. And he did, but in a way he hadn't comtemplated. Brought to New York, he worked his way up through various departments.

It was no eight-hour day: "If you're in a business in which your future depends on your performance you put in extra time and effort." He worked with manufacturers after hours, cutting, sewing, learning their end of the business. I'd like to have seen Jim Love when he was in the infants' wear department, sewing tiny garments.

But his experience in developing rapport with his sources became invaluable as Brooker, Jim Lutz and Dick Abbott pushed the new procurement policy of choosing sources and working with them over the long haul. When Love became a shirt buyer he helped establish a known-cost type of operation with a shirt manufacturer in Tennessee. "It's like having another assistant."

Bonnie was of course more interested in women's fashions. Used to shopping several stores but eventually finding just what she was looking for, she was most impressed by what Ward's shoppers do, buy today what the fickle, unpredictable public will want next year. Their job is even more difficult during this period of fashion revolution, when the clothes worn by men and women are no longer dictated by designers, but are influenced by the crazy styles—gypsy look, handcrafts, appliqués, macramé—the young people go for.

At the same time, women have the tendency to be copycats. The day of the absolutely exclusive dress is gone; women like to wear what other women of good taste wear. This is the secret of the mass market. Ada Shalit, who helps dress buyers decide what will sell through the catalog all over the country, told Bonnie that she likes to sit at Radio City and watch middle America go by. It's not only fun, but an important part of her job. Here was where she saw the very first tie dyes, for example. She recommended that the buyers stock up on tie dyes. They did, and Ward's customers showed their appreciation by buying them.

We hear about — and sometimes see! — the growing tendency of women to be free and unfettered, doing away with bras and girdles. Janet Bowen, of the foundations department said not to believe it. Today's women want to *look* unfettered, true, but they like to eat, too.

"Young girls with superb figures can wear panty hose without panty girdles," Miss Bowen said, "but most women can't. They just don't have the willpower, and they can't hold their tummies in by themselves. Woman are going to keep right on overeating and underexercising, and they'll still need girdles and bras."

Now they can have it both ways. Bras and panty girdles today are made of soft, easy-care tricot, with hardly any seams and without the hooks, bones and straps of yesteryear. One of Ward's best selling items is a brassiere that's so well made it received the company's hard-to-get Excellence Award. It's a copy of the nationally advertised Playtex cross-your-heart bra, but sells for less, thanks to Ward's high-volume orders from its source, the respected Warner Division of Warnaco. Incidently, the most popular bra size is still 34 or 36B, but with more women taking the pill, the C cup is catching up.

In purchasing wearing apparel, just as with automobile tires, the customer of the private-brand merchandiser benefits. For years one of the most popular walking shoes on the market has been nationally advertised and sold under a well-known brand name. Ward's customers can buy the identical shoe, made on the same last of the same material by the same manufacturer to the same specifications, but without the nationally advertised brand name. The only difference is that the pair with the Ward label costs a couple of dollars less. Obviously the manufacturer is pleased to have the additional business and customers go on happily buying both brands.

Occasionally the close relationship of merchandiser and

Unfettered look is featured in catalogs.

supplier can result in an unexpected savings to the merchandiser at the expense of lost business to the manufacturer. Mrs. Leigh Lubasz, an assistant shoe buyer, liked the looks of an Italian platform shoe. She made all the arrangements for a manufacturer which has a close relationship with Wards to make up a large order. After a couple of weeks, the manufacturer's representative called her. "We've made platforms for several shoe distributors and none of them are selling," he said. "I don't think you should go ahead with this one."

It was indeed a bad season for platforms, but at least Wards wasn't stuck with that model.

The street between merchandiser and source runs both ways. Rita Perna's designers frequently come up with excellent ideas which just aren't right for Wards. She, members of her staff, and buyers in general often see things which are intriguing, but not yet ready for the mass market. They all pass on these tidbits, sometimes in sketch form, sometimes in actual merchandise bought and paid for, to the sources they work with. A Danish design may be turned out by a Hong Kong manufacturer after having been passed on through a New York buyer purely as a favor.

I've been involved with people in the rag game before. (Although it had been a dozen years since I wrote the book, Rita Perna remembered several of the things I said in "Bergdorf's On The Plaza," the story of the swankiest women's store in the world.) I've never really understood the wild enthusiasm these people have for copying each other's clothes, but I accept it. They go about their jobs with the same determined abandon that Dick Butkus goes about his. In the Montgomery Ward building, Bonnie and I found this enthusiasm even more pronounced. They had an additional motivation: they had already come a long way, but they wanted to go farther. In the Big Three rivalry, the Ward A line people felt that they had long surpassed Sears in style and quality, and had caught up, in some lines, with J. C. Penney. (Penney, which originally marketed only soft goods, had a head start.)

One reason for wanting to improve the quality of the product is that higher prices bring higher profits. "The customer wants better goods today," William F. Ryan, the merchandise manager for soft goods, told me, "and Wards is willing to give it to her—and profit from it. Selling quality merchandise is good business. When people buy something that won't perform they don't remember how cheap it was, only that they are stuck with something they don't want. When they get quality merchandise, they come back."

"The goods we sell today would have been totally unrecognizable at Wards ten years ago," W. R. Wineman, whose sportswear department sells more units than any other, said. "We've moved up in taste as well as price. How do you move up? You do it by doing it. Year by year of adding better price lines, finding and developing resources and working with them. We buy our garments on a long-term contractual basis a year in advance all over the world."

The pride has rubbed off on members of the Ward family all over the country. In Chicago Bob Guelich's teenaged daughter, Janie, came running home one day to say that she and her friends had just been in one of the Wards boutiques; "And Daddy," she cried, "our prices were just as high as anybody else's!"

Bob had mixed emotions.

The world of fashion is by no means restricted to the female of the species. The lion has a ruff, the peacock has a fan and men have multicolored flares. Wards has a wildly dressed young man named Steven Van Leer.

When I talked with Steve he was wearing an Edwardian jacket, tapered at the waist and flared out over the hips, a broad-striped shirt and a five-inch tie. His tapered trousers fit inside his three-quarter length boots. Because of its snub toe it's called a snoot boot.

As men's fashion coordinator, Steve works with buyers in passing on new fashions and approaches. He studies trends and hangs out with other guys who love to talk clothes. Every summer he goes to what at first thought seemed to be the craziest place in the world to do fashion research—National Guard Training at Camp Drum.

"There are 10,000 of us there, from all over the northeast, wearing fatigues all day," he said. "Off-duty hours we talk about girls and clothes. They're connected: the groovy chicks dig what I wear. National Guard duty accentuates what we all know—everybody's just a number. One way to be an individual is to wear the latest thing in clothes."

Steve is a perfect example of the purchasing agent for the young men of middle America. They aren't ready for the extreme fashions of the Greenwich Village mod shops, but they don't want to be too far behind.

"Wards can't be an innovator," Steve said. "Our customers don't want to be first with a new style. My job is to see to it that they are *second* first."

While I was getting the low-down on what I'll be wearing next year, Bonnie was talking to Mrs. Sylvia Barnes, who buys best-grade dresses. "We try to give people good value without snob appeal. We're aggressive, alive—oh, it's a wonderful business."

In the midst of all this enthusiasm Bonnie broke down and admitted that she had seen something she liked in the catalog— a knit suit. Mrs. Barnes's eyes lit up. She got out a catalog and sure enough, there it was, on page 110.

"That's mine!" Mrs. Barnes cried happily. She had first seen it as a two-piece ensemble, jacket and pants, manufactured by Kimberly, an excellent name in moderately expensive clothes. She liked the lines, which were stylishly simple, but she was afraid that not enough Wards customers across the country were ready for a pants suit. So in addition to the pants she had a matching skirt designed, and also a shell—a sleeveless knit blouse—of a contrasting color. (The final colors decided on were gray with a cream shell, red with a white shell.) For a manufacturer, she went to Italy. She gave the factory there meticulous specifications.

"We are very particular about the fit of a garment," she explained. "After all, the customer can't try it on when she's buying it through the catalog. We leave nothing to chance."

At this point Carl Boyer, whom Bonnie describes as a very tall, good-looking, rather elegant-appearing young man wearing oxford-weave buttondown shirts, steps in the picture. Boyer is with the import department, the liaison between the buyer and the foreign offices of Wards. He travels over the world looking for reliable sources of goods. Bonnie thought the job sounded glamorous, but he said it was exhausting. You don't do a lot of sight-seeing when you are traveling from one factory to another, studying their operations. But he liked his job and he was

*Bonnie Herndon, the author's wife and a style-conscious New Yorker, was
so surprised to see a suit with this styling in a mail order catalog that she
traced its production from idea to completion for the benefit of other
clothes-conscious readers.*

57

proud of his accomplishments. In 1968, Wards imported $14 million worth of wearables; in 1971, $30 million.

In regard to any adverse effects on American employment, Boyer said that the great quantity of merchandise Ward imports ($99 million in all lines; 6.6 per cent of all goods purchased) couldn't possibly be produced in this country. "We don't put people out of work," he said, "we put them *to* work, all over the world."

Members of the Ward Italian office worked with the quality control people at the factory to make sure that the knit suit was manufactured absolutely to Mrs. Barnes' specifications. Any skimping would result in the garment's being rejected on the spot. The four pieces were packed tightly in plastic bags which were again packed tightly into large containers. This saves space and shipping cost. At the major ports of entry Wards employs customs brokers to facilitate moving them through customs. On arrival in America, the suits were removed from the plastic bags, and shaken out. Each one was then placed on a hanger, and put in another plastic bag.

But before the customer could buy the suit, it, like all other garments, had to pass a final inspection in Chicago in the week-long critique of all garments, held twice a year. A sample of each suit, in each color, was put on a live model. A group of the most particular people in the whole world—department managers, buyers, resource representatives, inspectors, catalog sales managers and other specialists—scrutinized the ensemble. It had already been checked many times in the factory, but not with the same attitude. These people were deliberately trying to find fault with it, in every way from material and workmanship to the way it looked on the model. Fortunately, it passed.

The original Kimberly, jacket and pants only, cost around $100. The Ward four-piece ensemble cost $75; $55 without the pants.

After all this, the story has an unhappy ending for Bonnie. She ordered too late. They were completely sold out.

Buyer "sells" new fashions to store and merchandise managers.

For all the excitement and innovation of the New York scene, it isn't enough; many trends begin on the west coast and spread eastward. The large operation Wards maintains in Los Angeles to take advantage of this phenomenon began, ironically, with misfortune.

A few years ago a delightful, big-hearted man named Greg Young, a department manager in New York, contracted muscular dystrophy. He planned to retire but Tom Brooker, who thinks everybody is happier working, talked him into a less demanding job: managing the small west coast buying office located in the catalog building in Oakland.

Greg's increasing physical handicap could not decelerate his alert mind. He caught the mood of the vibrant environment and noticed how many trends in American living styles begin on the west coast. Greg believes that in retail, everything begins with merchandise. To get a jump on southern California fashion trends, he proposed setting up a bigger buying office in Los Angeles. Brooker, thanks to his own familiarity with southern California, agreed and approved. Thus the big Los Angeles buying office got started through the efforts of a physically handicapped man sent to the west coast to take an easy job.

Brooker has a fascinating knack for maneuvering people into their appropriate slots. When Dick Abbott went to New York, he took over from a tall, suave New Yorker named Fred Giersch. Fred graciously showed him around the office, then left for a lesser job in the midwest. Dick and I both agreed that under such circumstances we would have kissed Montgomery Ward goodby forever.

When I talked with Fred Giersch about it, he admitted that he had been hurt. "But Brooker's a funny guy," Fred said. "He's great at telling you why you should be where you don't think you want to be. He told me that I needed broader national experience, and then when I had my ducks in line he would have a new spot for me."

In Los Angeles, meanwhile, Greg Young's physical condition was deteriorating. When Fred was sent in to run the show with Greg's assistance—Fred is Mr. Outside, Greg Mr. Inside—everybody understood.

"Brooker was right, dammit," Fred admitted. "I love this business, I know my job, and this is a wonderful place to do it. It's testing you constantly, and you have a tremendous rapport with the people you work with. Merchandising is a great challenge. We can procure the finest things imaginable, but we don't make a nickel until the purchaser takes it home and keeps it."

One of the major operations of the Los Angeles office is to choose swimsuits for Ward's customers. Each year the buyers look over some 800 styles presented to them by the major manufacturers, including Jantzen and Catalina, and narrow the selection down to about 50 models for their customers to choose from.

Another big buying operation ties in with a program Greg Young started in 1959. In hindsight his proposals look pathetically obvious but in those days the Ward management was so uptight that he had to present it to the board of directors before he could proceed. In its moldering days, Wards had lost an entire generation of customers, and Greg's Junior Miss program was designed to catch up.

Teenage customers, he said, deserved to be treated with respect, no matter what their life-styles were, and to be able to buy the things they wanted, no matter how weird they might appear to be. Further, earning the loyalty of the youthful customers today means having that loyalty tomorrow, when they are adults in the market for a great variety of merchandise.

With a strong go-ahead from the new management, Greg's program has flourished. Bonnie and I saw the buying end of it in operation in Los Angeles.

What teenaged girls want the most, of course, are wild jeans and colorful tops. Next come coordinates, which include pants, skirts, tops and jackets. Bonnie, who like most other women shops on a kind of budget, was fascinated by the way Sue Howry, a junior miss buyer, procures these coordinates. Sue begins at the beginning. Instead of looking at garments already made up, she looks at swatches of materials dyed to match. If she doesn't like them, she gets the mills she works with to try more colors—anything she can dream up. Once she's happy with both the colors and the match, she buys the material by the truckload. Then she goes to the manufacturers with her designs and specifications.

But Sue, like any customer, must operate within a budget; Wards can't sink its entire bankroll in junior misses coordinates. By operating within the policy of selecting the best sources and then working with them with mutual trust, she is able to get the most for her money. Her source will give her an estimate for a simple sleeveless top, for example. She compares it with her budget—Hooray! Now she can add a tie, or buttons down the front, or more special features.

Betting on her taste, anticipating the demand, she can give the manufacturer six months' time in which to deliver the order. This enables him to plan his work program in advance, perhaps fit her order into a slack period. He can keep his employees busy all year round, avoid shut-down and start-up costs, and pass the savings on to Wards and its happy teenage customers.

One day I noticed that both Fred Giersch and Greg Young were wearing double-knit slacks, and commented on it. Both of them immediately started talking about the advantages of double-knit fabric; for one thing, you can travel in it all day, bundling up your coat and throwing it up on the rack if you want, and still look good when you arrive. The material stretches, is comfortable and bounces right back into shape.

When double-knit suits first came on the market, however, they cost $200 or more. Wards had a good relationship with a clothing manufacturer in San Diego, and through the benefits of this rapport and large-volume buying, was able to bring out a double-knit suit for $80 when others were selling for twice as much.

Another west coast innovation, far removed from coordinates or suits, was a funny looking thing called a beanbag chair. Really, that's all it is, just a big bag filled with plastic pellets. The original model was made of leather, and was pretty expensive for a funny looking gimmick. By specifying vinyl instead of leather, however, and ordering it in quantity, Wards was able to get the cost down to $20 for a chair. A larger model, one you can stretch out in, cost $56. I would never have even thought about the expensive, leather beanbag, but I couldn't resist the $56 one. I can fall backwards into it, scrunch around until it fits just right, and then the next thing I know I'm drifting off into a nice little nap. Come to think of it, it looks mighty inviting right now. . . .

Your Invisible Interior Decorator

My black vinyl beanbag sprawls on an orange carpet between a 100-year old Morris chair upholstered in red and a bright blue arabesque desk. Frankly, I like it, but this eye-shattering clash of colors, periods and styles would send some people up the walls. Others wouldn't know enough to care; still others would feel uneasy and unsure.

The home and its furnishings comprise the American status symbol today, Gordon Farnsworth, manager of Ward's furniture department, says, and he wants his customers to feel secure in their surroundings. His department—largest in Montgomery Ward—procures furniture for you from some 250 manufacturers, but it goes far beyond just putting the stuff out on the floor for you to buy. The company is your invisible home decorator.

Suppose, for example, you're starting out completely fresh, as so many of Ward's young married customers actually do. You can sit down with a catalog and, in an hour or so, choose all the items you need with the positive assurance that they will all go together in style, period, and color. You can do your entire house in any style classification offered, such as Modern, early American, Mediterranean, or, if you're daring, a grande melange.

After the big decision on period comes color. Do you like gold? Well, along with your sofa in Goldenrod you can buy Goldenrod carpet, Goldenrod bedspreads, Goldenrod wallpaper, Goldenrod draperies, Goldenrod towels—until you sneeze. Or would you prefer Clove, Green Mint, Terra Cotta, Parrot Green, Space Blue, Pineapple, Pink Pink or Real Red?

As next year some watery-eyed copywriter may decide to change the name of Goldenrod to Margarine, Wards uses a nationally recognized numbering code which not only keeps each color constant, but relates it to others. Whatever its name, Goldenrod will always be No. 126, and will always fit in tastefully with other tones from 120 to 129. A young couple just starting out in a two-room apartment can, as they move up in the world and about the country, add roomfuls of furniture and furnishings with complete inner security, just by checking the furniture department or the catalog.

Wards became the pioneer coordinator in the mass merchandising field almost by accident. It began in the bathroom. To go with the paint suggested for bathroom walls Wards had to bring out a line of matching towels. Next came the carpet. And then the company went out and hired a coordinator to tie the whole house together, from wash cloth to refrigerator.

"A coordinator is part consumer, part merchandiser," Dave Farrar, who coordinates the design of all home furnishings, said. Farrar himself is a young man of ingenious taste. He is so far out that he has a *black* telephone in his office instead of the elegant pastel shades the other executives sport. (Tom Brooker has a black telephone, too, but for another reason—it's twenty-five cents cheaper.) His conference table and chairs are of clean and simple lines. They're a dinette set.

"The coordinator begins with the various buyers, working with them on their purchases, and carries right through to the customers' purchases. We're particularly interested in the twenty-two to forty-four-year-old bracket, because that's the largest group in our society.

"We want to know everything about this customer—how she thinks, how she wants to live, how she is going to be forced to live because of space limitations. We already know she is better educated and more traveled than the past generation. She lives with a communicating factor that we've never experienced before, because history is made right before your eyes on television.

"So this customer understands technology like our generation did not. We're on the threshold of a breakthrough. We're going to be using products and materials that we've never used before. Like plastics. The word 'plastic' has meant something inferior. But the customer of the immediate tomorrow understands plastic. She is as happy with it as her mother was with a piece hand-crafted of fine wood. She knows plastic will last, it's easier to use and it's easier to clean."

With its tremendous buying power, Wards has been able to go to the largest American manufacturers, with their research and technology, and the new foreign manufacturers, with their exciting designs, and get the best of both. The heavy, hand-

crafted wood-grain Spanish look in plastic that will take a beating, or the bright futuristic shapes—take your choice.

Though a veteran of many years in furniture, Gordon
Farnsworth welcomes the new trends with fresh confidence.
He had already been in charge of the furniture department of
a group of large quality department stores for 15 years when he
was approached by Wards in 1960.

"I knew I wasn't going any farther with department stores—
they're ready-to-wear motivated," he said. "I thought it might
be interesting to fight windmills once more in my lifetime and
I came to Wards. I knew I was running a personal risk. To
change over from the department store mentality to the completely different marketing policy of Montgomery Ward was
going to be difficult. It's a good thing I didn't realize *how* difficult. But to be successful in the merchandising business you've
got to be the type of person who likes challenges. This is a
challenging business. As I tell the younger people that our
personnel department sends up, if you're the kind of person
that has to clean up your calendar, and settle every issue every
night, don't think about the retail business. We're on the end of
the string of the consumer. She dictates what happens. But I
happen to enjoy it. I wouldn't give anything in the world for my
years with Wards."

Today the once stodgy old company which used to have the
image of 9 x 12 linoleum for farm kitchens is heading into the
unknown future of new designs, new materials, for an unpredictable generation.

"It won't be long," Dave Farrar said, "before you'll be going
to Jack's pad for dinner and instead of a ten-room house you'll
find a condensed plastic room with different levels of foam to
lounge on. There's a movement of honesty in home furnishings
among young people, and we'll just have to see where it takes
us. We'll be ready."

Though then and now the customer can furnish her home out
of a retail store or through the catalog, with no more knowledge

of interior decorating than is routinely provided, Wards conducts courses for those who want to develop their own appreciation of the art. Part of the Ward Consumer Education Program, they are offered in most of Ward's major market areas.

An interesting feature of the courses is that they have undergone constant upgrading since first inaugurated as more and more women of college background and higher income level began taking them. In addition to a basic course, Wards offers a more advanced study of design, and a third class devoted entirely to space planning.

Man the Toolmaker

The secret of man's success as ruler of the planet boils down simply to his use of tools. A bear can scoop a salmon out of a swift-running stream, but even if you put a dip net in his paw he wouldn't know what to do with it, or hold it if he did. On a higher level, a monkey can pick up a stick with one hand, using his oppositional thumb, and knock a banana out of a tree. But that's as far as he can go. The stick has got to be handy; he can't plan ahead and have it ready when the banana's ripe.

It took us humans millions of years to develop our use of tools to a sophisticated degree. We had to learn to walk upright; then we could chase a small animal and hit him with a club at the same time. We learned to use a jagged piece of rock to skin him with, then, *wow!*—we learned to look at a smooth stone and visualize the jagged edge that would result from breaking it. This was brainpower, and along with the ability to pass on the information to somebody else, it eventually resulted in such things as color TV and the hydrogen bomb.

I doubt if a heavy-set Irishman named John J. McGivern ever thought of himself as an anthropological exhibit, yet one day in a cluttered office in Chicago, he demonstrated in 15 seconds the development of mankind.

McGivern was standing by a sample side-by-side two-door refrigerator—freezer on one side, refrigerator on the other—explaining a new idea to a factory representative. He strode to his desk, picked up a roll of masking tape and came back, walking upright and tearing off a strip of tape with his oppositional thumbs at the same time. He plastered the strip across the left hand door, about 18 inches from the top.

"There," he said. "That's what I mean." Thus John McGivern demonstrated the unique ability of the human race to conceptualize a new tool for a new purpose.

John is aggressive and ambitious. "There has never been any doubt in my own mind that someday I will be president of Montgomery Ward." To get there he has to go up a step at a time. An important part of his self-advancement parallels the advancement of mankind and the big-brain theory. At the end of the working day, instead of rushing to the elevator in order to bump fenders with the other commuters on the way home, John shuts the door to his office, sits down, puts his feet on his desk and thinks.

What he thought about in 1966 was refrigerators. He was the buyer for the refrigerator department. Under the profit-center system brought in by Tom Brooker, this department, like the 40 others in Wards, was now operated like a company on its own. McGivern's job was to procure merchandise to be sold to catalog and retail outlets, which in turn would pass it on to the customer. McGivern liked the profit-center system. He'd played professional baseball, in which a healthy batting average means advancement, and the comparison was obvious.

It was also obvious that Montgomery Ward needed something new in refrigerators. The line was static. This situation is particularly bad in the private-label chains. When you go to Wards or Sears or Penneys all you see is the private label line of refrigerators; the salesman can't drag you from a GE to a Frigidaire to a Whirlpool.

The latest thing in all refrigerators was the icemaker. It had been around for some years, but only began to take off in the early sixties. In the affluent society people were drinking more, whether highballs or soda pop, and consequently wanted more ice cubes. With everybody running for ice — and the kids running for ice cream — the door to the freezer compartment was now being opened 35 to 40 times a day.

Back in science class at Drake University McGivern had learned the inexorable law that cold air is heavier than hot. Everytime you open the door of your freezer cold air spills out the bottom and warm air flows in the top. The freezer has to use more electricity; John figured it added $2 or $3 a month to the bill. What could be done about it? Well, if he added a third compartment containing only the icemaking machine and a small storage space for ice cream and popsicles, with its own special door, then he'd conserve a lot of cold air. That would save people money. People buy things that save money.

So John McGivern stuck a piece of tape on one of the doors of a side-by-side refrigerator to show where the third door

John McGivern, more than happy with the success of his three-door refrigerator.

would be. Later the design department worked it out esthetically, and now Frigidaire makes the refrigerator. The three-door model was unique with Montgomery Ward. People looked at the new refrigerators, talked about them, and bought them. It gave Wards a winner. As for John McGivern, when I talked to him five years later he had taken two giant steps: he was the head of two departments doing a total of $80 million a year.

It's in the nature of man to improve, refine, perfect. Nothing is ever good enough, not even when it's the best of its kind. Being Number One may even provide an extra stimulation to be even better.

According to the July 1969, issue of Consumers Union, the Ward lawn mower was judged to be the best buy. Wards sold a lot of those best-buy lawn mowers. But the manager of that department, Robert T. Jackson, determined to develop an even better product and assigned the project to John Gutenkunst and John McCarron, his buyers.

He gave them two and a half years to do it. Their only restriction was that the lawn mower had to look like a lawn mower; consumers don't seem to like revolutionary products. They were certainly successful in following out this directive. When I saw the prototype, after going through a procedure about like gaining admittance to the CIA code room, I blurted out the first thing that popped into my mind: "It looks just like any other lawn mower to me."

"That's just the point!" Gutenkunst cried happily. Then he pointed out the differences I hadn't seen.

A rotary lawn mower is a dangerous tool. More than 140,000 people are injured each year by lawn mowers; I know a half dozen of them personally and I bet you do, too. A lawn mower can pick up a stone or a nail and throw it with murderous force, often hitting an innocent bystander. It can roll back on your foot, or you can pull it on your foot when you start it. Lord knows why, but people are always sticking their hands or feet into the chute through which the grass is expelled. The blade whirls with such rapidity that by the time you feel the first contact, you've been hit six times more.

The safest mower, of course, is the one that won't cut anything, even grass. But that's not very practical. Next comes the old-fashioned hand mower, but people just won't buy it. Ever driven through a low-cost subdivision and seen people cutting their tiny lawns with a roaring gasoline machine? Or tried to get your son to cut the grass with a hand mower? A power mower is a status symbol.

The compromise is to build a power mower that will cut grass but not the person who's pushing it, or just walking by. This is what Gutenkunst set out to do. Tests showed that an object picked up at the rear of the machine is thrown out with greater velocity than something picked up at the front. Working with factory representatives, he designed a mower the bottom of which is covered in the rear, but it still cuts grass. Inside the chute are baffles which not only make it almost impossible for you to stick your hand in far enough for the blade to hit you, but also decrease the velocity of the grass and foreign objects being thrown out and direct them downward in a fan-shaped pattern. He put heavy teeth on front and back so it won't run over your foot. Many injuries, believe it or not, are caused by people sticking their hand underneath a mower in order to lift it and adjust the height. Gutenkunst put handles on the new model.

Finally, it's a proven fact that no matter how much research goes into safety features, some joker is always going to mess around and take them off—especially things like a plate on the bottom. Gutenkunst designed a one-piece shell, including deck and bottom plate. To die-cast this odd shape in a magnesium alloy required special equipment imported from Switzerland. The Modern Tool and Die Company, which worked with Wards on developing the mower, built a new plant to house the equipment. All that to keep you from removing something put on to protect you. Even so, thanks to Ward's gamble that enough people will buy it to justify a big order, the price of the new mower is $109 — $20 less than the CU best buy.

Inflation is a fact and I'm not going to attempt to refute it, but, as in the case of an improved lawn mower costing no more than its predecessor, mass merchandising provides some positive exceptions. Jim Lutz was bragging at dinner one night, for example, of an excellent new 12-inch TV set for $68. I remember spending that much for a secondhand set so my oldest boy could watch George Gobel instead of doing his homework.

One of Edward Gudeman's proudest accomplishments at Sears in the thirties was to bring out an electric refrigerator for $129.50. Just for curiosity I checked the 1972 Sears catalog and found a refrigerator — with defroster — for $132.50 It's small, 5.3 cubic feet, but I don't imagine Gudeman's pride of 40 years ago had much more storage space.

The most dramatic cost reduction brought about through mass merchandising I know — and in a most inflationary period — was about 90%. The product is not something like hoola-hoops or 78 rpm records, either, but one zooming in popularity, the microwave oven.

If any one man can have the major responsibility for both the popularity and the reduction in cost of the microwave oven it's William E. Kiesel, manager of the Montgomery Ward range department. When he first became interested microwave ovens were available in this country only as high-voltage vending machines costing around $2,000. He dreamed of a microwave oven which the ordinary customer could afford.

Statistically, he should have kept on dreaming. For all the inventiveness of man, and the natural desire to try something new, only about six out of ten new products ever make the grade. It takes time, money and promotion to put a new product over. The electric refrigerator was on the market for ten years before it reached sales of a million a year; color television was available in the fifties.

In spite of the gloomy potential Kiesel jumped into the

nonexistent market. He was ready when Litton Industries made a breakthrough in the magnetron tube, the most costly element. Litton welcomed him. "Working with a mass merchandiser was the only way we could possibly break into the market," Dan C. Cavalier, Litton's vice president of marketing, said, "because, frankly, the market wasn't ready."

The concept of cooking with microwave energy was so new that no safety specifications were in existence. Kiesel knew that the government would establish standards at some future date, but he had no idea what those standards would be. All he knew was that before sinking a few million dollars into microwave ovens, they had better meet specifications that nobody had started thinking about yet. He even tried to anticipate them. Foolproof switches to cut off radiation instantaneously on opening the oven door comprised an obvious precautionary measure. As for the door itself, should it open from the top or from the side? Well, if it opened from the top, when you removed food from the oven it might spill on the inside of the door. That meant a side swinging door.

A metal screen in the door would provide adequate protection against radiation, but suppose a small child stuck a sharp object through the screen? He had it covered with plexiglas. As for radiation emission, he demanded a maximum of one milliwatt per square centimeter on production, no more than five milliwatts during the life of the product.

But all this cost money, and Ward's first microwave oven — a countertop model made by Litton to Ward's specifications — sold for $470. That was less expensive than any other but it was a lot of money for something which at that time was just a gimmick to the public.

Cooking electronically is no better than cooking with heat, it's just quicker. But to some people, the tremendous savings in time are worth the price. Say, for example, you meet a nice couple at a cocktail party — or maybe it's the boss and his wife — and you impulsively invite them home to dinner. You can pull a roast beef out of the freezer, pop it in the microwave oven, and it will be ready by the time the glasses are empty. Kiesel cooks his eggs in it in the morning—45 seconds. The gadget is great for the working wife or bachelor girl, and if I were a young man about town it's the first thing I'd put in my playboy pad. Instead of inviting a cute chick up to see my etchings, I'd invite her up for a gourmet dinner turned out in a half hour from scratch.

At the beginning, however, Kiesel had to face the fact that the buying public had not yet gotten the word. He took a bold step.

"If we're going to capture the market on this," he told his staff, "we've first got to bust $400. Then we've got to shoot for $350."

He did. By sticking his neck out and buying in quantity, and by needling retail outlets into pushing and promoting the product to the public, he was able to get the price of the microwave oven down from $470 to a no-frills model at $200 within four years. By that time the government had issued specifications limiting emission to a maximum of one and five milliwatts. Kiesel had hit it right on the nose.

He had blazed a brand new trail. With the market now established, Litton introduced its own model. "We give full credit to Wards as innovators," Dan Cavalier told me. "They recognized the market potential early, and aggressively promoted it. We're glad they picked us to work with. We had the opportunity to learn from each other for two years while the market was developing, and their orders made it possible for us to maintain a year-round operation and bring down the cost. Now the demand is here, we're beginning to build a marketplace. It won't be long before there'll be 25 to 30 brands of microwave ovens on the market, and while they can all thank Wards, we've got the jump. I'll tell you one thing: it took the electric refrigerator 10 years to get a million sales a year, but it's not going to take that long for the microwave oven."

You and I, as consumers, rarely have to look far into the future. We may compare one brand with another in terms of how well each will stand up over the long haul, in style as well as technology. But we still buy what is available. The merchandising people of the big chain-catalog houses not only plan far ahead, but dare to prophesy.

William Hunter, one day, was reading an article in *Fortune* about the generation of electricity by nuclear plants. He put the magazine down and started dreaming.

Dreaming may at first thought seem out of character for Bill Hunter. He worked his way through college as a refrigeration service man and just happened to apply for a job at Wards when they needed an assistant refrigerator buyer. Four years later, at the age of 26, he was department manager of refrigerators and ranges, and at 29 took on freezers, room air conditioners, humidifiers and dehumidifiers. You don't normally get to be Ward's youngest department manager, the equivalent of the presidency of a big company, by dreaming, but Bill is not a normal corporation man. He wears his hair a little long in back, and holds up two fingers and shouts "Peace!" when you walk in his office.

Suppose, Bill was musing that day, electric power becomes so cheap that it replaces fossil fuels—coal, oil, gas—in homes of the future. In that case, instead of a central heating plant, we may well have zone control. We'll heat or cool rooms or areas when we need them. The principle is already partly in effect; Bill has four air-conditioners in his house and he, his wife, and their three kids automatically turn them on and off, like lights.

While we're controlling temperature, how about controlling the environment as well? That is, purify the air we breathe. Something has to be done to air conditioners anyway. Though they are the largest selling appliance—more than refrigerators —they are also archaic. Most air conditioners sit in a window, instead of being mounted like a picture frame on the wall.

Thinking about improving air conditioners, Bill toyed with the idea of combining them with air purifiers. The method— electronic precipitation—already existed, and it's simple.

An electronic precipitator charges all dust particles either positively or negatively, then blows them through a screen charged the other way. They stick. But though the principle is simple, the contraption is expensive. You may like the idea of clean air—but do you like it $300 worth?

About this time the Tappan Stove Company, one of Ward's suppliers, bought a company which had developed a less costly and more efficient device. Tappan thought of it in terms of kitchen ranges; Bill thought of it in terms of environmental zone control. He took the first sample home with him. Bill has sinus trouble; his wife and son have hay fever. After the sample ran for a couple of hours, they all felt wonderful.

The immediate result was a full-scale air purifier. Then Bill combined it with air conditioners and humidifiers, and eventually came up with a complete temperature-moisture-purifier environmental zone system. Beginning with the spring of '72 you could buy it; Bill Hunter started buying it for you years before.

In the meantime, of course, buyers have to continue their pragmatic jobs of taking what already exists and making it better—at, not so incidentally, a better profit for good old Monkey Ward. Just about every fisherman in the country, for example, knows the name Mitchell 300. It is *the* spinning reel. All sporting goods stores, including Wards, carry it. They have to.

Because of its popularity, stores use the Mitchell 300 as a come-on. It lists for $29.95, but you'd have trouble finding a store which would relieve you of that much cash. My local independent sporting goods store sells it for $19.95. The mail-order discount house I use (which gives the retail price as $45) charges $14.95 plus shipping. It's $17.77 in the Sears catalog, $16.99 in Wards. But all these prices are meaningless because sooner or later you're going to find it at some store marked down to $12.88 on the weekend special. The store loses money, but hopes to get it back on the things you buy to go with it.

Ed Lennox, who not only buys fishing tackle for Montgomery Ward but uses it successfully, was positive that he could procure a reel similar to the Mitchell 300 which Wards could sell for a comparable price with a higher profitability. And while he was at it, he thought he might just be able to supply Ward's customers with a better reel. He chose Europe for his fishing expedition; spinning reels had originated there. He visited several manufacturers in Germany and Italy with whose products he was familiar but eliminated them all. Then the head of Ward's buying office in Florence, Ezio Nocentini, suggested he visit the Ofmer company in Bologna.

Ed had never heard of Ofmer, but the visit proved to be a pleasant surprise to both. He was satisfied with the workmanship of its open-face reels and Ofmer was happy to increase his volume courtesy of Montgomery Ward. But that was just the beginning. With Nocentini acting as interpreter, Lennox spent four days explaining to Ofmer not only how he wanted the product improved, but why.

He insisted, for example, on having all the parts, including the tiniest screws, finished in rust-resistant chrome. Ofmer thought the added expense ridiculous. Ed patiently explained, through Nocentini, that many of the reels would be used in salt or brackish water. Ofmer still thought it ridiculous. Impasse. Finally Ed realized that cost-conscious Europeans carefully rinse their reels after using; Ofmer realized that crazy Americans do not.

When the first samples arrived in Ed's office, he set about having them tested. The most demanding usage he could think of was bone fishing, and the best bone fisherman he could think of was Tom Brooker. The chairman of the board accepted the assignment and came back to report that the reel was fine except that it was just slightly out of balance. The tip of the rod wavered when he brought in a big one.

Ed was glad to get the report even though it was unfavorable in one respect. A major advantage to the consumer in buying from an outfit like Wards is that the product gets an extra check, if not always from the chairman of the board. The defect was corrected, the contract placed and the reel, called the Hawthorne 3000, was placed on sale.

On Lennox's suggestion most sporting goods managers in Ward's retail stores displayed the Mitchell 300 and the Hawthorne 3000 side by side at about the same price. The Hawthorne's gears are made of rust-resistant steel, the Mitchell's of aluminum. The Hawthorne has ball bearings in the spooling which gives it smoother action; the Mitchell has no bearings at all. The Hawthorne has a double disc drag which is more effective, smoother and lasts longer than the Mitchell drag. Sounds like a better reel, doesn't it? Did people buy it? No, they bought the Mitchell 300.

Why? Well, the Mitchell comes in an extremely handsome and ingenious package. It may be difficult to accept this, but the next time you see a hardy fisherman using a Mitchell 300 the odds are good that he bought it because it comes in a pretty package. Lennox called in the design people and they came up with an equally fancy package for the Ward reel. Now, displayed on sporting goods counters right next to the Mitchell 300, the Hawthorne 3000 outsells it. Ofmer has built a new plant with new machinery in order to turn out more, at less cost to Wards. Ed Lennox's efforts have resulted in an item that provides Wards with a markup of over 40 per cent, and of superior quality measured by the ultimate test; less than 3 per cent are returned, for any reason.

I hope that, even though you may not even like to eat fish, much less catch them with a Hawthorne 3000, you've stuck with me this far. Because the Hawthorne 3000 epitomizes the seemingly incredible contradiction that can be accomplished through integration of manufacturing and sales. You pay the same, or less, you get a better product, and the company makes a nice profit. Everybody wins.

4

Selling the Goods

One day, like a damn fool, I suggested to Bonnie that she make an excursion to the Montgomery Ward store in a nearby city to see what it was like. She was off in the time it took to find her checkbook. She came back furious. The store was poorly lit, the restroom was dirty, and when she saw something she wanted to buy the two clerks were so busy talking to each other they didn't pay any attention to her.

This would turn off any customer, but Bonnie was particularly annoyed. She'd spent some time in Ward's buying offices and knew how those people knocked themselves out procuring merchandise. All their efforts were negated by those two silly gossiping salesgirls.

My wife and her friends are typical of the average shopper. They have three major interests. First comes the merchandise, which covers everything from price and style to repair service. This eliminates many stores, in our case both the cheap and the very expensive.

Next comes accessibility—how far you have to drive through what kind of traffic and where you'll park the car. We never go downtown anymore. Then comes the atmosphere of the store, its overall appearance and the attitude of the personnel. I have to admit we're a little spoiled in my home town. The people in the stores where we like to shop are friendly, helpful and often even call us by name.

We average consumers don't care much about how these things happen. Persons directly interested in the world of retail, however, dig deeper. Take Vic Sholis, for example, a most unusual young man. Two weeks after joining Montgomery Ward in the corporate office in Chicago, fresh out of graduate school, Vic found himself on a project reporting to the chairman of the board. You can't beat that for getting to the top fast, but in Vic's case it was almost natural.

Vic was Super-Trainee. He came from *Harvard*, personally recruited by the vice president in charge of personnel. Landing a Master of Business Administration from Harvard was like getting the President of the United States to come to dinner. Of 700 candidates for the MBA degree in 1968, only five condescended to an interview with the vice president of a retail organization, and four of them weren't really serious. (That year Harvard MBA's wanted, and could get, nine-to-five positions with prestigious financial institutions in New York; not for them the long hours with a retail chain headquartered in the midwest.) Further, though Sholis had his choice of some 20 corporate giants, he had chosen Montgomery Ward. Wow.

For three months Vic acted as a liaison man between a high-powered management consultant firm studying a far-out approach to an arcane problem in retail accountability and the top management of Wards. It took a Harvard MBA to interpret the study. Then one day he dropped the bomb. He asked the personnel director to send him out to work in a store with the rest of the peasants. When the stunned executive recovered, he asked why.

Because, Vic said, although he'd been engaged in this top-level study of retail operations, he really didn't have any idea of what the hell was going on out there. If he was going to be of any value to a retail chain, he ought to know how merchandise gets sold to customers.

A few days later Victor J. Sholis, Vanderbilt '66, Harvard MBA '68, was unloading a truck at the back end of a retail store. A few more weeks and he was managing the lawn and garden center. Christmas was coming on, and he said he'd like to get inside the store for the annual rush. He was given the stationery department—now he had two departments to manage. The store is open 72 hours a week, but Vic did not have the luxury of such short hours. On mornings when a management meeting was scheduled he'd get in at eight, and he usually stayed on an hour or two after the store closed to straighten up and take care of the paper work. After six months of that he had a general idea of what life is like in a retail store. I asked him for an example of what he had learned.

Vic paused a moment before answering. A poised, personable young man who is used to people asking him questions, Vic always pauses a moment. Then he gives an answer that's right on target.

"Well," he said, "something that came as a shock to me was the tremendous amount of back office work there is. You go into a department store and you never see the office back in the back where they have to fill out the orders. Tremendous amount of paper work. The size of the staff it takes to handle it is just staggering."

There we have two views of retailing. The average shopper knows what he or she wants a store to be, but doesn't know or care how it gets that way. The young man with a future in retailing is impressed with what goes on behind the scenes in a store—*one* store.

I'm impressed by something else. John Kenneth Galbraith, in "The New Industrial State," calls it *Technostructure*. This is the collection of talented people it takes to run a large corporation properly. Or, to reduce the definition to retailing, the large number of talented people required to enable the individual sales clerk to separate you from your money in such a pleasant way that you'll come back for more of the same treatment.

All corporations have an organizational chart which looks like a pyramid. Actually the retail chain is composed of many pyramids, all upside down with the point of each resting on the individual sales clerk. The next time a salesperson treats you right, it might interest you to contemplate for a moment on how many people you don't see are responsible. I'm talking specifically about Montgomery Ward, but the system applies generally to any large store in any large chain.

To begin with, the salesclerk in any department, whether it's ready-to-wear or sporting goods, is directly under the manager of that department. Each department manager reports to one of two managers next up the line; one is responsible for A and B lines (wearables and home furnishings), one for C and D (hard goods and appliances). There is also a personnel manager, operating manager, credit manager, and advertising manager. And then there is THE manager.

The manager is the coach of the team, the duke of the realm. His position is the one ambitious young men in retailing first shoots for. He's got it made — if he makes it.

The difference between the store where Bonnie found disillusionment — and Montgomery Ward lost money — and the store in Tucson, Arizona, which has the highest rate of profit in the entire chain — where Wards makes the most, percentagewise — is the two managers. We'll pass over the first, as the poor devil did not make it and has been transferred. The second is Lylan "Pete" Pederson, No. 1 in profitability. We went to Tucson to see this paragon in action.

Pete and his wife, Roberta, met us at the airport. It turned out there'd been a mixup over lunch, and a quick little frown passed over Pete's forehead. That meant that if he had handled the matter it wouldn't have gone wrong, and a mental note was being made to do something about it. After the frown, Pete and Roberta proved to be pleasant, unruffled and well-

rounded. They'd started out in Minnesota, had been transferred 13 times in 17 years on the way up, and were now
happy in Tucson and with each other. They knew the history
of Arizona and the southwest, and discussed it interestingly.
They knew the personality of the town, the nature of its
people—Pete's customers. Both are active in civic affairs—
"you put back into a community what you take out of it"—
but not particularly social. Pete plays golf on the public course,
as does the manager of his tire department, an unlettered but
hard-working Chicano whom Pete had encouraged and
promoted.

When we arrived at the store the wind was blowing and a
piece of newspaper sailed by. Pete ran after it and grabbed
it. Walking through the spotless, shining store, he simultaneously gave us a pleasant little guided-tour type of lecture,
straightened out things on counters and swept the store with
his eyes like an eagle hunting for prey. He nodded and smiled
at the sales people on the floor and they smiled back. They
weren't afraid of him; they were all making money together
by taking good care of their customers under his direction.
"It's like driving a car—only one person can do it."

Pete reviews every phase of operations with the appropriate
managers, analyzes the problems with them, delegates the
authority to them to do something about it—and sees to it
that they do it. His staff works on a percentage of profit—
"my operating manager is probably the highest-paid in the
company." Although some managers don't like to fool with
trainees, as the income they produce is not commensurate
with their salary and the store profitability suffers, Pete has
put through more than a hundred. Two of his assistant managers started out in his store.

He makes managing a store look easy; Jascha Heifitz makes
playing a violin look easy. It's the same thing, which is why
there are only a few Pedersons and Heifitzes in the world,
and why they both do all right. It is a pretty safe bet that
if you are an intelligent and personable young man with an

enthusiasm for merchandising, emotional stability and understanding, good physical condition and a lot of energy, its
possible to be a store manager and a millionaire by the time
you're 50 —unless the company pushes you further up the
ladder and you become a multimillionaire.

The store manager has a degree of autonomy, but that
doesn't mean that he and his personnel are just plopped
down somewhere and told to carry on. Determining whether
a community is a good market for Wards, finding the proper
location for the store, making the deal with the developer
and building the store to proven specifications takes years,
and millions. Once built, each store is furnished a basic list
of merchandise to keep in stock, along with detailed instructions and procedures as to how to replenish it. Regular ship
ments come in by truck; Wards has its own fleet. Each of the
buying offices, located in Chicago, New York and Los Angeles,
has a sales manager who keeps everybody posted on new
products, improvements and trends. If an item is selling
well elsewhere, push it; if it's a dog, unload it.

Headquarters sends out bulletins, manuals, brochures, telling
everybody from manager to sales clerk how to do their jobs.
They go into minute detail. The booklet on fitting men's clothes,
for example, tells the salesman to make sure the customer isn't
pulling in his stomach when trying on a pair of pants. He'll
buy a pair too tight for him and then blame it on Wards.

Chicago and New York also furnish advertising copy and
mats covering everything from swimsuits and water skis
to parkas and snowmobiles.

It looks as though your friendly local manager should be
able to run your local store pretty well, doesn't it? Well, maybe
he can, but just as the salesperson is covered by layers of
technostructure within the store, so is the manager at the
bottom of more strata of talent. Each store is located in either
a zone, which may comprise several states, or in a metropolitan
district. The metro districts have several merchandise managers, an operating manager, a personnel manager, a credit

manager, an advertising manager, and, of course a district manager. The zones have several merchandise managers and an operating manager, all of whom maintain a constant monitoring system by reports, by phone, and in person. They're on the road most of the time.

Now we get up to the regions. In this high altitude the boss is a regional vice president and a member of the board of directors of the company. His staff includes managers of personnel, merchandising, operations, credit, real estate, budgets, taxes, repair service, and traffic, as well as a controller and a legal department. The regional offices are located in Baltimore, Chicago, Kansas City, Oakland, and Orlando, Florida, and their people travel, too. When Charles W. Wagner was promoted to vice president of Region 3 with offices in Kansas City from metro manager of Dallas–Fort Worth, he contemplated moving there immediately. Then he figured that in order to keep 30,000 people from Louisiana northwest to the Canadian border on the ball he was going to have to spend most of his time on the road anyway. What difference did it make where home was if he wasn't going to be in it? For some time he and his wife kept their home in Fort Worth and he rented an apartment in Kansas City to be away from.

From the regional offices all roads lead to Chicago and a dozen more vice presidents including executive vice presidents, each with corporate staffs. They, too, stay on the move. One day Charlie Wagner mentioned that Sidney A. McKnight, executive vice president, was flying down in one of the company planes next day. The two of them were then going down to Houston to see William D. "Wild Bill" Davis, the Houston metro manager who was being transferred to metro manager of Los Angeles, the most vital group of stores in the company. One of the purposes of the visit was to tell him when he got to Los Angeles, to cool it.

It is true that Wild Bill has had his rambunctious moments. Once, to attract people to a special sale, he bought up all the watermelons in the area and gave them away to customers. Another time, when one of his assistants was accused of a financial irregularity and the auditor got nasty about it, he knocked the auditor cold. Any management expert would agree that a word of caution would be called for in this instance, but some might suggest a simpler means of communicating it, like a postcard. They overlook important characteristics of the successful retail manager: possessing the sixth sense of the artist, he has correspondingly thin skin and impressionability. Handle him with care, and in person.

McKnight and other three-star vice presidents report to the president and chief executive officer, Edward S. Donnell. He doesn't just sit around in his office, either. I mentioned one day that he looked a little tired, and he said well, he'd just come back from visiting eight stores on the west coast in two days. And when Donnell visits a store, he visits every department, asking questions and making comments right down to the sales clerk level, which is where we started.

Is all this supervision necessary, and if so, why? Why can't a nice lady sell you a spool of thread without all this brass breathing down her neck? I've asked this question of dozens of people at Wards, including the president and all the vice presidents, and they just look at me, then at their watch. I finally found the answer in "The New Industrial State," written by a man who, as far as I know, never sold anything in his life except his own intellect.

Galbraith, former advisor to presidents and Ambassador of India, is an economist. Rarely has such a personable individual and master of the language stirred up such controversy. Conservatives criticize him because he is an avowed liberal; liberals decry his espousal of the large corporations. Whatever you think of him, he has the explanation of why the chain store sales clerk is like the pea under all those mattresses and the Princess.

The power of a large corporation, Galbraith says, lies in the decision-making ability of its group of specialists who make up the technostructure. Its chief ingredient is the talent of the individuals who comprise it. The large corporations must have this talent in order to survive, and only the large corporations have the resources to hire it.

Translating this into the simple language of consumerism, the reason you can walk into a well-kept store and buy what you want or need from a knowledgeable and courteous sales-person is because of the talent which the mass merchandiser can afford to hire. If, with all this technostructure, it still sometimes doesn't work out to your satisfaction, just try to imagine shopping without it. The goods procured by the sophisticated buying departments would never get on your back or in your house; you'd never get waited on.

Structuring the Technostructure

When Tom Brooker took over Montgomery Ward, he knew that he had to see to it that you, and millions more consumers, *would* get waited on. This is the other, and equal, half of the philosophy of integration of mass manufacturing with mass merchandising. We have seen how he went about getting things to sell, now let's look at how he went about selling them.

At the time of his first report to the stockholders, six months after joining the company, Montgomery Ward had 521 retail stores, 9 mail order plants and 679 catalog stores. Let's skip the catalog operation for the time being, as did Brooker; he had to get the retail show on the road. Some 60 of the stores were new, but they were of different sizes, shapes, and inventories. Four were large department stores in the Chicago area, bought in a lump from The Fair Company.

It's interesting to note in passing that, so different are the operations of local department stores from chain stores, it took The Fair personnel a long time to make the transition. In retrospect Brooker says it would have been more economical to close them down and start them over from scratch with chain-oriented people—if he'd had them.

Nine out of ten retail outlets were from 20 to 35 years old. They were small, located in the downtown section of small and middle size towns, and crummy.

The retail personnel fit in well with their surroundings. Some of the old-time salespeople had a staunch loyalty to Wards, but in general the sales force was a demoralized bunch, just hanging in there. As for the technostructure, its chief ingredient, talent, had either departed, been fired, or gone underground. During the first half of the fifties hundreds of managers had left the company.

What with established Sears, growing Penneys, local department stores—many of them grouped in national consolidations—and the new discount stores, Wards was at a disadvantage in almost every major market in the country. After long deliberation, Brooker decided on a plan to move existing stores to more favorable locations and build new ones in metropolitan centers. He figured the budget would permit 20 relocations and eight new stores a year, for a total of 28.

These stores would be all alike. It was suggested that they vary from city to city. "I know that the prototype system works because I've been involved in it," he said referring to his experience with Sears. "I don't have time to research other methods."

But stores neither build nor run themselves. Brooker had to have knowledgeable people both to develop a prototype and to make up the technostructure. He began with the tall thin man.

When Ed Donnell arrived in Baltimore to take over Montgomery Ward's eastern region, he immediately set out to look over his domain. One of the wonderful things about being in retail is that these people get paid to do what they, and millions of consumers, love to do—go to the store. They even go on their days off. They get the same reactions you do, only more so.

They are more appreciative of a well-run operation, more critical of a sloppy one.

Even in this bunch of storephiles, Ed Donnell stands out. He admits his mania. "I like to get out and feel the merchandise." On his first assignment he had a lot of merchandise to feel: his area took in the entire east coast, extending westward to Ohio and upper New York state in the north and bulging almost to the Mississippi, then to Florida in the south. In it were more than a hundred stores.

Ed is blessed with a super abundance of physical stamina, mental energy, and optimism. Nevertheless, after he'd visited a few of the so-called "green awning stores," which dated back to the days when Main Street merchants let down the awnings on summer afternoons, he wondered what kind of a mess he had let Tom Brooker talk him into.

The stores had been built in the late twenties and thirties, and they looked it. Located in dying downtown areas with little or no parking, they were all built to the same general plan: 50-foot store front, 150 feet deep, three stories with a mezzanine on the first floor. Some had no elevators; some had the kind you pull with ropes. They were poorly lit; many had not been painted since before the war. The wooden floors were smeared with oil; that's cheaper than wax. Air conditioning? Don't be ridiculous. Many a Ward's manager began the day by stoking the coal furnace.

The stores looked alike, but there the consistency ended; Ed could not have imagined that there were so many ways to misrun a business. In Huntsville, Alabama, walking through the sporting goods department one day, he noted a preponderance of national brands, rather than Ward's own private label. Curious, he and the department manager took their coats off and proceeded to list every item—description, stock number, price. It turned out that only one out of every four articles had been procured through the central buying office; 75 per cent of the merchandise had been acquired outside the company, bought from any traveling salesman who happened to be passing through.

This, Ed Donnell found to his horror, was one type of store he was in charge of. Built in 1928, it was still the same in 1961.

How can you offer the consumer a bargain that way? A major advantage of a chain is the capacity to buy large amounts of goods at volume prices and pass on the savings to the consumer. Ed had a pleasant little chat with the people in the store and fired off a report to the buying office suggesting that it make its presence and function better known.

After prowling the stores all day, Ed dictated letters and memos to concerned personnel most of the night. Those were 7 A.M. to midnight days, week after week.

In Baltimore and Washington, he had a totally different problem. The decision had been made to enter the two big metropolitan markets. Three new stores were actually under construction. Ed looked at the sites and plans, and it was like seeing snakes. I asked him later if he'd had a fit, and he replied, "I think that's properly phrasing it."

Ed admitted that there were many things about operating rundown downtown stores that he did not know, but when it came to groups of big stores in metropolitan areas he had a proven record. The new Washington and Baltimore stores, under construction, representing an investment of millions of dollars, were all wrong. They were of different sizes, shapes and styles, and all too small. Stopping construction in progress means money and headaches—long-term financing, interim financing, contracts with builders—but that's what Ed did, dead in its tracks. Then he hurried to Chicago. Brooker listened and backed up his decision; he had gone after the Donnell expertise and he was smart enough to use it.

At that time in the retail industry there were many different approaches to the problem of store location, all involving getting out of downtown. Some retailers, including department stores with local dominance, and Sears with its eminent position in the field, were moving out to individual or free-standing perimeter sites, confident that their customers would follow. Others were beginning to cluster together in shopping centers. Another approach was to maintain a large central operation downtown and scatter smaller stores in centers and suburbs. Some grocery chains adopted the intercept principle—place stores between the main masses of population and the new big stores or centers.

Donnell believed in the shopping center or mall principle, in which two or more major retailers provide a strong nucleus for a great assortment of merchandise and services. "People go where the power is," he says. In the metropolitan areas there should be several of these power centers, with Wards in a reasonable number. But regardless of wherever and how many the locations, the stores should be uniform in size and layout.

"What he wanted was big prototype stores," Brooker told me later, "and he was 100 per cent right. Of course I knew we had to have them, but I didn't know how to do it. Ed had the knowledge. He got all of our regional managers, our display people, our engineers, and we sat down with them and made them agree as to what we should have.

"The operation of a metro district was the same thing. I knew we had to have such an operation and I could study the essential elements with the technicians, but we needed someone who had run a metro district to give that final approval and flavor to it. That's what Ed had."

With plans and backing, Donnell went back to Baltimore and started up construction on the three stores again—his way. By 1972 the Washington and Baltimore metros contained a total of 14 stores, and were the most profitable in the company. In dollar volume, either one would rank above many corporations listed on the stock exchanges.

While Donnell was beginning a new concept for Montgomery Ward, built from the ground up, in the east, a pilot program based on existing stores was underway in the west. In San Diego Wards had three stores, but each was so different from the others that it might as well have been a part of another operation.

To straighten out the San Diego mess, Brooker chose Elwood Powell, one of a small group of top-flight executives who had stayed on with Wards during the horrible years. At the time he was a 30-year veteran, with experience both at headquarters and in retailing on the west coast. He also had Brooker's backing: "We'll send you all the help you need."

Some of the problems in San Diego were technical. There was no central warehouse, no central credit, no central repair service. Each store was on its own. With experts flying out at his request, Powell centralized those operations.

A major problem was advertising. As each store carried different inventories of merchandise, the managers could hardly get together on which items to push in one ad. You'd see a good buy advertised, then go to the store nearest you and not find it.

Powell inaugurated weekly meetings at which he announced how many inches of advertising the budget would stand, and then threw the selection of what would be featured to the group. They wrangled and hassled. One week, after the usual bitter argument everybody finally agreed to advertise toasters except the housewares department manager of one store. His mother must have been frightened by a pop-up toaster, because he refused to carry them in stock. Powell sat back and enjoyed the fun as the previously divided factions joined forces and overrode the anti-toaster manager. Once they were all agreed, they were all involved. From then on there was less wrangling, more positive and concerted action on what to promote and how to make sure it was available in each store. A basic inventory common to all was agreed upon. Within less than a year Montgomery Ward was no longer losing money in San Diego, but making it. And a pilot program had been developed which could be transferred to other localities.

A city with a unique problem was Houston. For decades the only Ward store in Houston was located in a downtown section which gradually turned into a black ghetto. During the short period of expansion before Tom Brooker took over, three new stores had been built on the outskirts of the city. They were practically empty. The white folks continued to think of Wards as the black man's store, and the handsome new buildings frightened away the old Ward customers. The store managers didn't seem to know what to do. Houston was losing a million dollars a year.

Into this seemingly hopeless situation Brooker sent the new golden boy, Frederick H. Veach. Blond, with white teeth that blind you when he smiles, which is most of the time, Fred was 41 years old—younger than any of the managers he would supervise—and he came directly from one of Sears' largest and most successful stores, San Jose, California. Veach had been doing a bigger business in that one Sears store than all four Ward stores in Houston combined. He didn't realize it, but he and Houston were selected for each other for bigger reasons than salvaging one metro district. He was being thrown to the Ward wolves to learn to survive.

For three-fourths of his life, ever since his father went to work for Sears when Fred was nine, he had been a rootin' tootin' member of the team. After graduating from UCLA, Fred was sent to the Sears store in Beloit, Wisconsin. The manager took him to the receiving department, said, "It's all yours," and left.

Fred was all alone with about a ton of just-arrived merchandise. He knew exactly what to do with it. He could quote any sentence out of the 110-page shipping and receiving manual. He worked in receiving—six in the morning until one the next, six days a week—for about five months, then handled the office for a while—daily order report, sales report, cash, office procedures, advertising—then managed the sporting goods department. He was the only person in the department; he ate lunch and dinner on the job.

The zone manager came by and criticized his paper work. "Don't you know how to delegate work?" he asked. "I'm sorry, but I don't have anybody to delegate it to," Fred said. The zone manager chewed out the store manager, and Fred got a part-time assistant—"the greatest luxury I ever had in my life."

Fred was 32 years old when he got his first store—the youngest store manager in Sears. He was still in his thirties when, three managerships later, he took over San Jose, Sears' ninth largest store. He had everything: an eventful past, an exciting present, a future to dream on. With the encouragement of the enlightened Sears management he participated on a leadership level in many civic activities. He liked the idea of volunteerism, of people taking care of themselves and each other, rather than leaving it up to the government. He got a special kick out of taking over a sloppily-run agency and making it efficient. His wife, Peggy, told him, "Oh, it's just your superego."

Into this paradise came the shattering announcement that Ed Donnell was leaving Sears! It affected Fred deeply and emotionally, even personally. *How can he do this to me?* There just couldn't be any valid reason why a man like Ed Donnell would leave Sears, Roebuck. And for Montgomery Ward!

A month later, at 6:30 in the morning, the phone rang. Fred was sound asleep but he woke up fast when the call turned out to be from Tom Brooker, calling from the east coast. He suggested they get together for a chat. Fred, flattered by the call— after all, Tom Brooker had been a vice president of Sears when Fred was bouncing boxes in Beloit—agreed. On Brooker's next trip to the west coast they had dinner together in Brooker's suite in the Fairmont Hotel in San Francisco. "It was a beautiful big dinner brought up there for the two of us, wine, and me a little country kid, you know, and Tom Brooker, for crying out loud, unbelievable."

So Fred began rationalizing: Brooker had assured him that Wards had a great future and offered him more money and it was a big opportunity and he had the Sears store in San Jose at the point where he'd have to stay up nights to figure out how to hurt sales and profits and he was only working about 30 hours at the store and putting in another 30 for the community and maybe beginning to get a little lazy. Brooker asked him at least to go to Baltimore to see Ed Donnell, and he did. Ed impressed the daylights out of him with his regional office and staff, and reconfirmed all that Brooker had told him about the future of Wards.

As for the immediate job, he would be in charge of a metropolitan district, consisting of four big stores: status plus challenge, for Houston was losing money. Brooker said he thought Veach could turn the situation around in three years. Fred instantly began wondering if he couldn't do it in two and a half years, maybe even two. He didn't realize that he was being manipulated by a master; Tom Brooker is as skillful at playing men as bonefish. Veach had snapped at the bait and was hooked. He traded gods and went to Houston.

I once asked Fred what he thought of Wards during his days with Sears, and he replied, instantly, "Utter contempt." After the war, Sears had sprinted forward dramatically, moving out into big new stores, while Wards remained mired in the same old locations and let them go to pot. The managers he knew were frightened and insecure. They could be, and were, fired on the spot for trivialities. Fred did not know of any who participated in community affairs; they didn't even attend service club luncheons.

But these were green awning store managers. In Houston's new stores Fred expected to find a different type. He did not. The stores were not well managed. Though there's a lot of behind-the-scenes activity in running any facility that serves the public, to the customer the important thing is your contact with the sales person. Merchandising departments in Chicago, New York and Los Angeles can knock themselves out procuring the finest of goods at the lowest of prices, but all their work goes for nothing if you're turned off by the sales clerk. That person must really want to do a good job, for personal incentive, for Wards, and for you. That feeling has to come from the top, and if those at the top are themselves living in fear, they can hardly inspire those on the firing line.

One of the managers was J. M. Burns, who had started with Montgomery Ward in 1928, served the company with intelligence, loyalty and enthusiasm for 25 years, then been fired brutally and without real cause. The new management had prevailed upon him to come back. Now he was manager of a handsome new store in Houston and in comes a new hatchet man from Sears on top of him. Here we go again.

After studying the overall situation, Veach concluded that the acceptance of Wards by the people of Houston was only a matter of time. Managing the business properly, promoting and presenting good values, would bring in the people. The important thing was to make sure that they were made welcome when they did come in. His greatest contribution to the Houston metro therefore, would be to instill mutual trust, respect and confidence between all the layers of personnel, right up to the managers and himself. He had to overcome both the long-term fear and the immediate resentment against this young squirt from Sears.

Fred Veach came equipped with one necessary attribute: he is a natural, likable, warmly candid human being. Over the years he has added another: he has studied human nature and management in the classroom and special institutes, and in person-to-person relationships. He's an enthusiast on psychology and motivation and to replace fear with inspiration, he used every trick in his extensive repertoire.

He recognized Jim Burns as being potentially one of the finest merchants he had ever seen. The manager of the appliance department of Burns' store, another veteran of the harsh years, was also most capable. His appliance department practically kept the store alive, but he had an aversion to service contracts. Veach talked Burns into a big program to sell service contracts. They set a modest goal and constantly prodded the appliance manager with persuasion rather than threats until he finally reached it.

On that day Veach hired a special messenger in a gaudy uniform. He had a small pillow covered with gold cloth. The messenger was driven to the front door of the store and from there, carrying the gold pillow in front of him, attracting everybody's attention, he walked through the store to the appliance department and proffered the gold pillow to the appliance manager. On it rested a telegram. In front of the gathering crowd, the appliance manager lifted the telegram off the gold pillow and opened it. It was from metro manager Veach, congratulating him and expressing Veach's personal appreciation for an outstanding contribution.

Word of the golden pillow spread through the Ward stores in Houston. It was the symbol of a new era, management appreciation. As for the appliance manager, from then on he sold service contracts like crazy.

One year from the time Fred Veach arrived in Houston it was out of the red. Veach jumped to vice president of the western region, in charge of almost 100 stores extending from Arizona to Alaska, and then to a post created just for him, vice-president–organization administration.

In their successes in three separate parts of the country Donnell, Powell and Veach contributed much more than profit, much as Montgomery Ward needed it. Whether you're putting together a team, a technostructure or a bowlful of mayonnaise, selecting and blending the ingredients requires expertise. In making his selections, Brooker had only two places to go, Sears and the existing group at Wards. Department-store people had already proven themselves incapable of adjusting to the catalog-chain type of merchandising, and Penneys had not yet matured. But Tom could not buy all the talent he needed at Sears, nor could he rely exclusively on the talent he found at Wards; there wasn't enough left. That meant he had to take the best of what he had on hand at Wards, and blend in the Sears infusion, drop by drop.

He himself had been the first drop. His million-dollar investment started the process of acceptance, and his quiet, patient, thoroughgoing activity on the company's behalf completed the blending. Almost without straining, Tom Brooker staged a marvelous performance. In meetings the country over as well as in Chicago he demonstrated two contradictions. He showed himself to be a firm boss who was setting the policy and wanted no argument. But he also came to be accepted for what he was, a benevolent chief executive who desperately needed and would welcome advice and cooperation in making that policy work.

The next drop of Sears oil was Ed Donnell. Through his knowledge of the metro market and his own personable manner of selling it to Ward's regional managers, he earned their respect. Once he had it, Brooker could bring him into headquarters as executive vice president, the second ex-Sears man to take a position of power over the old timers.

There the first power struggle occurred. It was waged in the corporate arena before sophisticated spectators who knew every trick in the game, and who also knew it could only end in complete victory for one gladiator, bloody defeat for the other.

The prize was the presidency. The position became open when John Barr resigned after 10 years as chairman of the board and was succeeded by Brooker. In commending his service, the board noted that he had "accomplished his objective of bringing into the company an effective, capable management team." In a sense he had accomplished that objective too well. For all of Brooker's patience and tolerance, he was shocked when he read in the paper that Barr had sold a large block of Montgomery Ward stock. He sympathized with Barr's need for money to purchase a new home, but he couldn't comprehend that manner of raising it—selling stock in his own company. Barr's long association with Montgomery Ward ended in a most amicable way. He was offered the position of dean of Northwestern University's graduate school of management and accepted it.

Thus Brooker became chairman of the board—but who would be president? People involved with any national organization can understand the basic issue, for it represented the classic conflict between the home office, as represented by the merchandising department, and the field. It is a civil war which rages incessantly.

To the people at Wards, who, as Brooker noted from his own intense personal experience "were brought up in turmoil," the struggle was of direct, personal interest. The internecine battle for survival was a part of their lives, just as violence is a part of the life of a professional football player. They had lived with it for years. Now they were witnessing the most exciting episode yet. The identity of the gladiators contributed to the interest; they were men of two completely different styles.

Charles W. Wood, vice president of merchandising, was entrenched in his position. Though not a Ward veteran — he had been brought in by the Barr administration — he had the characteristics which enabled him to seize power and hold on.

"Charlie would stop at nothing in his fight for power," Brooker said of him. "That was one of his values. A fierce sense of competition is good in this business. It puts people on their mettle, forces them to say what they're going to do and then do it. Charlie had a department store background and never really understood our type of operation, but he was a great merchant."

In the other corner of the championship ring was Ed Donnell. He was an entirely different type of gladiator. To the old Ward crowd, who accepted the knife in the back as a fundamental weapon, his style was puzzling. He didn't seem to know he was in a fight. Though a major portion of his duties was to travel extensively, training and encouraging his managers during long stretches of 18-hour days, the onlookers were amazed when he actually did it. One of the established precepts of corporate warfare is, never turn your back on your opponent.

Yet Donnell would not only disappear from the home office for days, even weeks, he would make his absence known by pouring in communiques from the field. At that time Ward's merchandising techniques were in pitiful shape by Donnell's standards, and the critical reports he fired in from afar triggered counterpunches from Wood — delivered to Brooker in person.

"I'd come in on Monday after being out for a week and find

that Wood had spent that time pouring venom into Tom," Donnell said later. "I didn't like it, but I didn't let it keep me from doing my job of trying to build this company in the field."

The impression of the onlookers that Donnell didn't seem to know he was in a personal fight for survival was correct. He didn't. He had come to Montgomery Ward with the firm impression that he would be president if he delivered, and he had a quiet inner confidence that he was delivering. Nor did he ever think that even if he did not deliver, Wood was a qualified candidate for the presidency. Wood, of course, had other ideas. And the spectators, who had seen men with less on the ball than Wood bulldoze their way up in the old Ward arena, were not about to write him off.

As for the referee, Tom Brooker, he was not ready to declare a winner. True, he had personally sought out Ed Donnell and brought him into the company. But was Ed ready for the presidency? As for Wood, Brooker considered that he was making a contribution to Wards. His forcefulness was an asset. Further, Brooker wished to instill a sense of security in the company. Finally, if Wood did go, who would take his place? His successor would have to possess both great ability and the trust, confidence and respect of those he would lead. That combination doesn't come along often.

Rather than end the battle by booting out one of the contestants, Brooker tried to bring about a cessation of hostilities. He sent the gladiators off to Florida for a week of sensitivity training. They played golf together. "They were less hostile for about six months," Brooker said later, chuckling.

That ended the first round. Donnell could be considered the winner; on Brooker's recommendation he was elected president of Montgomery Ward.

But the fight was not over; indeed, it was intensified. Donnell had the coveted title of president, true, but his direct authority covered only field operations. Wood, as vice president of merchandising, continued to report directly to the chief executive officer, Tom Brooker. Apparently he continued to report in the same way. Once, in a rosy mood at a social gathering, he asked Donnell if there weren't some way they could work together in a more friendly fashion. "One thing that would be helpful is to get that knife out of my back," Donnell said.

The sense of hostility spread throughout the building. "Wood was trying so hard to cut Donnell's throat that he disrupted the entire company," one of the outside directors said.

But all along Donnell was building rapport with the people in the field. They were mass merchandisers, they spoke his language, they saw what he was accomplishing. Away from the arena a significant development was taking place: Jim Lutz was winning friends and influencing people. His success as a national merchandise manager demonstrated both his personal capability and his thorough knowledge of mass procurement. With that record, Brooker could then safely elevate him to the vice presidency of the north central region, headquartered in Chicago. There, too, he earned the respect of his teammates.

Though there must be a sense of competition between merchandising and operations, there must also be cooperation and balance. The field had now come to the conclusion that they had no confidence in the situation. The four regional vice presidents wanted firm and clear balances between merchandising and operations. They demanded a statement of policy. Wood took it on himself to write it, and presented it to them at a meeting held in Donnell's office in September 1966.

The statement was too strong. It would tilt the balance in favor of the merchandising department in general, Wood in particular. The four vice presidents rejected it. The shouting went on all day long. Brooker looked in from time to time. He had no intention of making a corporate decision based on the recommendations of the field, but it would be wise to get a reading. And the reading indicated that the situation had become intolerable.

At the end of the day Donnell went in Brooker's office. "I've reached a conclusion," he said. "We don't have the support of

Jim Lutz and his vice presidents, clockwise from top, John Marchese, Bill Allred, Curt Ward, Dick Abbott, and Chett Eckman.

the merchandising department. If we are to work together as a team, we can't go on like this."

"Are you thinking corporately?" Brooker asked.

"I have to be," Donnell said. "The success of the corporation depends on its ability to pull together."

"What do you suggest?" Brooker asked.

"Wood has got to go."

"Hmmm," Brooker said. He made no commitment. Corporate decisions of such sensitivity are not made under pressure, but in the loneliness of the mind. . . .

About ten o'clock next morning Ed Donnell was sitting in his office when Jack Foster, vice president–personnel, walked by after leaving Brooker's office, and stuck his head in the door.

"He's out," Foster said. Ed Donnell had won the battle. Jim Lutz, with Donnell's strong endorsement, became vice president — merchandising.

Everybody loves a good fight, and a victor had emerged in a clear-cut decision, if not a knockout. But perhaps of more significance to the thousands of employees of Montgomery Ward, and its millions of customers, the discrete elements of the technostructure had become united. The group which forced the showdown was divided right down the middle: half had a long background with Wards, half had come from Sears. They supported the winner, regardless of his Sears background, because they thought he was the best man for Wards.

Of the four regional vice presidents, two, Lutz and Fred Veach, had like Donnell been dropped into the Ward blender. The other two needed no blending; they had a combined total of more than a half century with Montgomery Ward. They were Sid McKnight and Marty Munger.

One of Sid McKnight's earliest memories from his childhood in Brinkley, Arkansas, was wanting to be governor of Arkansas when he grew up. That ambition was sidetracked in favor of becoming an admiral in the Navy, but though he won the competition for appointment to Annapolis, a mild case of astigmatism prevented his accepting it. He wound up at Louisiana State University on, of all things, a music scholarship. Sid must have been surely the most aggressive baritone in the chorus. On graduation he had several job offers, but although he knew nothing about retailing, he liked the idea of competing with other trainees.

At that time, '37, Wards was expanding, and there was something to compete for—manager of his own store. To the aggressive young retailer this is the territory it is imperative to reach and to hold. More than any mockingbird declaring his dominion from the top of his tree, more than any chimpanzee shrieking defiance at a potential intruder, the store manager posits the territorial imperative. You can see it in his every action, hear it in his every word.

For all his competitiveness and strong baritone, McKnight is a likable and soft-voiced territory holder. He has always believed that he should leave a town better off than he found it, and in his jump from store to store in the south and midwest, he tried to put his belief into effect through working with Chambers of Commerce, civic organizations, Boy Scouts, and of course, music clubs. He likes to remember Emporia, Kansas, where he had his first store at age 27. He'd come home at night tired, and maybe a little out of sorts because of something that had gone wrong that day. His wife, Jean, would suggest that they go downtown and walk around. They'd check the store windows, and Jean would comment on what some of the other stores were featuring in their displays. Ideas would start churning around in Sid's head and he'd forget that he was tired and cross in his eagerness to get down to the store early next morning.

He loved the responsibility of managing a store, of being in charge. Wherever he was, he tried to hire the best people, and attract the finest customers. He also attracted offers at higher salaries from other organizations, and, being human, he considered them. Years later, talking to me in his big paneled office on Mahogany Row on the eighth floor at head-

Sid McKnight, left, and his regional vice presidents: Wayne Matschullat, Bob Harrell, Bob Elliott, Charlie Wagner and Marty Munger.

quarters one day, he suddenly closed his eyes at the pain of what might have been. "How close I came to walking away from all this."

Why he didn't, during the terrible fifties, he really doesn't know. It's a corny thing to say, but then Sid is a corny guy in a nice way—anyway, I think Sid McKnight stayed because he really loved Montgomery Ward.

He was a regional manager with headquarters in Kansas City—the position is a vice presidency today—when John Barr took over. Sid saw the department store people come and go, and it was with no great hope that he went to Chicago to meet the new Moses, Tom Brooker. In one session he realized that here at last was The Leader. He hurried back to Kansas City, called a staff meeting and told tham all about Tom Brooker. "He looks like Gary Cooper!" he said. He didn't care where Brooker came from, and he didn't care how many people Brooker would bring in from where he came from. Sid had had competition before.

When Donnell became president of the company, and a new man was needed to be in direct personal contact with the people out in the field, Sid McKnight's years of loyalty paid off. He was brought to Chicago and became senior vice president to deal directly with the people in the field. By 1971 he was an executive vice president with a salary in six figures and stock options. It couldn't happen to a nicer guy.

Like Sid McKnight, Martin D. Munger went with Wards on graduation from college, in his case the University of Michigan. As a farm boy outside Batavia, New York, Marty had bought his first shotgun through the Montgomery Ward catalog. It cost $12, and he put a lot of game on the table with it. Seven years later, when the Ward sporting goods department in Batavia needed extra help for the hunting season, Munger went to work selling shotguns. He left Wards for a while to be an insurance salesman, but he didn't like the idea of making money selling people more high-cost insurance than they needed. He had a little trouble sleeping at night, and he came back to Wards. He slept soundly.

Tough talking, positive, ambitious, Munger has had his run-ins at Wards. Once he was demoted from manager to assistant manager. Another company offered him three times his salary, but he was too mad to quit. He stayed on to prove who was right and who was wrong, and, well, the other man is no longer with the company. Years later, during the regime of the department store people, he was regional manager in St. Paul when he had a disagreement with the vice president. Nothing personal, just technical differences between running chain stores and department stores.

This time he was demoted all the way down to store manager. "It was a destroying experience, a traumatic experience." He spent a month in Florida recovering. Again he had offers to go with other companies. Why didn't he take them?

"Because I had confidence in Montgomery Ward, that's why," he said. "And I still do."

Marty managed the Denver store with such relentless efficiency that he made more money there than he had as regional manager. When Brooker came in, bringing with him people from Sears, Munger welcomed them. "At that time we had the fewest number of capable administrators or merchants in the history of Wards. We'd reached the lowest point. Sears had been able to get good people because they were opening new stores, expanding their business, offering challenge and opportunity. I'd been suffering a communications problem for years and now we had people I could talk to. It was no problem, it was a thrill."

All the time, after being kicked out of his job as regional manager, Marty was determined to get it back. When Donnell left Region 1 Munger was sent in, not as regional manager, but as vice president. He's a corporate officer, member of the board of directors. He's proud and happy. "Sure, I aspire to be president of the company, but I'm not praying for Ed Donnel to be killed in an airplane accident. I'm where I can make a contribution to the company and I'm making it."

Tom Brooker, seated in front of a composite photo of the team he put together, tells author Boo Herndon how he did it.

The Price of Talent

Tom Brooker admitted to me that one of his severe under-estimates when taking the presidency of Montgomery Ward was the number of people he could rely on. He had to go out and get more. Dick Abbott, musing one day, gave an example why. "The first meeting I attended, with Mr. Brooker and the regional managers, you could cut the air with a knife. Nobody spoke up. It was a one-way street. Mr. Brooker got almost no communication out of those men. They had learned the hard way to keep their mouths shut."

Fear permeated Wards all the way through the techno-structure down to the salesperson. Brooker had to import men of bold capability into procurement, service, credit and every major corporate function as well as into retail operations. His enticements were challenge and opportunity, and, of course, money. As he was buying people who not only made good salaries but had built up personal equity in Sears' liberal fringe benefits, he had to pay through the nose to get them.

It is not wise to let two people with comparable responsibilities and positions know that one is making a lot more dough than the other, and as a result Wards has the craziest payroll system I've ever heard of. In the military, in civil service, in big corporations like the Ford Motor Company, executives have numerical designations with salary ranges. Henry Ford II, for example, as chairman of the board, is in grade 28 with a salary bracket of $181,000–272,000. He was, incidentally, most interested to read this in my book on Ford and checked up on me to see if I was right. Nobody had ever bothered to tell him that he had a number.

Wards had a personnel classification with commensurate compensations, but it also has the Executive Payroll. What its members make is known only to the very top echelon of management, the Internal Revenue Service and a lady named Lucille De Coster. She is a tall, cool-looking well-dressed blonde, and, oh boy, has she got status. She is in charge of the executive payroll and not only knows exactly how much every executive is making now, but who's going to get a raise and who is going to get fired. You'll never find Miss Lucille De Coster standing alone at an office cocktail party. There was so much talk about her at the beginning that even John Barr, the chairman of the board, was curious. He asked her to come up to his office just to take a look.

To keep the payroll clerks from knowing too much, individuals on the executive payroll are designated by a special code to which only Miss Lucille De Coster has the key. She has never missed a day at the office, not even when she had a whiplash injury. At income tax time she fills out the corporate tax forms listing the compensation of members of the executive payroll, totals the amount and writes it on the outside of a brown envelope containing the forms. She seals the envelope and delivers it personally to the tax department at Wards. There the figure is entered in the proper place, and the brown envelope, still sealed, is delivered to the Internal Revenue Service. Until the envelope is opened by the IRS, only the eyes of Miss Lucille De Coster have seen the compensation plus reimbursed expenses paid each member of the executive payroll.

When the executive payroll began, the minimum figure was $20,000. Since then it has been raised to $25,000, and again to $35,000. On occasion executives have received raises which put them over the old minimum, and have come charging in to Miss Lucille De Coster to raise hell about not being put on the executive payroll. She must tactfully explain that they haven't made it yet. On one occasion an executive received a raise which put him almost, but not quite, to the executive payroll minimum. He haughtily turned it down, preferring to wait until he got enough to put him among the ranks of the exalted.

Even in her position as goddess of the payroll, Miss Lucille De Coster remains human. She loves Montgomery Ward. She drives to work in the morning, in her convertible, sometimes wearing a mink coat. "On clear days when I see the white building gleaming in the sunlight, with the statue of that crazy lady on top, I feel good all over."

An unusual salary negotiation occurred in the case of Joseph L. Brannon. Joe, a man of distinctive physiognomy and taste in neckwear, had built up 34 years' worth of retirement benefits and 8,000 shares of stock when he had a disagreement with the Sears management. A fixture of Phoenix and a crap-shooting crony of Senator Barry Goldwater, he wanted to stay there and could well afford it. But Joe isn't happy unless he's working hard for more money. "It's a vice," he explained.

But Tom Brooker and Ed Donnell knew Joe well, and knew what he could contribute in any capacity in Phoenix or anywhere else. But they also knew he could afford not to work. Donnell wrote him a tentative letter asking if he'd be available on a consultant basis. Joe wrote back in the affirmative — provided the consultation required 60 hours a week. Brooker, unflapped by unorthodox characters, then called Joe and asked him to take over the Ward stores in Phoenix. He named a figure. "I'll take it," Joe said immediately.

For years Joe and Brooker have had a standing bet on the outcome of the game between their respective alma maters, Notre Dame and USC. Some time later, settling the bet, Brannon said, slyly: "I'd have taken the job for half as much."

"I'd have given you twice as much," Brooker said.

It had been Brooker's intention to bring in only key people to provide guidance and expertise. But this was repeated on every level. Joe Brannon, for example, for his three Phoenix stores, hired executive personnel in store management, merchandise management, district merchandising and department management. "I wanted people to spread the gospel: *It ain't no sin to make a profit.*"

Corporate executives go overboard just like everybody else, and some hired Sears personnel just to get in the act. Sears became known as The Academy. "I thought of quitting Wards and going over to Sears," one bitter veteran commented.

"Then they'd hire me back for the money they won't give me now."

He was not the only Ward veteran who resented the Sears influx. Some schism remained, and will probably continue. Nor did all the Sears newcomers work out. In an expanding organization so well structured, so deep in advisory personnel, individuals could make a reasonable advance with only a fair amount of talent. But Wards was only beginning to develop a technostructure of talent, and some Sears alumni couldn't cut it on their own. Many Ward veterans, on the other hand, after grim years of using the utmost ingenuity to keep customers coming in to green awning stores, surprised even themselves with their performance in selling consistently good merchandise in handsome new stores under capable guidance.

Many observers of the battle of the retailers have wondered how Wards was able to obtain so many managers from Sears. Instant advancement was a big reason, of course. But another reason was the sheer luck in staging the raid during a period when Sears was suffering dissension. It had begun when the board of directors was faced with the choice of a new president. The contenders were vice presidents Austin Cushman and Edward Gudeman. Eddie Gudeman was the senior and a a man looked upon almost with reverence by the people I know who worked with him.

Of all the people I talked to in this great industry, only Eddie Gudeman articulated with intense fervor and sincerity a sense of altruistic service to his fellow man through mass merchandising. Gudeman, from a cultured family, had literally drifted into Sears. It was one of the first companies to actively seek college graduates and Gudeman just walked in one morning, said he was one (Harvard '27) and was hired.

He doesn't think he would have stayed in retailing if he had been connected with, say, a Fifth Avenue store clothing wealthy women, but at Sears he believed that he was helping to provide the highest standard of living for the American people. He didn't fully realize this himself until the early thirties, when he was a refrigerator buyer. Popular brand electric refrigerators were then selling for $220 up. Gudeman and his supplier developed a refrigerator that was functional and sold for $129.50. "Frankly," he told me, "it was beautiful. I looked at that refrigerator, and I thought of the people who would be able to have the comfort and benefit of electric refrigeration, and I was *proud.*"

But for all his dedication to mass merchandising, and his ability to put that dedication into black figures on a balance sheet, Eddie Gudeman never had a chance to be president of Sears. General Robert E. Wood, the ruler of the empire, though he himself had hired Gudeman in the first place, did not want a Jewish president. To avoid a division in the board of directors, he canceled out Cushman too, and made Charles Kellstadt, a dark horse, president. Many of the Sears people resented the treatment of Eddie Gudeman, others the arbitrary elimination of Cushman. Kellstadt's own blunt manner didn't help things. Eddie Gudeman was not the only executive who resigned, nor did all those who left go to Wards. But a climate was established which enabled Brooker to have somewhat easier pickings.

All this is now past history. General Wood is dead; Kellstadt and Cushman, who later jumped the presidency to become chairman of the board, retired. Eddie Gudeman's resignation enabled him to fulfill his self-imposed obligation to serve his country, as Assistant Secretary of Commerce, then become a partner with Lehman Brothers in New York. Brooker asked him to join him at Wards—"you be chairman and I'll be president or I'll be chairman and you be president, it doesn't make any difference"—but he chose instead to serve actively as consultant and member of the board.

Instead of displaying rancor against Montgomery Ward, Arthur M. Wood, president of Sears, discussed the rival operation in sincerely complimentary terms. "They're making a good turnaround," he said. "And we wish them well, especially since their success can largely be attributed to Sears alumni."

Although Wood knew that I was writing a book based primarily on Montgomery Ward, I had had no trouble reaching him, and he was most pleasant. I expressed some surprise at his equitable attitude and he said, "Well, they've got a right to live too. We much prefer a viable competitor than one retrogressing. Competition is good for all of us, keeps us on our toes, encourages us to do better market research. We've learned a lot of things since Wards came on the scene. Sure, it would be nice if we had a monopoly, but life under such circumstances wouldn't be very interesting, and it wouldn't put as great a demand on our ingenuity. The consumer benefits from both of us working hard. It results in a combined reputation for quality and service, one we can stand on. It's good for the customer."

Wards and Sears do not compete against each other in many major markets, and in others they and Penneys compete together, in effect, against discounters, particularly those dealing in low-end merchandise. On occasion two of the chains will go into a new shopping center together. They operate on the theory that together they will attract more customers to the center, and each is confident that with more potential consumers milling around, it will get its share of the business.

Further, Ed Donnell points out that Sears is a $10 billion business, Penneys $4.8 billion, and Wards $2.5 billion. It is not Ward's policy to play catch-up ball even with Penneys, let alone Sears. "We're not shooting to be the biggest," he said, "but the best. Our goal is high profitability."

The Invasion of Los Angeles

One major marketing area where Sears and Wards have come closest to locking horns is Los Angeles. In this vital, growing area Wards is making a determined effort to increase its markets in the face of a preponderance of Sears stores. Its charts of the L.A. metropolitan area resemble military maps,

with population areas and sites of present, future and contemplated stores plainly marked. Sears surely has similar
maps.

The decision to go into this market was made by Tom
Brooker with both planning and boldness. In Ed Donnell's
first week at Wards, he and Brooker discussed Los Angeles.
Donnell said that it would take a lot of courage and cost a lot of
money to enter the L.A. market. Both factors should be taken
into consideration before committing the company to that
course.

Brooker looked at him with his I-dare-you expression. "Well,
Ed," he asked, "isn't that a market you want to be in?"

"It's a market I'd like to be in, but I don't like the cost of
entering."

"Well, we're already in it," Brooker said, "and I think it
will be worth improving our position." In Brookerese this
meant *Charge!*

Why was it necessary to be in Los Angeles? First, that's
where the money is. If it is not the best market in the United
States, then it is second only to New York—and New York
is impossible. The number of stores it would take to make any
impact at all in New York is out of sight. And even if Wards
had unlimited money and could plop down stores from Con-
necticut to New Jersey, from Long Island to Westchester,
would the customers pour in? Maybe not. New Yorkers are
committed to national brand names sold by existing department stores and discounters. They never heard of Ward names
like Signature and Riverside and Brentshire and Carol Brent
and Airline and Powr-Kraft or, for that matter, Montgomery
Ward—and they don't want to hear of it. New York is out. That
leaves Los Angeles. Four per cent of that market would bring
in $150 million.

Second, style and style leadership emerge on the west
coast. New York is two beats behind southern California in
style. Los Angeles is definitely the greatest market for women's
sportswear in the world. It's the test tube of fashion. Wards

has to maintain a buying office in New York, but, since the L.A. buying office gets an immediate feedback it can be relatively more effective.

When the invasion began, Wards had three stores in the Los Angeles metropolitan area. Sears had twenty, each about ten miles apart. Obviously the perfect location for the new Ward stores would be midway between the existing Sears stores. The first question that popped into my mind, and into yours, too, I bet, was suppose Sears would put in additional stores midway between their existing ones. Tom smiled tolerantly when I asked it.

"Well," he said, "in business you expect your competitors to be sound. A customer will travel about five miles to shop. If Sears put in a new store midway between two existing ones, the customers in that area would simply transfer from the old stores to the new."

Within eighteen months after the march on L.A. began, Wards put in four new stores. Then came the realization that they had pushed too fast. The slow conversion of The Fair stores in Chicago was still costing money. The stores in Los Angeles were also operating at a loss. Wards had neither the capital for more stores, nor instant personnel to staff them properly. About this time Sears clamped down on the exodus to Wards. The invasion came to a slowdown.

That left the company in a bind. In retailing, newspaper advertising is vital. It's vital to the newspaper, too. Fred Bliesener, Ward's national advertising director, is convinced that many newspaper subscribers don't pay much attention to the news columns. They get their information on current events from TV and radio; what they really look at in the papers is who's selling what for how much. But that's another story. In Los Angeles, Wards must advertise in the *Los Angeles Times,* and its rates are high. Wards was paying to reach a lot of people who had no convenient store to go to. The heavy advertising budget—7 per cent of sales—kept the stores from making money, but new stores would get a free ride. Sears, now up to 25 stores, was getting its advertising for only 2½ per cent. Wards had no choice but to blow the bugle and resume the invasion. Donnell recommended a new commander, Robert M. Elliott, for metro district manager.

Elliott came into Wards straight out of Washington and Jefferson in 1949. Other men's poison was Bob Elliott's meat, for at the time the company was deliberately lopping off experienced, high-salaried managers and putting in younger fellows who'd work for less. Bob was one of them.

"I'm in love with the retail business," he said. "I got my first store in three years. I was making $8,000 a year and I was a big man in town. Even during the worst years I was enough of an egotist to think I was going to keep going right on up."

In less than 20 years Bob Elliott made it to the most crucial Ward metro district. By 1971 Wards had ten stores in Los Angeles with two scheduled to open each year from then on. The advertising budget was $4 million, with each additional store reducing the average and reaping the reward. "We're gonna make millions here," Bob said.

Los Angeles is way out. People in the huge sprawling area talk differently, wear their hair differently, dress differently from anywhere else in the United States, and from each other. One store, in a Mexican-American area, has Spanish speaking people in every department. Another is slapped down right between the wealthy community of Beverly Hills and a black neighborhood. Elliot sent me out to see it during the mad months before it opened.

I found Walter Golden, who turned 30 just two days before, and had been with Wards for only two years as director of the hard core unemployment program, happily and enthusiastically building his territory as manager of C and D lines. He'd been successful in attracting and training young blacks and this was his reward. He was a militant, all right, but not just a black militant.

"I never wanted to be a black manager of a black program,"

Videotaping interview training session for hard-core "unemployables."

he said. "I wanted to help everybody get a chance. We've got some white people who are on the wrong side of the economic boundary, too. The program I ran was successful not because I was black but because I knew the retail business. It's a rare occasion when a man gets a chance to do something for his country, for society in general and for his own particular ethnic group, and I made the most of it. Now we're going to make this store a success."

Back in Elliott's office, he beamed happily at Golden's optimism. "That's the kind of spirit we've got here," he said. "This is an area of vast geography and great retail growth. We can't overstore it. The important thing is to build up the confidence in the department managers. They've got great merchandise to sell. Let them determine what to push in the big advertising specials, and how and when to do it. All these layers of people are here only to provide the department managers with advice and help. They have the pride of authorship. This company rests on them."

Elliott did not stay on to see his metro district make the millions he predicted in 1972, because by that time he was running the entire western region as a corporate officer and member of the board of Montgomery Ward. But his method of building business in Los Angeles still typifies what the whole thing comes down to: the vast procurement of merchandise, the technostructure of talent, all directed down to the pride of territory where you, the customer, make the purchase.

Wired For Hunting

Some of us, involved in what we choose to think are more sophisticated pursuits than buying something for a dollar and selling it for 40 cents more, may not immediately understand the enthusiasm of those we buy from. I confess that, after talking with hundreds of men and women from trainees to chief executive officer, I appreciated their fervor without really understanding what the hell they were so fervid about. But I got a strong hint from two anthropologists with the improbable nominal parlay of Robin Fox and Lionel Tiger in their book, "The Imperial Animal."

They see modern man as a hunter, product of 70 million years as a primate, and half a million years as a modern predator. The 10,000 years we've spent in settlements based on agriculture, two centuries in an industrial society, aren't enough to wipe out that hunting background. "We are wired for hunting," say Tiger and Fox "—for the emotions, the excitements, the curiosities, the fears, the social relationships that were needed to survive in the hunting way of life."

In the sales and management personnel of the big stores, in the layers of talent up the line, I have seen these very attributes. If you look sharp, next time you buy a dress or a lawn mower, maybe you'll see them too. The retailer is a hunter. We are his prey. Advertising is his pack of dogs.

Does this mean he's going to eat us up? Not at all. Although the hunting instinct may be programmed deep within mankind, surely the thoughtful anthropologist will agree that we've put on a few veneers of civility over the millennia of social co-existence.

In just the past few years of concern over the preservation of wildlife, for example, a friend of mine who's a hunting guide in Alaska has changed his outlook completely. "I used to take hunters out to shoot bears with guns," he explained. "Now I take conservationists out to shoot them with cameras. Hell, man, I'm selling the same bear over and over."

Just as there remain hunters who'd kill off the last eagle in America, so there are still plenty of salesmen who get their kicks, and their livelihood, out of overselling, or downright cheating, their prey. But they don't last long in the stores wise shoppers frequent, *because we don't go back.* They did shoot us dead; they did eat us up. The people I know at Wards, and they are like the people at many other responsible establishments, want to sell us over and over, like the bear. Frankly, I think it's a nice arrangement.

For now the enthusiasm for the hunt, the satisfaction in bagging us at the cash register, is tied into mass merchandising. The more pelts the hunters deliver in the form of sales receipts, the more money the tool makers in the merchandising departments have to improve their products, the more extensive the service department can be to keep what we bought in working order.

Receipts are fine trophies, but the technostructure pool of talent dreams up many more incentives to gratify the hunting instincts of the people in sales. You wouldn't believe the thing in Charlie Wagner's office. It's about five feet tall, with a polished wood base and a gold-plated body reminiscent of Medusa's head. It's surmounted with a purple velvet crown.

Charlie and his wife are independently wealthy. He's the chieftain of an area covering a third of the United States, and including 132 stores, but he's as proud of that monstrosity as a big game hunter is of the tusked elephant head on his wall. It's Charlie's trophy. He got it because his Region 3 tribesmen sold the most blankets in July.

A hunter gets his trophy.

Wards gives all kinds of prizes. A crusty veteran named Grady Byrnes was telling me of his career with the company one day. He had a couple of bad breaks as a manager—his store burned down, for one thing—and he was fired.

"When I walked out that door I thought the world fell on me," he said.

"Why'd you come back?" I asked.

His jaw shot out. "To make 'em eat dirt," he snarled, "and I did, too."

"Gosh," I said. "How?"

"I put on a big promotion, sold more freezers than anybody else, and won a trip to Italy," he said.

I don't think I've ever heard a happier ending.

Prizes and trophies typify only one form of the hunter's reward. He'd get bored stiff chasing the same type of game forever. Nor would an ambitious retailer be content with selling blankets or freezers for too long in the same place. Man must have new hunts, new challenges.

120

Chuck Higgins, manager of Wards paint department, who likes to think about many things ("Paint is the least interesting thing I do around here"), expresses personnel incentive on a graph. The horizontal line represents financial compensation, the vertical what Chuck calls psychic compensation.

Suppose an individual is constantly given new challenges and opportunities but no money at all; his line runs straight up. With regular salary increases in the same old job, his line advances horizontally. The optimum line of the Higgins graph runs up at an angle of 45 degrees, but in actuality it's more like a staircase, jumping up with a new assignment, scooting sideways with raise or bonus. When the line stops advancing in any direction, the man is ready for the headhunter.

For all his interest in psychic compensation, Higgins admits that money is more important. So does Tom Brooker. When he came to Wards he had his personnel people set up a makeshift bonus system. Later, when he brought in John D. Foster from the New York Port Authority as vice president, personnel, Foster was shocked to learn that the chief executive officer had had to initiate an incentive program. "We're supposed to think of that first," he said.

In this new climate, a young man named Bruce Mathews, director of benefits and compensation, took it on himself to work out one of the most radical bonus plans in industry. Mathews had been with Ford and Celanese, both exciting industries, but he found retail fascinating, and more complex. To him one of the key groups in the company is composed of the retail store managers. He set out to uplift them through the prime motivation, money.

"What we want is an entrepreneur who's willing to take a risk," Mathews said. "He expects to be rewarded if he's successful. He knows he won't be if he isn't, but he's the type of individual who is confident that he can come back and make it up next year."

It would be easy to work out a bonus system to reward store managers if it weren't for one unfortunate fact: in 1967, when

Mathews started working out his plan, 170 stores were losing money, and some, because of circumstances beyond the manager's control, were going to continue to lose. This upset the promotion schedule. A promotion to manager of a bigger store should be a great advancement. But a promotion from a small profitable store to a large unprofitable one could raise hell with the line on his Higgins graph.

So Mathews worked out a formula under which a store could lose a potful of money and the manager would still get a bonus. Tom Brooker approved it personally.

The catch was, of course, that the store would have to lose *less* money than before. A modest reward for reducing losses had been incorporated in the existing system. Mathews made a drastic change in it. He weighted the loss-reduction factor three times over the profit-making factor. In short, if a manager of a store losing $150,000 a year reduced those losses to $50,000 a year, the $100,000 he saved the company would be figured the same as a $300,000 profit made by another manager. At 6 per cent, both would receive a $12,000 bonus. One manager actually received a $19,000 bonus and his store still lost money—but nowhere near as much.

With this incentive, the manager-entrepreneurs took off. In the first year of the new bonus plan Wards net operating earnings nearly doubled—from $17.4 million to $34.3 million.

For a quiet fellow jiggling figures around on a yellow pad far from the hunting grounds, Bruce Mathews sure had the entrepreneur pegged. But what had he gotten out of it? Well, people in staff functions in Montgomery Ward, those who support the hunters, also get a bonus. But what pleased Mathews most was that when the plan was first presented to a group of store managers, they all stood up and hollered.

"It's the only time I ever heard of that a plan read out at a meeting got a standing ovation," he said, embarrassed but proud. That was *his* trophy.

After four years the bonus system had to be changed again

in order to effect a more stable balance between base pay and bonus, but it was great during the bonanza years.

Many retailers will probably disagree with my hunting analogy; some may even disagree with Mathews' assessment of them as entrepreneurs. People in the business are themselves divided; some say running a store is a science, some an art. To people like Ed Donnell it's just a joy. Though he prefers striding with his long legs from department to department in an actual store, he can still make a game out of presentation of figures to the board. Instead of playing golf, or curling, on the Sunday preceding board meetings, he goes to his study with his papers and his electric adding machine (you know which brand) and happily punches away, working up the report himself.

To Tom Brooker, the slipstick man, retailing is strictly a numbers game. Yet for all his faith in arithmetic, Tom has shown several examples of creativity in marketing.

One of his projects with Southern California Edison Company in the early thirties was selling light bulbs. He sent his men out in company uniforms, equipped with fuses and 150-watt bulbs. They'd install the fuse free, then while they were there, replace the overhead kitchen light, usually 25 watts, with the bigger bulb. "You don't have to pay a thing for this," the salesman would say. "We'll just add fifty cents a month to your bill for four months."

"Oh, that's wonderful," the housewife would say, bathed in all that light. With commission, the company came out about even on the cost of the bulbs and made money on the extra wattage.

Even this virtuoso performance did not assure advancement in the utility field in the depression and an executive in the company helped the young man out—right out of Edison into Firestone Tire and Rubber company's retail stores. He didn't know anything about running tire stores so before reporting to work he visited a Western Auto store in Los Angeles. He'd stand around all day watching, and talking with the clerks—until the manager got curious. It's typical of Brooker that he still remembers the manager's name, and that they became good friends.

With this secondhand information Tom found a Firestone store that wasn't doing well, sent the manager off on a month's vacation, and put himself in charge. He pumped gas, changed tires and gave himself a short course in store management. He learned to reduce problems to "the numbers." From then on he could pick up a store statement and, computing each item sold in relationship to the expenses of cost, installation, labor, gross profit, overhead and credit, determine what was wrong in a store 500 miles away and figure out what to do about it.

The tire business was seasonal: people bought tires before taking off on summer vacation trips. It was Firestone policy to cut down on personnel and expenses after Labor Day. Tom observed that when other stores were cleaning up in November and December, Firestone stores were practically out of business. Why not sell appliances, radios and similar items in the Christmas season? He worked out a program and asked for $150,000 to implement it. The idea of selling things to people at Christmas time was so far different from tire people's way of thinking that Brooker had to go to headquarters in Akron to get approval. But he did get it, and it paid off. Brooker left Firestone for Sears in 1944, but people are still buying the same type of goods he first put in at Firestone stores across the country.

You may wonder, or at least I often have, how so many stores of all kinds and ownership manage to stay in business if so much talent is required to run them. According to the ebullient Charlie Wagner, getting us consumers to buy is the easiest thing in the world. ("It's so simple to get business that it's pathetic.") If all the stores in the country suddenly conspired not to take our money, they'd have to fight us off with clubs.

The manager therefore—department, store, metro, zone or

region—has the responsibility not only to see that things go right, but that things don't go wrong. He is in constant revolt against the Second Law of Thermodynamics, which says that all systems must break down into chaos: if anything can go wrong, it will—and it can.

How many times have you gone into a store to make a routine purchase of an ordinary item and been told they don't have it? Yet if everybody had done his simple, normal job, the job he gets paid to do, it would be there waiting for you—and the store would make its 40 per cent markup.

Most of the mistakes made in retail are just plain goofs, but some are wingdings. Although he's been in this business since he was 18 years old, even Charlie Wagner was surprised at some of the things that turned up in a recent project. He selected the 16 worst stores in his region and set out to find the causes and correct them. In every store but one he achieved the objective without changing managers; firing the manager is easy but getting a replacement isn't.

Wagner maintains that success in retailing boils down to three basic principles: people, merchandise and display. People, particularly people in retail, have to have their egos fed regularly, like day-old kittens. Every manager in Charlie's region, or a member of his staff, stands at the door at the end of the day and gives the sales people a figurative pat on the back as they leave. Charlie has rewards for just about everybody except the janitor and he's working on that.

As for merchandise, keeping it in stock requires both the routine of order checking and the talent for sensing the future. A young trainee fresh out of the Navy, where he had followed the structured and boring schedule of a junior officer, told me he enjoyed his new life in retailing so much that he dreaded his vacation. "The Christmas rush is just starting," he said, "and here I am staying on after hours trying to second-guess the public on how many spring coats to order."

As Charlie Wagner found in his study of 16 problem stores, stocking the merchandise you want goes beyond both routine and talent. In three stores located in towns only 50 miles apart, he found a wide variation in the number of electric blankets carried. Stores are suppose to carry six types of electric blankets; that's the basic number. One store carried seven blankets, and sold 20 per cent more than the prototype figure derived from stocking the basic list. One of the problem stores carried only four blankets, and showed only 61 per cent. The third store wasn't carrying any electric blankets at all. The department manager didn't like electric blankets. With a percentage of zero, he found it possible to overcome his dislike.

In an extreme case of personal prejudice Charlie found that one store's lingerie department wasn't carrying nursing bras. He asked the department manager why not, and her answer was, honest to God, "Why, Mr. Wagner, I think it's just indecent for women to nurse babies."

All that Charlie could say was that in retailing it's the customer who's the final judge on all merchandise, and if Ward's customers want nursing bras, they ought to be able to get them.

In another store the manager of the paint department was not stocking a basic white paint in gallons, even though this produces 4 per cent of all paint sales. The department manager explained that there was more profit in selling paint by the quart. "My God," Charlie said, "our competitors sell paint by the gallon and there's no profit at all if our customer goes to them."

This is a particularly interesting example of the necessity of technostructure. That man had been managing the paint department for 20 years, and the store manager assumed he knew what he was doing. Wagner assumed the store manager knew what *he* was doing. "I don't blame the paint manager, and I don't blame the store manager," Wagner said. "It was our fault up here on top. We've got to teach them."

One of the most interesting programs in encouraging sales

people to be what you and the store want them to be is in
Joe Brannon's district in Phoenix. Lives there any lady who
would not love to walk around a store with someone else's
money in her purse, make purchases with it and then be able
to tell everybody off? Well, all you have to do is move to
Phoenix and join the Glendale Junior Women's Club. Sixty
members of the club are in the Courtesy Shopper program.
Each month Helen Tilton, who is in charge of it, gets the
group together, gives them each $25 and turns them loose.
The only guidelines are to avoid the busiest periods, be nice
and not look for trouble, and ask for the lowest-priced items
in each department to see if the salespeople will try to sell
them something better—trade up.

Their reports are printed each month in Handsome Joe's own
company magazine, *The Phoenix Planner*. Salespeople with
perfect scores get a $10 prize; those who fall short receive
caustic comments in print, from Joe himself. He doesn't print
the names of the malefactors, but just about everybody knows
who they are. While I was in Phoenix everybody was talking
about the department manager who got a zero. He was known
to pride himself on his usually well-run department, but one
of the Courtesy Shoppers must have caught him at a bad
moment. His name was not given, but when you're the only
male in a department, how can you hide? His pride was
hurt, and everybody was very happy when, the next month,
his department got a perfect record.

Sales people are graded on courtesy and helpfulness, which
is good for the customer, and on their attempts to sell higher
quality, more expensive and therefore more profitable merchandise and to suggest related items, which is good for
Wards. In addition, every salesperson in every Ward store
in Phoenix is supposed to push credit by asking if the customer
has a charge account and, if not, recommending it and offering
a credit application blank.

A shopper bought a can of paint, for example, but the

salesman neglected to suggest a brush. Brannon's comment: "Was the customer supposed to put the paint on with her fingers?"

Some typical reports and comments:

The saleslady asked, "May I help you?" I inquired about men's shorts. She explained the three grades of merchandise and explained why the best quality was worth buying. I selected them and she asked if I needed T-shirts or socks. She asked if I was putting the items on my charge and when I said I didn't have one, she asked if I would like to open one. She gave me a form to complete, thanked me and said, "Come again."

Grade: 100 per cent. *Comment:* It is superfluous to comment on perfection.

The salesman was very friendly. I asked for some good car wax and he showed me a brand telling me how good it was and how easy to apply. I said I would try it and he rang up the sale and thanked me. He failed to suggest related merchandise or credit. He was very polite and helpful.

Grade: 50 per cent . *Comment:* How can the shopper describe this salesman as helpful? Car wax needs an applicator. You can't apply car wax with some old toothbrush. If the shopper were really going to use this on her own car, she would be furious with the salesman, after she started to work on the car, because he had failed to suggest the additional equipment necessary to apply the car wax. Always remember that you are doing the customer a favor when you suggest merchandise that he needs to complete his job.

The saleslady asked to help me. I picked out some washcloths and said I would take them. She said, "Will that be all today?" When I said, "I guess so," she asked if the sale would be cash or charge. I said, "Cash, I don't have a charge." She rang up the sale and thanked me.

Grade: 40 percent. *Comment:* This "selling" effort does not rate more than 10 per cent, if that. This is the type of "salesman-ship" which causes the operators of our company (and all companies) to study the feasibility of coin-operated dispensers.

I looked around and no one approached me. I finally selected a pair of socks and took them to the salesman. He told me the amount of the sale, rang it up and thanked me. Did not greet me, suggest better merchandise or related items or credit.

Grade: Zero. *Comment:* This salesman is an experienced department manager. Everyone should study his technique. But do not consider his technique as a method to follow for advancement in the company. We do not promote people into department managers because of their pretty brown eyes or because they play golf with the boss. Then just how did this guy make it to department manager?

The salesman asked to help me. I asked for a sink mat, which he got for me. He suggested a matching divider mat and when I commented it might cover the chip on the sink partition, he pointed out that Wards had a patching compound for covering chips in porcelain. He showed it to me and told how to use it. He asked if the sale was to be charged. When I said I didn't have a charge, he invited me to open one and gave me an application. He thanked me and invited me back. Excellent service—you could use eight more just like him.

Grade: 100 per cent. *Comment:* It is superfluous to comment on perfection, but we have to agree with the customer. The customer is always right and we just wish that we had eight more just like him.

The saleslady was talking to a friend and after about ten minutes she asked to help me. I asked for a pair of ladies' briefs. She got them for me and said, "Will that be one pair?" I said, "Yes," she rang up the sale and thanked me. She didn't suggest related items or credit. We seemed to be interrupting her visiting.

Grade: Zero. *Comment:* And it rated zero. With the economy the way it has been, how can any of us be so thoughtless as to ignore a customer. We need all the customers we can bring into the store and we can't have anyone irritate a potential customer. Remember, when we ignore a customer in one department, she will be mad all day and if she remained in the store she could be mad at 44 different departments. Does any one person have the privilege of making all of her fellow employees unhappy because she chose to insult one customer?

In fairness to the salesperson, some customers just can't be completely satisfied. Kitty Breen, who is in charge of Ward's personnel training program, makes a point of telling new salespeople that the customer is not always 100 per cent right. "We use a lot of part-time help, many of them educated women who are just looking for something to do. These people are human, their feet hurt, they've got their own problems, and I just can't stand up in front of them and tell them that the customer is always right. They wouldn't believe me. In our culture today the salesperson who waits on you this morning may be your bridge partner tonight. People know that customers aren't perfect, because they're customers themselves. Some customers nobody can please. Instead of giving our new salespeople this kind of malarkey, I tell them frankly that our job is to please the customer, but we realize that it isn't always easy. Let's just keep our cool and hang in there, and do the best we can."

You may well on occasion have been given short shrift by a salesperson because it was humanly impossible for her to have recovered from the hard time the last customer gave her. You may be kept waiting an inordinate length of time because of something which you couldn't know anything about.

One of the most dramatic examples of this occurred a few years ago at the Washington's birthday sale in one of the Houston stores. There was a large number of customers in the lawn and garden department and an obvious shortage of personnel. If you were there that day, fretting and impatient, you would have had no way of knowing that one of the salesmen was in the men's restroom, crying.

Working had always been Thomas Miles' hobby. From the age of 12, and all through high school, he clerked in a grocery store. Summers he worked on a construction job by day, jerked sodas at night. When he finished high school he got a temporary job working part-time at Wards, opening boxes. He worked fast, finished and looked around. Other employees, better paid, were matching the contents of the boxes against the order slips, and Tom went to help. "You're not supposed to do that," a box buster told him, but Tom did anyway.

One day a rumor swept through the store. Mister Donnell, a

company big shot, was going to visit the store next day. In the excitement everybody but Tom forgot the receiving area. He took off his shirt and went to work. Late that night the manager, Jim Burns, came in. Tom was still there. Burns looked at him, then at the matched orders. "Who did that?" he asked.

"I did, sir," Tom said.

Burns looked at the spotless floor. "Who swept up?" he asked.

"I did, sir."

"Who straightened the bins?" "I did." "Who got rid of the trash?" "I did, sir." "Who helped you?" "Nobody." "How much are you making?" "A dollar an hour." "Well, you're making $50 a week now."

The day before the big Washington's birthday sale Burns dropped by the unloading area and said, "Come in neatly dressed tomorrow."

Tom floated home on a cloud. "It was the most inspiring thing that ever happened to me," he said.

Next morning he came in, neatly dressed, and was sent to the garden shop. Somebody showed him how to ring up a sale. The doors opened and the crowd came in. Tom got up his nerve and approached a lady. She wanted some climbing roses, on sale two for $1.22. Tom was real courteous—"I'm always real courteous"—and he made the sale. He made another sale. It was the happiest day of his life. He saw a customer looking at garden rakes and hurried over. "May I help you, sir?" he asked.

The man looked at him, up and down, and then said, "No, nigger, *you* can't help me."

Tom Miles, neatly dressed, real courteous, on the happiest day of his life, went to the restroom and cried.

That's why some customers were kept waiting that morning. Tom knew they were there, and he pulled himself together and came back. He also came back prepared.

"Not everybody's a tiger," he explained. "People can change their spots. Some come in, see a black salesman and blow their stacks. I just treat 'em nice and sell 'em a tractor. I'm not any black militant, but I'm not any Tom, either. I'm just positive.

If I deserve something, I want it no matter what my color is."

You may be interested in Tom Miles' career with Wards. In his second year he sold more than $100,000 worth of merchandise. Some weeks his commissions, on items like garden tractors, totaled $700.

In the meantime he was going to college at night. The Houston metro manager, Bill Davis, noted his performance and asked him to manage the paint department.

"Think I can handle it?" Tom asked.

"I wouldn't ask you if I didn't," Davis said.

The job paid $125 a week—at least 50 per cent less than he was making. His wife thought he was crazy for even thinking about it.

But he would be A Manager, responsible for an entire department—sales force, paper work, profits. In almost every society, whether it be of chickens or cheetahs, of monkeys or of men, there are always individuals who have the drive to be leaders. They will fight, work and sacrifice to achieve leadership. Such men have changed the world.

Tom Miles became manager of the paint department, then the hardware department. "I've got the largest number of items in the store, and I know what everyone of them is for and what to do with it," he said. "I don't mean to be boasting, but not every man can run a hardware department. And I'm not stopping here."

Ambitious men of all types find a home in the constant challenges of retailing. Sorting these hunters out, categorizing them by skills and inclinations, is one of the challenges of the technostructure. Placement of people has an effect on both stockholder and consumer. In retailing it takes all kinds, but which kind goes where, and how can you tell?

Not all store managers are entrepreneurs; some are operations-minded. Kitty Breen, who has studied the nature of the human male from within Wanamakers, Saks Fifth Avenue, Penneys and, of all places, as the only woman on the roster of the New York Fire Department, has noted both types in her personnel work at Wards. She has learned that with all her training aids—manuals, films, one-on-one sessions—the end result reflects the attitude of the manager.

"Nothing takes place in a Montgomery Ward store unless the manager wants it to happen," she said. "If he's operations-minded, he might be more interested in training people on the registers, and making sure they know their clerical work. Others lean toward sales training. I try to get the point over that you've got to make the sale before you ring the register."

If you look sharp, you may be able to tell the managerial orientation of the next store you're in. At the beginning of this chapter I related how my wife, Bonnie, came back disheartened from a shopping trip to a Ward store. Later, talking with an executive high up in the technostructure, I mentioned some of her comments. He smiled, reached into his drawer, and pulled out a file on that very store.

"You wife has a pretty good eye," he said. "What she saw is represented here in numbers. Some changes are going to be made."

Not long after I noticed in the list of transfers in the company paper that a man named John F. Lee had been transferred to Staunton, Virginia, as manager of the store there. That was the change. We gave him a few months, then took the day off and drove over to see him—and the store.

"It's so much brighter looking," Bonnie said when we first went in. "The aisles look bigger." As we strolled through the salespeople smiled at us, and asked if they could help us. I stopped in the appliance section to look at the microwave oven. A young man charged up and came within an inch of selling it to me.

"I use it myself," he said, "right here. I heat up my dinner in a minute and sneak back and eat it. My whole dinner hour only takes ten minutes and I can be back on the floor. Oh, excuse me a second." He'd seen Bonnie looking at a three-door refrigerator and dashed over to sell it to her.

I dragged her away. In five minutes we'd caught the flavor

of the store. We went in to see the manager. We expected a ball of fire, but we were still surprised. To begin with, his name was not John F. Lee, but Sean Prionsius O'Laoi. He'd come from Ireland as a teenager, gone to college in New York, worked briefly for Sears, then joined Wards with all-out Gaelic enthusiasm. He was manager of a catalog store at 23, a small store handling C-D lines at 26, and now here he was, all of 30, in charge of a full-line store that had lost $112,000 the year before.

Sean was full of himself, as well he might be. Marty Munger, head of the entire eastern region, had just come through, looked over the store and the figures, and told him the store looked alive for the first time.

"My predecessor was operations-minded," Sean said. "He went by the book. He's now the operations manager of a large store and doing a good job, but here he'd argue with a customer over $10. I'm sales-minded. There's no such thing as a useless sale. I want that customer to come back."

Sean had brightened up the store by replacing all burned out lights with brighter ones. He'd cleaned all merchandise out of the aisles. He'd put in the boutique presentation of fashion items. He'd made a fetish of presentation of merchandise. He was presenting a strong image through advertising, and backing up that image. Technically, that means that, instead of including many items in an omnibus ad, his policy is to devote an entire ad to one item or a group of related items, and make sure that sufficient quantity was in stock.

He'd sent out a letter to all credit customers asking them to let him know personally if they had ever had cause to be dissatisfied. He received 600 letters, and a couple hundred more phone calls and personal visits. He was muttering about one visitor who'd just left.

"Six service calls on one refrigerator!" he said. "I go on the basic theory — how would I feel in the same situation? I did the same thing with this fellow that I do with any dissatisfied customer — asked him what he thought would be fair. They nearly always ask for less than I would suggest myself. I took in this man's old unit and applied the price to a new, more expensive one. He's happy and it didn't cost anything. I reconditioned the old unit, sold it and broke even. And now I've got a regular customer who brings in his friends."

But the real secret of Sean's success is what he calls people power. "My department managers should function as department managers, with pride and authority, not as computers doing what somebody tells them to do. 'You make the decision and I'll back you,' I say. Sure, I argue with them when I think they're going overboard but if they win the argument and sell the goods I'm delighted. I told one department manager he was crazy when he wanted to push $400 stereo consoles. Well, he showed me — he increased sales 200 per cent. Then he got enthusiastic over TV. Let's see, I've got the figures here — he increased TV sales from $2,866 to $10,000.

"The manager of the appliance department quit to go into business for himself. Roy Ensminger, the manager of the paint department, said he wanted the appliance department. Roy was an excellent paint man, and transferring him would be going against company policy in a way, but what the hell. Then the manager of the shoe department, Gary Corbett, said he wanted the paint department. He hated waiting on women who couldn't make up their minds. Well, that's two problems — hell, it was three problems — I had to put somebody in the shoe department. I wound up with a 19-year-old kid running the shoe department, boy named Stewart Graham, but he liked selling shoes. Well, paint's up 23.6 per cent, appliances up 52.5 per cent. The shoe department didn't do that well, but gosh, Stewart inherited a lot of ladies' shoes that were so old they were out of style."

Sean wasn't sure whether he'd cut the year's losses by the full $112,000, but in just nine months on the job he knew he'd come close. And he knew he'd make a $15,000 bonus for nine months' work.

This is great for Sean Lee and Montgomery Ward, but what

about the people of Staunton? What about consumers everywhere? Well, first of all, it makes shopping a pleasure. You know you're going to do it anyway, why not enjoy it? (You can go to the ladies' room, too; Bonnie says it's spick and span.)

For the occasional consumer who buys a faulty item, the attitude of the managers removes the anguish and bickering of getting it exchanged or returned—and you know you can continue to buy with confidence. For the extremely cost-conscious customer, it enables you to save money; Sean's department managers have to reduce prices on selected items in order to get people in the store to buy other things at regular prices. (We'll go into this subject later.)

But most of all, this 30-year old Irishman is making his store a profitable operation. Add his efforts to those of Pete Pederson, Handsome Joe Brannon, Wild Bill Davis and all the others up through the technostructure to Ed Donnell and Tom Brooker, and the result is the profit which makes mass merchandising possible. Mass merchandising is the key to mass manufacturing. One cannot exist without the other. Integration of the two provides us consumers with the products of our times.

5

The Wonderful, Wonderful Catalog

Catalog sales surely play a profitable role in mass merchandising, else they wouldn't continue to give those massive, colorful books away. Each big catalog costs Wards about two dollars, and employees say proudly that the catalog desk makes Wards the biggest store in town.

One year, one company, a dozen separate catalogs—even a bikini cover.

But to millions of us, particularly those who grew up with the wish book, the catalog is not just a sales device—it's an emotion. Watching a child look through a catalog is one of the world's most beautiful experiences. I'm doubly fortunate in that I have been that child, looking with wonder at glories which actually existed, although I knew I couldn't have even a fraction of them, and have also been the parent of children experiencing the same emotion. Making some of my own dreams come true for them—and the catalog helps—is really what life is all about.

For all its nostalgia and parental fulfillment, the catalog is far more than a wish book. It's entertainment: The most cosmopolitan intellectual, the most rural tiller of the soil and those of us in between, all derive hours of pleasure scanning pictures and detailed descriptions of the world's production.

And it's practical: The big catalog is the most comprehensive consumer guide on earth. It is at the same time the poor man's Consumer's Union and the rich man's Consumer's Union. It gives us detailed coverage on many more items than any consumer organization could possibly provide, without our spending an extra nickel, yet in order to continue to receive it we must make annual purchases totaling several times CU's six-dollar subscription. In this quality-conscious, cost-conscious society I honestly feel sorry for anyone who doesn't have the brains or the income to have and to use the catalog for comparison shopping. It's a crying shame that those who need it the most are often completely unaware of it.

Although one company, Montgomery Ward, has taken steps toward making the catalog available to the needy (I'll go into this later), the fact remains that catalogs are expensive and no company can afford to give them away without positive hope of return. The catalog is not just one book, but an annual total of twelve listing more than 100,000 items—and an entire line of shoes is one item. (The largest stores carry 30,000 to 35,000 items.) The two big basic books, fall and winter, spring and summer, run around 1,300 pages each and weigh almost five pounds. (Six of the books I've written are in paperback; if you bought one of each they'd cost you $7 and all together they weigh only half of one catalog.)

In addition to the two big books Wards puts out ten more special books, including the holiday wish book and the farm and garden catalog, and several booklets telling you about things you always wanted to know but were afraid to ask, like hydronic heating, sauna baths and parts for your Model A Ford.

The twelve basic books total 86 million copies a year, 28 billion pages. The paper, in a sheet six feet wide, would go around the world four times; that's 50,000 tons of the stuff, or 900,000 trees. To cover that blank expanse with words and pictures requires two million gallons of ink, and to stick the pages together 125 tons of glue.

As for the people involved, some 140 copywriters and editors hammer out descriptions and exclamation points, 53 full-time artists plus several outside free-lancers add their touches, and photographs come from the central studio employing 56 people and from ten outside studios. Printing, binding and shipping require 750,000 man-hours annually. If you want a steady job, you could do it in 400 years.

With this expense, you can see why the name file of Montgomery Ward's 10,000,000 customers is being constantly updated to see if they deserve the newest catalog. The new, potential customer can probably get one free by writing the company or asking at the nearest store, but if you want to keep the books coming you've got to meet the standards of a complex formula which boils down to a minimum of two orders totaling $20 or more.

The company you'll be in as a catalog customer may surprise you. More than 25 percent of Ward's customers are in the $7,500 to $10,000 household income bracket, as compared with the national average of less than 20 percent. Forty-nine per cent of catalog customers make more than that; the national average is 42 per cent. Fourteen percent are in the manager-executive category, as opposed to only 7.8 per cent nationally.

In spite of the urban shift in population, the farmers hang in there with the catalog; though the national percentage has shrunk to less than 4 per cent, Ward's farmer catalog customers are almost 9 per cent of the total.

The income bracket and career status of the catalog customer, in short, is higher than the national percentage, which surprises even the people at Wards.

What surprised me was the identity of a catalog customer whom I found in my own house. When our daughter Sue reached the car-driving age of 16 we gave her a fixed amount to pay for her own clothes at the beginning of the school year. She blasted off, delighted with the project but aware of the responsibility and determined to be frugal. She went to the Army and Navy store and the thrift shop, of course, being a teenager in the seventies, and, because she's a girl, to a chic boutique where they sell cardboard shoes for a fantastic price.

We live in a town with a lot of stores, and I expected her to go on looking for days. Instead she came home, washed her hair and then, immobilized by the hair drier, she used the time to do her real research in the catalog. By the time the infernal machine on her head had done its job, she had her shopping list written down. She went to the phone and, in five minutes, ordered most of her wardrobe from the catalog store. Her mother and I were impressed — and surprised — by this management of time and money.

Her phone call put into effect a most complicated operation. First of all, Sue had to give her name, address and telephone number. She'd forgotten to get our credit card number before she made the call, but our local catalog store is a small operation and Ernie Duggins, the manager, and his assistants know us, so they good-naturedly got the number from the files. After the call, they then put her order in a form acceptable to the data processing machine at the catalog center in our region, Baltimore. All details for each unit ordered have to be translated into computerese by shading out the appropriate block in 37 columns on a card that only a data processing machine can look at without getting a headache. It's a tedious job which bugs the clerks, and which is the reason they're so crochety between four and five. This is a bad time to shop a catalog store.

About five o'clock on the day Sue phoned in, Ernie put all the cards in an envelope and walked a couple of blocks down the street to the mail box in front of Timberlake's Drug Store. A little later it was picked up by the mail truck and started on its way to Baltimore, arriving there at 11:30 P.M. Couriers from the catalog house make regular pickups at the post office around the clock (clerks take orders by phone all night, too) and Sue's order was being processed before dawn. The computer took a look at it and decided my credit was okay. By the time the fillers came in at 7 A.M. the list of items was there waiting for them.

They began bustling around the huge place, collecting items for each order. A huge spiral chute cuts through the building like a stationary corkscrew, and you can stand by its side and watch the merchandise go sliding down. At the bottom all these objects, which would be mighty dizzy if they were you or me, are loaded on conveyor belts and go out to the assembly section. They're put in great bins from which the packers take them and get them out to the waiting trucks. Those whose destinations are the farthest away leave as early as noon. We're only a couple of hundred miles from Baltimore, so Sue's order left later. Even so it was packed up within 24 hours after she'd called it in.

Some orders, of course, go through the post office. Only 12 per cent of today's catalog business actually comes in and goes out via the U.S. mail, but that's still a lot of merchandise

But Sue's order was not complete. Several of the articles she ordered were fashion items, and this type of merchandise all comes out of the Chicago warehouse. Numbers of these items were incorporated in the computer print-out and sent over leased wire that night to Chicago, where they were filled the next day and loaded on a truck that rumbled back to Baltimore that night. If any of those items had been manufactured in Baltimore it would be making a round trip. Sounds inefficient, until you try to think of a better way.

With so many steps necessary to fill an order, it's really no wonder that occasionally you may open your package expecting to find a dress and pull out instead a football uniform. The reason it doesn't happen more often is because inspectors are constantly trumping ACEs—Accuracy Control Errors. Fred Nordenholz, general manager of the Baltimore house, showed me a report on one department at the end of the day. Of 118 units checked, there were 6 errors. Three were the wrong items, two the wrong quantity, one poorly packed. One employee had made three of the six errors; she was extra help, brought in for the Christmas season, but after that extraordinary performance she was ex-extra help.

Fred isn't really all that tough, but better her than him. Back in 1935 Fred was working his way through law school by sorting packages in the catalog house. Wards offered him a chance to advance. He couldn't handle both his added responsibility and his studies, and, well, he has been with Wards ever since. Now he's where he wants to be, and he wants to stay there.

Furthermore, Fred has Exposure. His name, picture and address appear in the catalog, with a statement to the effect that if you are disappointed with Ward's merchandise or service, write directly to him about it. Not only that, but his home phone is listed in the Baltimore directory. Once he got a long-distance call at home at one o'clock in the morning. The irate customer had ordered a light fixture that didn't work. Fred tried to be diplomatic, but wondered why the fellow couldn't call him during the day.

"During the day I don't need the damn light," the man said.

People can be handled a lot more easily than the computer. No question but that it saves Fred and his staff a lot of time. For one thing, he can punch into the machine a Buy-point; when the number of units on hand gets down to that level the computer automatically orders more.

"But sometimes the goddam machine goes crazy and spits

out dozens or grosses instead of ones," he said. "It's great when it's working but when the son of a bitch fails here I am sitting with 600 people all waiting for it to get going again. Sometimes people make it do the wrong thing. One dumb guy put a whole batch of orders through twice and everybody got two of what he ordered."

Happily for both Fred Nordenholz and my daughter Sue, she got exactly what she ordered, one of each.

Though most of what she ordered were machine-wash and permanent-press clothes—today's youth does not want to stand over a hot ironing board—she did splurge on one item, a suede shoulder bag, $13.00. She saw it in the catalog twice, on page 181 where it was fully described, and on page 50, where a pretty girl in a tan tunic is carrying it.

Why twice? Well, to begin at the beginning, all buyers in all departments, whether their wares are shoes or coats, refrigerators or power tools, fight to get their items prominently displayed in the catalog. As the catalog must meet a budget, with each page pulling in its percentage of sales, it's a battle royal. A bedspread—bedspreads and draperies are the largest-selling catalog items—gets a full page with an illustration in color. A replacement TV tube gets one line. A page may show several similar items—coats, or lawn mowers, or TV sets.

Page 50 sells girls' pants and tunics, but the models are also wearing shoes and jewelry, and the one on the right is carrying a handbag. A note at the bottom of the page tells what pages these accessories are on. This is the work of a groovy young woman named Alice Shost, who coordinates the accessories. She gets photographs of the clothes to be featured in the catalog, then goes to the accessory bank. By choosing from this large selection of items—jewelry, shoes, handbags—Alice can make almost every page a small boutique from which a customer can order a complete outfit. You'd be surprised how effective a sales tool this is. If a $7.50 necklace is shown with a pants suit, about one out of three women who buy the suit will also buy the necklace.

For jewelry to go with the pants and tunic on page 50, Alice

A long way, baby! The 1878 fashion illustration at right was the first to appear in any mail order catalog. Below, a 1972 cover. Wards got a batch of complaints on it—from old-timers—but a lot more orders!

MONTGOMERY WARD CENTURY 2

OUR 100TH ANNIVERSARY YEAR

1972

SUMMER SALE

35 GREAT CENTURY 2 VALUES

1623 BIG PRICE CUTS
Some items at our usual low prices

Satisfaction guaranteed

a 2 value

The Plush Bikini

in soft 'n lustrous panne velvet— a terrific beach look— a sensational price!

788   Bikini and Sun Glasses sold on pg. 11

Chicago, Ill. 60607

SALE ENDS
Aug. 21, 1972
INDEX PAGE 216
CREDIT TERMS,
PAGES 301-2

took a $4 whistle on a chain, and the big suede bag. From her desk—piled high with catalog pages, swatches, accessories—a detailed list of everything to appear on page 50 went to the photographic agency.

Today's catalogs, especially the big beautiful books put out for Century 2, Ward's 100th year, sparkle with colorful and vivacious photographs. They've come a long way since that 8 x 12 inch sheet of 30 items ("1 New Style Balmoral skirt. . . . $1.00") Aaron Montgomery Ward mailed out hopefully from his 12 x 14 foot headquarters in 1872. Three years later the famous 1875 catalog, the one in which Ward stated the incredible guarantee to refund the customer's money plus postage if goods were not satisfactory, contained a few woodcuts.

By 1895 the catalog had grown in size and number to the point that its printer, R. R. Donnelley and Sons Company, installed the first rotary press for commercial printing. To keep busy between catalogs, Donnelley began printing telephone directories. The catalogs were profusely illustrated with artists' drawings.

During the years in which Sewell Avery was president the catalogs went from photographs of models wearing Wards garments to photographs of the garments themselves. Avery, in his ramrod integrity, felt that showing clothes on attractive models did not present them fairly—the customer might not be as pretty as the model. When he finally permitted the use of models again, he still insisted that such details as the number of buttons be plainly shown.

Today's catalog tries to strike a balance between magazine-style photography and a true portrayal of the item. Although some of the best known models in recent years have posed for Wards catalogs—go back far enough and you'll find Lauren Bacall—the truth is that most of these girls aren't as pretty in the flesh as they look in the book. The camera has only one eye and it broadens out the face and body. A good figure comes out on the plump side in a photograph. Those beautiful models in the catalog look like skinny bags of bones when you meet them in the street.

Recognize any of these former models from bygone Montgomery Wards catalogs? Susan Hayward, Mona Freeman, Lauren Bacall and Suzy Parker.

Scores of models, both women and men, make their living posing for the catalog. Add Sears and Penney, and you multiply the total by three. Wards pays more than the fashion magazines, but the girls work hard for their money and their career life is short. At the age of 35 even those who have stayed skinny are through. Customers, regardless of their own age, just don't want to identify with older women.

The photographers Wards uses might be classified as second echelon. It can't afford the big name photographers, but it still may pay $500 for one photograph. A simple photograph of a man's shirt, just lying there with nobody in it, is worth $50, but that photograph represents both art and science. Photographed as is, the way you buy it, a shirt doesn't look like a shirt. It has to be folded, puffed and pinned in shape. This is not just to make it look good, but to make it look real.

S. G. North, who supervises catalog layout for soft goods, and who has been with the company since 1936, when he was a 19-year-old paste-up boy making $12 a week, looks upon the catalog with a kind of reverence.

"It's a selling tool, but it's also a reference bible," he says. "When I buy anything personally I always look at the catalog first. It's a yardstick the American consumer can rely on."

Although you wouldn't realize it without looking at it carefully, each big semiannual book is made up of several sections equivalent to separate magazines, each devoted to the wares of the appropriate merchandise department. The catalog sales manager of each department has a tendency to get carried away with the essentiality of his product and the copywriters assigned to that department get carried away with their own prose. Just like magazines, therefore, the sections have editors who keep the writers in line, both within the letter of the law and the basic integrity of the company.

The department which merchandises various exercise machines, for example, would love to have you believe that working out with the latest gadget for two seconds a day will fill you out in all the right places, slim you down in all the wrong ones. Unfortunately, it's not quite that easy and the final copy as printed in your catalog makes no wild promises. Hints, may- be — they *are* trying to sell you something — but no promises.

The description of every item does carry one solid, inescap- able fact, the price. You never know when this information will come in handy. The other night, at the middle of rush hour in the rain, Sue called me to say that the car had broken down. A couple of fellows from a filling station had pushed her in off the street and tried to get the car started. One of them came on the phone and said that my alternator was com- pletely shot. He said a rebuilt one would cost about $40. Well, hell, I don't know what an alternator is in the first place, and here some guy I don't know from Adam wants me to authorize him to put in a new one over the telephone. I said I'd call him back.

I called a friend who said that the symptoms did indeed indicate the alternator might have burned out. Then I looked alternators up in the catalog and found that a rebuilt one would cost about $30, including postage. That's a $10 difference, but I'd have to wait for the part to come and I wouldn't know what to do with it when it did get here. The important thing was that the difference of only $10 between Ward's price and the station's price meant that they weren't robbing me blind. The people had been helpful, they'd have the car ready the first thing in the morning, and I told them to go ahead with no uneasy feeling that I was being taken for a sucker.

You can get an education in tires by consulting the catalog. What's the difference between radial-ply, bias-belted and bias- ply? How much do you pay for an expectancy of 40,000 mile tread wear, how much for 18 months? You can get the answers and make a decision in five minutes in your own home with- out the salesman breathing down your neck. Many tire cus- tomers living near Ward's retail outlets study the catalog first and then drive in to buy the tires. Some 120 catalog stores have tire, battery and accessory service, with more on the way. Other catalog customers have to go to the trouble of taking the tires to your friendly neighborhood service station to have them mounted, and put up with the static on why you didn't buy the tires there in the first place, but you still know exactly what you're getting.

Buying wearing apparel through the catalog occasionally presents a problem to both buyer and seller. In spite of the meticulous photography and descriptions, the item doesn't always look exactly the way you thought it would. And although the catalog gives full instructions on how to measure yourself, the item doesn't always fit. Well, don't feel bad about returning it for exchange for a different size or model.

Many women like to see two or three different styles or colors of a garment—or get the opinion of husbands and friends, not necessarily in that order—before actually buying it. You can do this through the catalog, too, just as in your favorite retail store.

Articles returned are checked in the reconditioning unit before being sent out again. Once, checking a man's suit which had been returned with the statement that it had never been worn, inspectors found a pair of theatre ticket stubs in the pocket and a greasy spot on the coat (buttered popcorn?). And another time a small boy's jacket was returned with a Sunday School attendance medal pinned to the lapel. But nearly always the clothes are returned in perfect condition and all the reconditioning unit has to do is pin them up and send them out again.

Wards does a big business in fashions and other soft lines through the catalog. The next category is in home furnishings, and then hard lines—home modernization, sporting goods, tires, automotive. Major appliances represent 10 per cent of total business.

It's hard to imagine it, looking at the handsome Century 2 catalog, but just as in the late fifties some consideration was given to liquidating Montgomery Ward in toto, so in the mid-sixties the possibility of closing down the catalog operation actually reached the study stage. It had been going steadily downhill and one year lost $26 million.

There were many reasons for its going into the red, one of them the profligate waste of expensive books, but as is the case in most losing operations the cause could be laid to management. Tom Brooker had had to get his retail show on the road before he could turn his attention to the catalog.

When Brooker had first joined Sears some twenty years before, he had been intrigued by the mail order business, and when Brooker is intrigued by something he goes after it like a hungry hunter stalking a deer. He figured out its mysteries— mail order is the most complex operation in retailing—and brought his department, automobile accessories, from 16th to 1st in Sears, where it still is.

He solved two of his major problems at Wards almost simultaneously. An inordinate amount of man-hours was going into manually restocking the inventory in each of the nine catalog houses. Brooker had a study made by a consulting firm and one of his bright young men named Robert L. Swanson, and came up with a plan to computerize ordering for each of the catalog houses from one central location. This would perform the job currently being done by some hundred people in each of the houses.

On a visit to Fort Worth he outlined his plan to the staff of the catalog house there and got no response at all. They just couldn't understand so radical an innovation in mail order merchandising. The manager of the catalog house, Chett Eckman, drove Brooker to the airport after the meeting.

After driving in silence for a while Eckman cleared his throat and said, "Mr. Brooker, what you're doing is going to eliminate the merchandising job in the catalog house, and it's just going to be a warehouse."

I wasn't there, and Eckman was looking where he was driving, but I'll bet a hundred to one that while Brooker kept his poker face his eyes began to sparkle. Brooker had noticed Eckman when he first came with the company, had assigned him to Ed Donnell in the eastern region to enable him to absorb some of Donnell's knowledge, then had moved him to Fort Worth. Now this human development was beginning to pay off. Eckman, by criticizing the plan, demonstrated that he understood it.

"That's right, Chett," Brooker said, "but you're smart enough to realize that if we can accomplish this, how much better off we'll be."

After thinking about it Eckman did realize the wisdom of computerized restocking. The next thing he knew he was in charge of catalog operations.

Brooker had also had his eye on Sanford W. Allred. While Eckman is tough and brusque, as a good operating man should be, Bill Allred is flamboyant and expansive. He had gone to work with Wards as a teenager in Kansas City, and was a buyer in boys' wear during World War II. A friendly and ingenious fellow, he helped a large mill with a marketing problem and came up with three million yards of broadcloth at a time when a buyer would cut your throat to get a yard of material.

That moved him up to men's wear buyer—a dubious promotion inasmuch as Sewell Avery had fired the last four. All had gone in for the low slope type of collar, which looked awful on Avery's long scrawny neck. He'd put one on, see a turtle in the mirror, and fire the buyer. Allred had the Arrow shirt people, whom he had befriended, design a special high band collar for him, and put it in stock. Avery saw some, ordered a dozen and was immensely pleased with the way the high collar tended to shorten his long neck. This gave Allred time to build up men's shirts and other lines, and he became manager of men's wear. This is a method of getting ahead not taught in graduate business schools.

When Tom Brooker took over Montgomery Ward he met Allred and was impressed with him. He put him in charge of the west coast buying office in order to give him greater breadth of experience, then brought him in as catalog merchandising manager. He and Eckman, whom Brooker describes as "a pretty hard-shelled guy," turned the catalog into a profit-maker. Both are vice presidents reporting to executive vice president Jim Lutz.

Another factor in the metamorphosis of the catalog from a loser to a winner has been the development of the catalog agencies. In some 650 locations, Wards runs catalog stores. There's one in my hometown but I'd never been in it until I began researching the Ward merchandising operations and decided to buy some of these good things the buyers were telling me about. When I did go in it I wondered what I'd gotten myself into, because it was the frowziest looking dump I've ever seen. I bitched about it to everybody in the company, and finally Fred Nordenholz sent one of his men down to help Ernie Duggins brighten it up a little. But it's still in a lousy location and apparently it's not going to be changed until Wards finds a shopping center location for a large, modern retail store.

Beginning in 1964, however, Wards has gone off on a new tack, with catalog agencies instead of company-owned stores. In eight years it opened more than a thousand of these agencies and closed down over 200 stores.

To people who don't mind hard work, the agency setup offers an unbeatable combination, independent entrepreneurship with the backing of a big company. It's a Mom and Pop, even an entire family type of operation. The thousandth agency, for example, opened in California, Missouri, in the fall of '71, is owned by a retired Navy officer, Donald Schenewerk, and his wife Shirley. They have six children, from eight to 23 years old. Schenewerk said that he spent 20 years traveling over the world with the Navy, and it was great to settle down in his own hometown with his family.

Agencies are located in 47 states, including Alaska. They are usually in small communities of 10,000 population or so. Fred Nordenholz drove me over to Chestertown, Maryland, so that I could see one of his tigers, Edmund P. Lusby, in action. Though it was early in December Lusby was already working from 9

A.M. to 9 P.M. to handle to Christmas rush. "It's physical work," he said. "I'm so tired I can't sleep at night. But we like it."

When Lusby, a former dairy farmer, heard about the agency he wanted to jump right in. He knew the area, knew the people, and knew Wards as an old reliable company. His wife, Harriet, was skeptical. A major shopping center, Dover, was only 50 miles away and she couldn't imagine people ordering things when they could drive over and get them. It took them two months to make the decision, and for a while there they wished they hadn't. Harriet hated it. One day Ed came in from an errand to find her sitting holding the phone with tears streaming down her cheeks. A customer was cussing her out. Gradually, however, she began liking it. The Lusbys have a family operation; their married daughter works full time; two daughters, both in college, work during the summer and on weekends; and their son comes in afternoons after high school.

Their day begins when they come in and find the bin of orders delivered by truck out of Baltimore during the night. Ed unloads it, straining with the heavy items, and inspects the merchandise. Monday is the big day for orders; people in the community apparently spend their Sundays reading the catalog. More than half of the orders come in by telephone.

Dealing with the public is never dull. One irate woman demanded that Lusby come out personally to pick up a linoleum rug she had bought a year before. "I don't want this junk in my house one more day!" she shouted into the phone. Lusby hopped in his car and drove out. The linoleum she was complaining about was the cheapest grade carried by Wards. It was in an unheated room, below freezing, and it had cracked over the uneven floor boards under the furniture.

"Wards is a lot more liberal than I would be," Ed said. "I'd have let the thing lie there, but the company made it good."

Lusby uses what he calls the cheapest form of advertising — none. He enjoys a personal relationship with his customers and sees to it that their satisfaction is guaranteed. They are his advertising; they tell their friends. He's constantly being surprised. He didn't want to stock automobile batteries, for example, because he didn't want to fool with the big heavy things and he didn't think he could sell them. But the Baltimore office talked him into putting a couple on display, and now he does a big battery business.

He wasn't sure about tires, either. He didn't think customers would want to go to the trouble to order a tire, pick it up and then take it somewhere else to have it mounted. However, he made arrangements with a filling station operator to have the tires mounted for $1.50, mounted and balanced for $2.00, and now he sells a lot of them. Oddly enough, the service station sells Firestone tires. The operator is one of Lusby's best customers; he even bought a battery.

If anything goes wrong with a Ward appliance, it's fixed by a repairman from the service center 60 miles away. A local shop handles emergencies. All in all Lusby has a good setup. Every Saturday he sends in a weekly remittance report, and gets his commission back on Wednesday. The commission, incidentally, is 11.5 per cent on sales up to $150,000 a year, 12 per cent thereafter.

It's hard work, and confining, but satisfying. And every now and then something particularly exciting occurs. One morning the driver of the truck, which comes through about three o'clock in the morning, came out to Lusby's house and woke him up instead of dropping off the delivery at the store. A local farmer had ordered a tractor and the driver had it in the truck. Lusby dressed, and the two drove out to the farmer's house. They woke *him* up, and the three of them unloaded the tractor. The farmer was delighted with the personal delivery.

Many agents go out in the town and countryside and sell their wares. With the big catalog, and the special farm and garden book, they have an almost unlimited supply of goods. Looking at tires on parked automobiles along the street becomes automatic; every worn tire represents a potential customer. One agent spent his slack time driving around the country-side looking for fences in need of repair. He sold so much fencing that he sold the agency and went into the fencing business full time.

Running an agency is no 40-hour-a-week proposition, and Wards is careful in its selection to make sure that its agents know what they are getting into, and can do it once they are in it. But for people, especially mature couples, who like to run their own business with the backing of a big business, it offers financial opportunity, togetherness, and a sure way to see friends and neighbors.

One of the criteria for setting up an agency is the existing mail order business in the area; $25,000 in mail orders usually increase to $125,000 when an agency is set up. Which proves

This independently owned and operated catalog sales agency offers Ward's full line of merchandise to inner-city customers.

that even with the accent on retail stores and catalog stores and agencies, people far from these outlets still go on ordering directly by mail. After all, Aaron Montgomery Ward's first list of merchandise was sent out by mail, to local granges of the national farmers' organization, and his first order came in by mail—from a postmaster.

"With Wards and the Post Office," says M.T. "Mac" Holloway, general traffic manager, "it was love at first sight."

For years, before the parcel post service was created, orders went out by express and freight. (Remember the line, from "The Wells Fargo Wagon" in *The Music Man*, "Montgomery Ward sent me a bathtub and a crosscut saw"?) Wards recommended that customers club together and send in combined orders. They got a discount plus cheaper freight rates on shipments of 100 pounds and more.

When parcel post was first proposed, private shipping companies opposed it bitterly, and accused Wards and Sears, which by that time had grown to comparable size, of lobbying for the service. A Montgomery Ward spokesman testified before Congress that it wouldn't help the company. When parcel post did go into effect in 1912, it turned out that he was right. One- and two-dollar orders poured in, and as it cost as much in paper work to fill a little order as it did a big one, they nearly broke the company's back.

Parcel post, however, led to a closer relationship between company and post office. Wards cleared out space in its own buildings, and the post office set up shop. The company turned over railroad sidings to the post office, and cars were loaded direct. Incoming orders were sacked in the mail cars en route to Chicago, and whisked into the receiving office on the arrival of the train.

Though today most merchandise goes out by Ward's fleet of trucks for more efficient handling, Mac Holloway says the love affair continues in intensity if not in degree. In 1971 Wards sent out a total of 305,770,000 pieces of mail, ranging from first class letters (bills!) to third class circulars and fourth class catalogs and merchandise. Ward's postal bill was $29 million and the customers paid postage on packages of $9 million for a total of $38 million.

What about service? Well, in spite of all you may hear, Holloway still considers it pretty good. He has read newspaper stories of letters being delivered years later, but as far as he knows it has never happened at Wards. The number of packages which are not delivered to purchasers is far less than 1 per cent of the total—and that includes the packages people *say* they don't get. Wards takes the customer's word for it every time. To insure packages would cost $600,000 more than all losses combined. In short, Wards saves money on the basic honesty and efficiency of postal workers.

We tend to take the post office for granted. I don't any more. One spring day I received a battered tube-like container in the mail. Ed Lennox, my friend the fishing supplies buyer, had told me that Ward rods were the best made, and had his supplier, True Temper, send me one to prove it. The rod turned out to be great, but what was more interesting was the fact that I got it at all. It had been shipped from True Temper's plant in Anderson, South Carolina, addressed to Booton Herndon (MW), 2422 Jefferson Park Avenue, Chicago, Ill., 22903. That's my street address, all right, but I don't live in Chicago; I live in Charlottesville, Virginia. Somebody had crossed out the zip, which was correct, and written over it a Chicago zip beginning with 60 ___. Somebody else had crossed that out. It was stamped "UNLOCATABLE" at Chicago. Somehow or other the package got to Charlotte, North Carolina, and finally to me. A half-dozen people must have been involved with that package, and I bet a lot of them would have liked to have a new Ward True Temper fishing rod. Nobody would ever have known. But I got it.

Yes, Ed, and Mr. True Temper, it's a great rod, and so is the postal service. But then Wards has known that for 100 years.

6

The Challenge of the Consumer

Now that we know something about the processes by which the big catalog chains obtain their merchandise and sell it to us, how are you and I, the consumer, going to use this information to our advantage? Although the people at Montgomery Ward had talked frankly to me, often telling me a lot more than I really wanted to know, I was nevertheless a little hesitant when I approached Robert M. Harrell, vice president and retail merchandise manager. I decided not to beat around the bush, and asked him, point blank, "How can the customer beat Monkey Ward?"

Harrell's reaction was unusual, but then he is an unusual person. Not everybody enters Miami University and graduates from Miami University, a thousand miles away; he went to both Miami of Florida and Miami of Ohio. Bouncy and enthusiastic, Bobby Harrell looks younger than most people born in 1924 and who've been with one company 24 years.

Anyway, when I asked him how to beat the company, a big smile broke out all over his face and he promptly proceeded to tell me. If you follow his directions, you'll save 15 to 20 per cent a year.

That's a pretty big *if*, however. The reason Bobby is so happy to give you and me a game plan to beat him with is because he's certain we won't follow it. He is confident that when we go in to pick up a special bargain, his merchandise, displays and sales people are going to make it impossible for us to resist buying something else that is *not* a special bargain.

Bobby is the perfect throwback to the hunter of the tribe. A couple of times during our conversation he said, "You gotta shoot 'em when they're flying." Any duck hunter knows what that means. Translated to consumerese, Bobby is telling us that when buyers flock to a Ward store, he's going to make a killing. You and I are the ducks. If we can get out of Wards —or any store—with sale-priced merchandise and without being shot down by another salesman, we've beaten him at his own game. We're pretty smart ducks.

With all its sales and special price reductions, 60 to 65 per cent of all Ward's merchandise is sold at full list price. The other side of the coin, of course, is the 35 to 40 per cent sold on an off-price basis. You have your choice, but to get in the off-price percentage on a substantial portion of your purchases, you've got to follow the game plan, and resist that impulse.

Wards runs sales on individual items the year round, of course, but wise buying requires a knowledge of seasonal merchandising.

The annual July blanket and pillow sale is an excellent place to begin. Here is one of those peculiar situations in consumerism in which everybody wins—you, the store, the store's employees, the manufacturers, all the way back to the manufacturer's employees. In the July blanket and pillow sale you can save about $4 on a $12 pillow, $8 on an electric blanket. During such an event the store spends money in advertising to tell you about it, and may even offer a special PM—pin money—of 25 cents an item to the salespeople. This PM goes not only to the people in the bedding department, but to personnel as far removed as the detached TBA—tire, battery and accessories—store. Drive in on a hot July day to look at automobile air conditioners and somebody will try to sell you a blanket.

Why should Wards spend money in advertising and dole out PM's to sell you something for much less money than you will pay three months later? The answer begins months before, when buyers go into the market to procure this merchandise. They offer to purchase huge quantities during the off-season lull. The manufacturer sees an opportunity to keep his plants going with full employment. This is not only going to keep him from losing money, but enable him to make some. He can give a good price for this order. Now Wards has carloads of stuff bought off-season, and can sell it to you for less.

You save money, the store makes money (and gets you inside its doors in hopes of making more selling other items), the newspapers get advertising, kids make money delivering circulars door to door, the manufacturer keeps his plant going at a profit smaller than that of peak periods but a lot larger than he would normally expect at that time of the year, and the factory workers stay on the job and continue bringing home pay checks. Everybody wins. You don't even have to clutter up your house with merchandise you don't need yet. For a few dollars, Wards will lay the stuff away until you want it. You don't have to pay the full price, nor is it put on your account, until you take it out of the store.

The July blanket and pillow sale is an example of how the retail industry passes savings on to you through advance planning and coordination. But it is also an example of a basic principle in consumerism: it's always cheaper to buy merchandise before you need it. May, for example, is the time for women to buy summer dresses, August to buy winter dresses. July is the time to outfit children going back to school in September. (Caution: parents are taking a chance on the early purchase of some back-to-school items. You haven't saved a nickel if your child goes back to school, sees that the other kids are wearing something completely different and kicks up a rumpus until you buy it.)

So it is that February is a good time to buy air conditioners, boats, outboard motors, garden tractors and lawn mowers and summer furniture. August is a good time to buy winter items, like snow blowers.

"You'll never be able to buy a boat in the spring and summer as cheap as you can buy it in January," Harrell says. "Oh, maybe some individual store manager will wind up with too many and will have to unload at a good price, but from the standpoint of our advance planning, the winter price is the lowest of the year."

If you are a suspicious type of individual, as I am, you may wonder why Wards wants you to buy something for less money before the season begins. One reason is that you are doing them a great big favor. In ladies' fashions, the reason is obvious. When the canny shoppers make their purchases in May, they give the fashion merchandisers a good fix on what is going to sell when the crowd starts coming in. If nobody buys a certain style, then the manager of that department won't make that mistake again. If there's a big run on an item, he will not only reorder it himself, but will alert the home office. If the model looks like it's going to run, the buyer may well dash back to the manufacturers for more.

Another reason for selling you something at a lower price this month than next, is, as Bobby Harrell puts it, to take you out of the market. He used pool tables as an example. Wards does a big business in pocket billiards; many families have tables in their recreation rooms both for their own togetherness enjoyment, and to entertain their friends. New customers, or devotees looking for replacements, usually start thinking about making the purchase in the winter. The weather drives them indoors, and it also coincides with the holiday season, when many families give themselves one big present. Knowing that this market is going to develop, and that potential purchasers are going to check the competition, too, Wards reduces the price in September to take the customer out of the market—to get him first.

This applies, too, to across-the-board reductions for those intelligent enough to do their Christmas shopping early. Retailers know that there are always going to be plenty of people like me (I remember Christmas about December 23) who come charging in during the Christmas rush. For us there's no need to reduce prices, except maybe on an item here or there to get us in that store rather than in some other store. But to take the early-bird shoppers out of the market in November the store has to make its prices on toys and other gifts attractive.

Retailers also know buying patterns, and meet the competition. One of the most popular types of Christmas presents is the entire line of hi-fi and stereo equipment, including record players and tape recorders. People also give money for Christmas. That adds up to a big market for records and tapes the day after. Wards cuts its prices sharply on records and tapes during the week after Christmas.

Many other items go on sale during this week, too. This type of sale is historical. For years merchants were deluged with customers right up through Christmas Eve, then looked out on a great expanse of nothingness the week after. The 13th month sale, the week between Christmas and New Year, was a natural result. Merchants could not only unload what was left over from Christmas season, but sell special merchandise at reduced prices to lure the shoppers in for another whirl.

Moving the January white sale merchandise up a couple of weeks was a natural development. Other lines include men's suits, women's foundations, shoes and outer wear for the entire family.

At this time of year people fret about the amount of money they spent for presents, whether to accompany the lighting of the Hanukkah candles or to go under the Christmas tree—

or both. Through some strange quirk in the human mind, some people salve their conscience for spending too much before Christmas by getting a bargain after Christmas.

"We know that at that time of year customers respond to price reductions on big ticket merchandise, on all merchandise," was the way Harrell put it. After Christmas Wards makes a big thing of reducing the price of bottom-of-the-line appliances—washers, driers, ranges—thus making a double pitch to the seasonal seizure of frugality. The customer buys a bargain at a bargain and feels good all over.

Most of what we've been talking about here depends upon your anticipating what you will want, and buying it before you need it. This is the surest way. Another possibility is to wait until after the season has peaked—July for summer dresses, January for winter suits—and get what's left over. The manager has to clear out his stock to make room for new merchandise, and he marks it down to get rid of it. You can get a bargain—if you can find what you want.

Sometimes, too, a buyer goes off on a tangent and procures way too much of something. A few years ago Wards got caught with thousands of Italian motorcycles at a time when the craze for that size machine had suddenly expired. The company had to unload them at a horrendous loss. If you had wanted an out-of-style but serviceable motorcycle at that time, you could have gotten one mighty cheap.

Twice a year the catalog houses clear out their stocks. Some of the items listed in the clearance books are dogs that nobody wanted; many are perfectly good articles of merchandise, ranging from underwear to tractors, for which the demand was overestimated.

So much for seasonal patterns. The game plan on this type of merchandise is either to buy it before you need it at reduced prices, or after the peak at *greatly* reduced prices—if you can find it.

Unfortunately for the future planner, the big-ticket line of appliances—refrigerators, freezers, ranges, washers, driers—

have no seasonal pattern. They are offered in special promotions which, depending on the item, may be more or less frequent. The Federal Trade Commission, for example, restricts sales on tires. You may have to wait two or three months for the tire you want to come around.

Wards itself restricts the frequency of sales on many lines. Excellence Award items, which meet such difficult criteria that the company feels they are good buys at the list price, are sold at reduced prices no more than twice a year, or once a season. If you just missed the sale on 4-Season hunting boots you'll have to wait a year to buy them at reduced prices. For the $500-plus three-door refrigerator-freezer you'll have to wait six months or so.

The only official way to find out when a big-ticket item will be on sale is to check the newspaper ads, circulars, or special sale catalogs. However, Bobby Harrell pointed out that a good relationship with a salesman in the proper department may well pay off. If you want a new refrigerator, for example, and can get by with your old one for a while longer, tell your salesman to let you know when a sale is coming up. He is on a commission basis and he'd like to sell you one at full price. But if you're adamant about saving money he'd a lot rather take your name and call you than lose the sale. That call is money in his pocket.

He may even drop by and see you. Wards does a big business in off-premises sales of commission items—floor coverings, custom drapery, furniture, tires, building materials, plumbing equipment, fencing, appliances. Salesmen are not permitted to knock down prices on their own, but if the only way they can sell you is to wait for a scheduled promotion in their line, they'll do it.

Especially in the metropolitan centers, where Wards is fighting for existence with Sears, Penneys, the other chains, discounters and local stores, it has to put on promotions every week—and so do all the others. All want to attract you on weekends—that's when the ducks are flying. Every store offers reduced prices on many items every week. They dare you to come in and buy sale-priced items without buying something else on which they make full profit. But you can do it if you try.

If wise buying according to the Harrell game plan is challenging, think how lucky we are to be living in these days of standardized prices for guaranteed items. When Aaron Montgomery Ward got the revolutionary idea of selling the same article to everybody at the same price, most Americans—at that time we were a rural nation—were at the mercy of their community's general store. The storekeeper himself was at the mercy of his suppliers, with whom his only contact was the traveling salesman who covered the area periodically. The local merchant had to pay cash for his merchandise; he might have to wait until the crops came in—if they did—for his money. What else could a fellow do but get the highest price from each customer. There was as much haggling in an American general store of the nineteenth century as there is in an oriental bazaar, or a used-car lot, today.

Young Montgomery Ward was himself a store manager in a small town, then a drummer, traveling through the midwest and south. Life was a succession of wooden railway cars, horse-and-buggies hired at the livery station, general stores and rooming houses. He had to drive hard bargains with his customers, and he saw them take advantage of theirs. There must be a better way. . . .

Off the road, clerking in a Chicago supply house, he thought of that better way. He saved his money, purchased some merchandise, rented a small room and Box No. 517 at the Chicago post office, had his list printed, and he and his wife addressed them and sent them out to locals of the National Grange. He had only recently gotten married, to the former Elizabeth Cobb, and the young couple could only sit and wait for some response. Their friends, and Elizabeth's family, thought they were crazy. If the people in the small towns couldn't trust their own storekeeper, how could they trust an unknown company in Chicago?

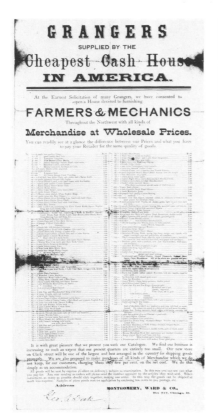

In 1872, when America was a rural nation, Aaron Montgomery Ward mailed out his first price lists. The family below, photographed in front of their sod house, obviously made good use of the new service. According to the Nebraska State Historical Society, the women's and boys' shirts were all made from the same bolt of Montgomery Ward calico.

166

It must have been discouraging. Few orders came in. The next year was even worse, for that was the panic of '73. But Ward figured that the harder the times, the more the people out there needed his prices. He continued to work at his job by day, fill what few orders he received at night. And, gradually, the orders increased. Elizabeth's sister's husband, George Thorne, who had been one of the first to predict that Ward would lose his shirt, brought in $500 and himself as a full-time partner. The business moved from a small room to a small store.

Then Ward got a strange break. The *Chicago Tribune,* in one of a series of exposés, called Montgomery Ward and Company "a swindling firm" and "dead-beats." Ward somehow prevailed upon the *Trib* to investigate his operations. The paper sent a reporter who must have liked what he saw, for it printed not just a retraction, but an out-and-out endorsement. Ward reprinted the entire article in his 1874 catalog —four pages listing 394 items.

But people are naturally suspicious, and still there were doubts. This was a period, remember, in which different people paid different prices for the same items. How could you *know* you weren't paying more than I? Ward settled this question in an ingenious and far-reaching fashion: the guarantee. This landmark of consumer protection appeared in the spring-summer catalog of 1875:

We Guarantee All of Our Goods

If any of them are not satisfactory after due inspection, we will take them back, pay all expenses, and refund the money paid for them. . .

This not only established quality, but price. If the refund was the same to all, the price was the same to all. Ward's friends told him that such a policy would result in his customers' robbing him blind, but it didn't work out that way. Then, as now, consumers appreciated fair treatment. The orders poured in. In the next catalog the number of items listed jumped to 3,899. To fill them the company moved to a three-story building containing an acre and a half of floor space. The consumer revolution had begun—almost a century ahead of Ralph Nader.

It is still no longer won, but today's consumer advocates at least receive more support from the people they're trying to protect. As Montgomery Ward, and later Sears, Roebuck, attracted more and more mail order business, local merchants whipped up campaigns against them. In many communities the very people who stood to benefit most from the convenience and one-price-to-all advantages of mail order shopping joined in the public outcry against it. In many communities demonstrations were held in which the people from both the town and countryside were exhorted to throw their catalogs into a bonfire. Local protection groups offered up to a dollar each for catalogs to keep the flames burning.

Some mail order customers played it both ways; they took the money, sent off for another catalog, and kept right on ordering from it. The campaigns had to hurt the mail order companies to some extent, but they prospered nevertheless. The catalog concept was just too economically sound from the consumer point of view to be defeated. Some merchants continued to gouge their customers, and probably always will, but many were forced by the mail order firms to meet the competition in price and quality. Aaron Montgomery started a trend which will last forever.

Before returning to consumerism today, let's touch for a moment on two other aspects of this farsighted man. At that time American business, like business the world over, was carried on under what sociologists call the Protestant Ethic. The guidelines of the ethic were to work like a dog and stay out of trouble, thus finding financial reward on earth and happiness in heaven. (In contrast, most enlightened businesses today operate on the terms of the Social Ethic, whose guidelines include working together, with incentives, fringe benefits and weekends, to achieve not only greater production but also some degree of happiness here and now.)

From the sweatshop misery of the cities to the drudgery of the farms piece workers and hired hands were expected to work from dawn to dusk, six days a week, to put money in the pockets of the owners. Wards created or fostered many exceptions to the industrial life-style of the times. The Clerks Benefit Society, formed to provide relief to employees and their families during sickness or on the death of a member, raised money by dues as well as company picnics and balls. Women employees, coming in soaking wet during the miserable Chicago winters, could dry their shoes and stockings at heating units before going to work. They left earlier than the men in order to get seats on the street cars. A medical department was set up with a doctor and a staff of nurses on duty full time; one of the nurses made follow-up calls at home. This was a time when tuberculosis took a terrible toll of city workers, and to keep up the strength of the employees Wards served 12-ounce glasses of malted milk at mid-morning and mid-afternoon. The work breaks themselves were unusual, let alone the free nourishment.

It wasn't easy to be a benevolent employer in those days. When the company tried to provide a blanket insurance policy for its employees, about 6,000 strong in 1910, it found there just wasn't any such thing as a group insurance policy. Insurance companies flatly rejected the idea of combining sickness, accident protection, old age pensions and life insurance in one package. Finally, after two years, the Equitable Life Assurance Society wrote a $5 million policy covering life insurance, sickness, accidents and old age. If you're in a group insurance plan, you can thank Montgomery Ward for getting it started.

Ward's other example of farsightedness was in the area of city beautification and concern for the environment. In 1887, when the expanding business needed still larger quarters, he and George Thorne bought a six-story warehouse on Michigan Avenue at Washington Street. The cost was high, $235,000, but the site had other values. Originally the location of Fort

Dearborn, the terms under which it was sold by the federal government specified that the grounds between the avenue and Lake Michigan would be forever public, with no buildings. Ward's $235,000 therefore bought not only real property but an unobstructed view of the beautiful lake, ventilation from its breezes and national light from the open sky.

For the next 23 years Montgomery Ward was almost continually involved in a fight to keep it that way. Offering to personally finance the beautification of the area, now known to Chicagoans and visitors as Grant Park, he took on a succession of foes. The city wanted to build scaffoldings to dump garbage into railroad cars between the avenue and the lake. The National Guard wanted to put up an armory with a parade ground. Marshall Field wanted to put up a public museum; trustees of the John Crerar library wanted to put up a building.

Some of these projects advanced to the stage where the land was filled in and building permits granted. In constant legal actions, Ward prevented them all. He was called stubborn and eccentric, and an obstructionist. He carried the legal battle to the state Supreme Court in four separate suits, at his own expense, winning each one. Instead of gratitude for preserving the beauty of the lake frontage, which he compared to the Bay of Naples, all he got was abuse. He was a premature environmentalist. Finally, in 1913, the *Chicago Tribune,* which had often criticized his efforts harshly, began an editorial: "Grant Park is Montgomery Ward's monument." But Montgomery Ward did not see it. It was his obituary.

Quality

To return to consumerism today, so far we have discussed only how to get the best price for what we buy. In consumerism price is the highly visible tip of the iceberg compared to quality, the murky mass beneath the surface. How can we be assured that what we buy, no matter the price, will give us good service?

Aaron Montgomery Ward, a pioneer environmentalist, was excoriated for his 20-year battle to save the Chicago lakefront. Top set of photos show the way it was. Below, Grant Park is today a monument to his perseverance.

171

How can we know that our clothes will fit, before *and* after laundering? How can we know that the many items we need, or think we need for twentieth century living, will do whatever it is that we bought them to do, for a reasonable length of time?

The answer, of course is that we can't be absolutely sure of anything made by man—sometimes even mother nature slips up. Though this book is based on Montgomery Ward, its execuives would be the last to claim that their products are infallible. In the world of consumerism they have double vision: they not only procure great quantities of merchandise and study the performance statistics, but they buy and use things themselves, just like us ordinary people. Ward's buyers have procured whole lines of merchandise for the company that proved faulty— adding machines that wouldn't add, chain saws that wouldn't cut—as well as individual items for themselves, made by the most reputable sources, which provided more headaches than service.

But we can learn a great deal from the collective experience of these men and women—more, in fact, than from any other group from just about any other retailer. For with the arrival of Tom Brooker in 1961, the company had to start all over again, almost from scratch, on the highest level of consumerism.

"You start with the consumer," he told me. "If you have a good customer, he has to be satisfied. We know that we have to have a good product. A good product is our best salesman."

You and I want to get a good product whenever we go shopping; Montgomery Ward *had* to get a good product—in 100,000 items selected from tens of thousands of manufacturers all over the world. It could be done only with good buyers, men and women with thorough knowledge of product, value, and cost. They represent us, the customers; they *are* us.

Although the total of their experiences, what they've learned from their goofs and their glories, would enable you to get the most in quality in just about everything you buy, it would also take the rest of your life to read it. We'll have to go mostly with generalities. To begin with, let's take the idea some people have that the catalog chains have their goods made to lower standards than items carrying the manufacturer's own brand.

I must admit I was surprised at how widespread this belief is. Of half a dozen friends who own stores which sell big-ticket items — refrigerators, ranges, TV, furniture — manufactured by the same companies which supply Sears, Wards and Penneys, every single one was sincerely convinced that his was the better product.

"Everybody knows that the original brand name is better than the stuff they turn out under other names," one said.

"Those big companies write their own specifications," another said, "but the quality is below the regular line, which I sell."

Some of these national brands represented here were Frigidaire (Wards), Whirlpool (Sears), Tappan (Wards), Corona Typewriters (Sears), Admiral (Wards), Bassett furniture (Wards), Firestone tires (Wards).

I personally don't believe this. Would it make sense for Sears, which owns a majority of the stock in and takes 70 per cent of the production of Whirlpool, to cut its own throat with inferior specifications?

I've noted in many years of reading Consumer Reports that Sears-Wards-Penneys merchandise seems to average out okay in comparison with name brands. Repairmen tell me the basic parts are interchangeable. It is true, of course, that buyers try to get the costs down but this can be done in more ways than reducing quality. John McGivern, when he was a buyer of power tools, took an electric drill to pieces, spread out its components and studied each individual part. The forward-reverse switch cost $2 — why not combine it with the on-off switch? The manufacturer said it couldn't be done, but McGivern, who's both persistent and big, said it could be done and that Wards would pay for it. It worked. Wards and the consumer now pay for only one switch on power tools, and the user gets the added convenience. Cutting corners isn't always a bad idea.

Finally, even if it were true that manufacturers make lines of inferior merchandise for the catalog chains, I wonder if it's good advertising to knock a product manufactured by the same company whose products you're selling.

But to get an official viewpoint, I went to John A. Marchese, vice president–merchandise procurement of Wards, who also spent 16 years with Sears. John's assignment, to develop products and improve quality, is as much a personal crusade as a job. From that standpoint he explained the benefits a major supplier gains by competing with itself—that's not the way *he* put it—under a private label. Most important, of course, is incremental volume. By selling more of its product, under whatever label, it can spread out and thereby reduce costs. Another benefit is additional feedback from more consumers on what they want.

And of great value is the technical and financial assistance furnished by the major retailer. Not every company needs this—Firestone and General Motors could probably make out without Marchese's staff looking over their shoulders. But in many cases Wards has provided financial assistance in building new plants and technical assistance ranging from design to final inspection, even assistance in cost-accounting techniques.

"Dealing with 7,000 sources," Marchese said, "we found that some were incompetent, some lacked integrity. Dropping them was easy. What's difficult, and rewarding, is working with the fellow who wants to do a good job, encouraging him, motivating him and his employees to do an even better job. We have been so successful that more than half of our merchandise is produced by 170 suppliers who have the Quality Assured Source label. To win this distinction a manufacturer must meet many demanding criteria. They knock themselves out to earn it. It's proof that they are tops in their field."

For years Wards sold the Simplicity line of garden tractors. With the increased market brought on by the back-to-the-soil movement, Ted Falen, buyer of that merchandise, decided to bring out a distinctive model. Falen bought, borrowed or leased every tractor on the market, complete with attachments. He studied them all, decided on the best features of each, and designed a super tractor. Arrangements were worked out with Gilson Brothers, a small, good company, to build it. This required a major expansion on Gilson's part; Wards helped, all the way. This tractor today carries Wards Excellence Award; Wards believes it is the finest made, by far. It is also available under the Gilson label, and Wizard of Western Auto.

Most major manufacturers maintain extensive laboratories to test their products. Wards has its own research laboratory which runs tests on top of the manufacturer's tests; its real value is its continuing contribution to product development and improvement. Every Excellence Award item, from socks to refrigerators, has gone through the lab, as has every product of the Quality Assured Resources. Its director, James C. Tielke, reports directly to Marchese.

Tielke was an excellent choice for the role of consumer protector. Starting out his business career in the family automobile dealership, he found he just couldn't take some aspects of the business. "It's hard to sleep well at night after screwing your fellow man all day." He gave up his share of a successful business and wound up at Wards. The company was then just barely muddling along; when asked where he worked he'd mumble. "Now I say it with pride. I can't make a contribution to a company without a deep personal conviction to it. Now I can. I get huge chunks of emotional income."

Tielke considers his work, taking a second look at the country's products, a service of the company to the nation. He tested an automatic garage door which was supposed to stop its descent if impeded, say by a child, but in tests it just kept on coming down. The fault was determined and the manufacturer notified. Now children, pets and toys are no longer in danger of being crushed, not just by Montgomery Ward doors, but all models made by that manufacturer.

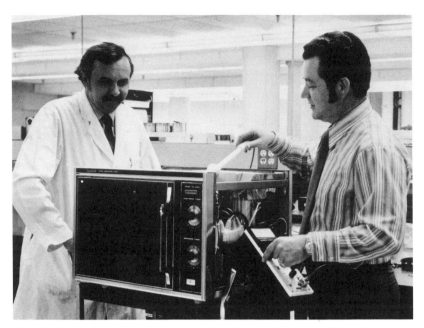

Jim Tielke, right, tests a microwave oven for safety standards in the Merchandise Research and Development Center.

To test brakes on kids' bicycles, Jim got employees to bring their children in to ride the bikes on the Ward parking lots, their fathers running along with them. Some of the brakes did fail, but, thanks to the quick action of the fathers, no one was hurt. Better there than on the street. Again the fault was corrected.

One product called for a moral decision. It was a tear-gas weapon, designed to be carried in a woman's purse for protection. The gadget functioned perfectly, but was it strictly a defensive weapon? Jim thought it could be of greater value—or danger—as an offensive weapon, and as such should not be offered for sale by Montgomery Ward. The decision went all the way up to Ed Donnell, who agreed. The item was not stocked.

Another service provided by Wards not only to its customers, but to the entire nation, is in permanent care labeling. Although several Ward buyers and quality control experts explained the situation to Bonnie and me, I'll use instead an unimpeachably

176

impartial source for background—Virginia H. Knauer, Special Assistant to the President of the United States for Consumer Affairs.

"Quality is just one of the consumer's concerns about clothing," Mrs. Knauer said in an address to the New York Couture Group in January, 1972. "Care is another. In the good old days when all dresses creased, and everything had to be ironed, you knew where you stood. Cottons went into the washing machine, wool went to the dry cleaner's, and delicate items were washed by hand.

"With the new miracle fabrics, and the endless possible combination of fibers, both natural and man-made, consumers no longer have an easy rule of thumb for how to clean clothing. A blouse that feels like the best silk may wash as easily as a terry cloth towel. But, unfortunately, the reverse is also true. A jersey that looks as washable as cotton may shrivel up in the drier.

"The new fabrics are a blessing. Just imagine the woman-hours that no-iron clothes have saved! But the new fabrics are also demanding. They need to be washed at the right temperature, dried at the right temperature, or drip-dried or blocked. Montgomery Ward, I am told, has 28 different sets of care instructions that are used on the apparel it sells.

"When there are so many different possible ways to clean clothes it is not surprising that women often make mistakes that ruin a garment, or at best, prevent their getting full performance out of it. The consumer needs full information on how to care for each of the innumerable items in her laundry basket."

Mrs. Knauer went on to point out that many of the clothes we buy today have washing instructions on tags hanging from the garment by a piece of string. The most conscientious of us tuck these instructions away in a bureau drawer; others try to tuck them away in our memory. But when it comes time to launder the item, who remembers whether the instructions about chlorine bleach apply to the lingerie you bought last week or the blouse you got the week before? When the labels are permanent a woman has the instructions before her when she needs them—at the washing machine.

Mrs. Knauer kindly omitted a more serious criticism of some manufacturers. L. J. Nolan, merchandise development manager in A lines for Montgomery Ward, bluntly said that he knew of cases in which garments made of material which could only be dry-cleaned went out to retailers with tags saying they were washable. When washed according to instructions, these garments would shrink. In most cases, people simply wrote them off. In the unlikely event that the customer would go to the trouble to return it to the retailer, and the retailer would go to the trouble to refer the garment back to the manufacturer, the manufacturer could simply say, "Where is the label that says hand-washable?" It would be a rare customer indeed who could produce that tag.

Mrs. Knauer announced that the Federal Trade Commission had issued a regulation to require all manufacturers to affix permanent care labels on most articles of clothing. They must be attached in such a way that they stay on the garment throughout its useful life, and they must remain legible. The regulations went into effect July 3, 1972. "They represent an enormous step forward in providing consumers with the information they need in order to get full satisfaction from the clothing they buy."

Mrs. Knauer pointed out that some companies, including Montgomery Ward, had not waited for the regulation. The actual facts were more dramatic. Many Ward's people, especially Dick Abbott, vice president in charge of the New York office, had long fought for permanent care labeling. The garment industry had long resisted. Dick, a pleasant, slender Christian Scientist who would normally rather serve his church than fight, can be tough when representing the consumer. He insisted that Ward's suppliers affix permanent care labels not only to the garments they sold Wards, but the garments they sold to everyone else. Before the government edict went into effect, there-

Virginia Knauer and Dick Abbott, both of whom are strong advocates of permanent care labeling for all apparel.

fore, Ward's customers, and customers of all other retail stores also buying from Ward's sources, had permanent care labeling.

The upshot of all this is that in the continuing battle of consumer versus supplier, a rule of thumb might be that the safer bet is to spend your money with the retailer which has gone into the marketplace, sought out the best suppliers, worked with them to maintain and improve the quality of the product, performed its own tests in well-equipped laboratories by dedicated people and described exactly what you're getting in a catalog which you can study either at home or on the counter in the back of the store.

As for the model you want and the price you want to pay, that's up to you. The catalog chains break most of their merchandise down into the categories of *good, better* and *best.* You get what you pay for, but this does not necessarily mean that you need it. Ten thousand commission salesmen of big-ticket items will gnash their teeth when they read this, but Tom

179

Brooker himself recommends to the average consumer that you consider first the item in the *better* category. It usually has the functional capability of the *best* model, without the frills. If you want to dazzle your neighbor with push buttons, exotic colors and fancy cabinets, get the *best*. If you want to save money, get *good*.

Some consumers will not be able to find everything they want in the mass merchandise establishments. Bill Allred, for example, says he'd recommend firing anyone who carried his size shirt in stock—16 neck, 37 sleeve. I'm eliminated for being at the opposite extreme—17 neck, 30 sleeve. As I'm built like an oversized dwarf, with a long body and short legs, I can't wear any ready-made suit, but I did entertain the wild dream of wearing double-knit slacks like Fred Giersch and Greg Young. I ordered a pair, but alas, they don't fit.

Just as mass merchandisers do not carry suits for odd-sized people like me, neither do they carry suits made of the more expensive fabrics. Few Ward executives wear Ward's suits; the fabrics in the clothes they need for the circles in which they travel are found only in suits that cost twice as much as Ward's finest. Bonnie tells me that the same thing applies to women's clothes. While she likes the style and worksmanship of Ward's suits and dresses, she prefers more expensive fabrics. The Ward dress buyers understand; they supply the mass market and they do it well. They also tell you whether or not you can put what you buy in the washing machine.

Some items supplied to the mass market cannot meet the wide range of individual preference. I have never had a better tennis racket than the ones we get from Wards and recommend them to the average player. But I prefer my rackets strung more tightly than the tension Wards specifies, and some players might want them strung more loosely. I pay a fellow $5 to tighten up the strings and I'm still ahead. For those who don't want to go to that trouble Wards is still doing you a favor; by buying its rackets from Chemold it is in effect recommending that brand. That's good enough for a lot of my friends, and both tennis pros in town now carry Chemolds to meet the demand.

For people who do not live near the mass merchandisers with their private labels, probably the next thing to buying that merchandise is to get a comparable line—not the lowest price line—made by the same manufacturer. Does it not make sense that if Wards or the other catalog-retail chains select a supplier and stick with him that the whole line of merchandise must be comparatively reliable? At least it gives you something to shoot for. There are so many brand names on the market that you can go crazy trying to pick one out.

The other day a local owner of an appliance store was showing me a dishwasher he had just received. The nameplate was enclosed in the shipping crate. The company makes it under so many brands that it doesn't even bother to affix a plate in the

Good, Better, Best . . . You get what you pay for. Wise consumers use comparative prices, given in the catalog and in retail display, not only to buy merchandise from Wards but as a consumer yardstick for prices of all merchants.

factory. Both of us looked the machine over carefully, inside and out, and could not find the name of the manufacturer anywhere. He knew, and told me, but I had never heard of it before.

Using the catalog to purchase the original brand of a manufacturer which supplies the private label of a catalog chain can produce another benefit I'd never thought of before. A friend of mine carries the brand name of a manufacturer which also supplies Wards, and curious as to whether he resented Ward's competition, I went in to see him.

At first he said he does not resent Wards as much as he does a discounter in town which sells the lowest-priced model built by the manufacturer, which neither he nor Wards carries, and represents it as a top-quality product. Then we got down to cases. We looked in the catalog and found a Ward model selling for $290 — (I'll round off the cents for this exercise) and an identical model under the original brand right there on the floor for $347. His price would include installation — all hooked up ready to go.

"Wards will charge you extra for freight and installation," he said, "and of course they can't offer you the service I can. They won't take in a trade-in, either. Just the other day I took in one that I'm going to take to the junk yard, but I gave her $20 off on it."

"Suppose I save you the trouble of taking my old one to the junk yard," I said. "Will you give me $20 for it?"

"Sure," he said. "I've got a good markup on this."

"How about $30 off?" I asked.

"Well, yes, I guess I could go that high," he said.

I then checked in with Ernie Duggins to find out what I would have to pay extra for freight and installation. "Twenty-five dollars" he said. "That includes freight from Baltimore, delivery to your house, and installation."

"What about service in case anything goes wrong?" I asked.

"We'll take care of it," he said.

So now we come to $347 list price installed from the local

store, $315 list price installed for the same model from Wards. But the local fellow was willing to come down $30 which made his price only $2 higher than Wards.

"I know that you have special promotions," I told Ernie. "Do you have one on this item?"

"Not now, but I'm sure we will sometime in the next two or three months," Ernie said. "It will be about 20 per cent off. I can let you know."

At 20 per cent off the total would be $257 as compared to $317. When I got home and recounted all these figures to Bonnie she had a fit. "That's terrible," she said. "I've always paid what the dealer asked, and I thought everybody else did, too. How much money have we been taken for over the years? It makes me mad. From now on we're going to let Wards do our haggling for us."

You can let Wards do your comparison shopping for you, too. That's one of the functions of the National Merchandise Comparison department headed by a big, heavyset Sears import named H. E. Bro. "This department has three consumer benefits," Bro said. "Competitive pricing, comparable values to other chains and standard brands, and ease of purchase."

Members of Bro's department shop other chains, discount houses and stores carrying standard brands in order to determine how Wards compares with the competition in quality, features, value, price, sales, packaging, promotional techniques, assortments, advertising and point-of-sales presentation.

It's hardly a precise procedure. Once Bro sent three men out to a K-Mart, each assigned to a separate department. One memorized as many prices and descriptions as he could, ran to the restroom and wrote them down behind closed doors, then returned for another brainload. Another used the same system, but went to other portions of the store to make his notes. The third simply got a shopping cart, put his coat in it, proceeded to his assigned department with paper and pen and brazenly worked there for four hours in front of the clerks and customers, writing everything down. Nobody bothered him at all.

Members of the Merchandise Comparison Department are having a ball testing lawn mowers of various manufacturers.

Bro's department also runs quality tests on Ward's merchandise, and if he finds quality and prices out of line, he prepares a report for the proper department. He presents the facts, pulls no punches. In the case of shag tile, a couple of years ago, tests showed that Ward's shag tile, advertised as being suitable for use outdoors, held moisture and shrunk. The Sears tile was superior; of small solace to the buyer, Penney's was worse.

Six months after such an unpleasant report, Bro checks back to see if suggested changes have been made.

Sometimes the comparison department finds that a line of merchandise is better than the buyer thinks it is. Shopping stoneware, Bro's boys found that Wards carried an excellent line, superior to the competition's in both price and value, but almost hidden from the public. Turned out the buyer, an older chap, preferred china even though surveys showed *customers*, particularly younger ones, wanted stoneware. Well, you won't have any trouble getting it now. Bro sprung it loose.

The research department, under Glenn H. Hoffman, studies

184

just about every phase of merchandising. One of its chores was to identify the Ward customer—age, income, etc. One statistic should be of interest to those concerned with the population explosion. Those clever Ward families manage to have one and a half children each.

The research department wants to know whether people love Wards or hate Wards—and where and why. In St. Paul, Denver and Detroit, for example, Wards is loved. But as recently as the mid-sixties, when Hoffman first began taking the popularity poll, the results were disappointing. At that time Wards had not successfully converted to the new Brooker program of procuring merchandise, and was still picking, choosing and discarding suppliers. Over the succeeding years buyers have proved more knowledgeable in procuring merchandise, and the steady rise in customer satisfaction reflects it.

Wards tests its acceptance through its own research department which makes tens of thousands of calls over leased lines from Chicago to consumers across the country. In one hectic period of two weeks telephone interviewers talked to 4,000 people. Good interviewers have to have a special knack, and a genuine liking for people, although they pay a peculiar price. Lory Murray, a pint-sized girl who directs the operation, has spent so many hours talking clearly and distinctly on the phone that she now sounds like one. A customer broke into the conversation one time to ask her, curiously but politely, "Am I talking to a recording?"

"They assign us the craziest projects," Lory said. "Once we took a survey on frost-free food freezers. Just try saying frost-free food freezers fifty times in an hour. When we called about boys' underwear a lot of men hung up on us. I guess they thought we were making obscene phone calls.

"Another time the subject was radial arm power saws. Here we were, a bunch of girls in Chicago, talking to women all over the country—usually it's the woman who answers the phone—about something neither of us knew anything about.

"People don't understand that we're using leased lines. I was asking a man in San Diego about ladders one time and he broke in and said, 'You mean you're calling me long distance from Chicago about a stupid ladder?' You can't get rid of a lot of people. When they realize it isn't costing them anything to talk long distance they go on and on.

"I called a woman once who had mailed in a check on her account and had just realized she'd made it for ten cents less than she owed. As soon as I said Montgomery Ward she said, 'You're calling from Chicago for one lousy dime?' We don't get much static on credit, incidentally. People usually use cash for small purchases, credit for large. They know they're paying a service charge. They accept it.

"I always know when I'm talking to an older person. They say Monkey Ward. Younger people don't. Big city people, particularly in the east, are the hardest to talk to. I hate to call Albany and New York. People in small towns in the mid-west and west are the easiest. When we talk to a man who wears Ward's work clothes he's always friendly. In five years I've never heard one criticism of men's work clothes. Or Skips— the kid's sneakers. I wish I could say the same about some other products. I've talked to Ward employees who wouldn't buy big ticket appliances even with the employee discount. But they're getting better now. Anyway, it's a wonderful job. Who's better to work with than people?"

Lory and her telephone girls ask direct questions. Some research projects are trickier. Robert N. Joffe, a research project manager, had the job of testing customer acceptance of a new shopping bag. It was a loud, iridescent blue. Joffe, a lean, dark-haired young man, hadn't studied that problem at Northwestern University. How can you get people to evaluate a paper bag?

He finally worked out a way. His assistants got 100 identical women's sweaters and put 50 in the loud blue bag, 50 in an ordinary, conservative bag, then asked women what they thought of the *sweater.* Most of the women thought the sweater in the blue bag was sleazy, of poor quality. They much preferred the identical sweater in the conservative bag. Out went the wild blue shopping bag.

In another experiment the research department hung an assortment of clothes in the teenage Junior Reflections department. They asked 800 women what they thought of the clothes. Answer, so-so. Then the decor of the department was changed completely. Lots of mirrors and chrome. Now the women thought the clothes were spectacular.

Girls under twenty weren't fooled a bit, however. There's a moral in there somewhere.

In a comparative test between the Sears and Ward washing machines, women said they found Ward's too noisy. The buyers, thinking women would put the washers in the basements where it wouldn't matter, had saved costs by not cutting down on the noise. However, many women put the machines in their kitchens, or utility rooms just off the kitchen, and it did matter. The users of the Ward machines also complained that they required more water, which was true—but they rinsed better. The Ward washer was made quieter, but instead of cutting down on the water the merchandising department accentuated the superior rinsing qualities in promotion and advertising. Through an advanced form of comparison shopping, a liability was turned into an asset.

In addition to encouraging improvements in the various lines of merchandise, the comparison shopping department constantly seeks to give the customer something incomparably better, a wonder of the world. This is why the Excellence Award came into being. It is of such prestige in the company that a buyer will do practically anything to win it for his product.

Only 100 items a year receive the Excellence Award label. It represents the ultimate in the buyer's art, and is commensurately hard to get. It must be demonstrably superior in quality, as attested by the impartial research lab, have exclusive features, be reasonably priced in relation to quality (though these items are nearly always in the upper half of the price range) and have a strong market demand. (A cement mixer was once on the list of excellence awards, but not too many people fell over themselves to buy it and it was crossed off.) It must be compared with similar items carried by Sears, Penney, K-Mart, discounters and national brands. It must be the best and it must remain the best; it is compared to the competition every six months and if anybody comes up with anything better, the Excellence Award label comes off.

Judges for the award include the top members of the merchandising operation, from Jim Lutz and John Marchese on down. They are tough. Just the paperwork required with the submission of the item is stupendous. The buyer describes his (or her, for women's clothes developed by the soft lines departments are also eligible) pet in sextuplicate and in detail, complete with every feature of the candidate, and full comparison with the competition. Then the buyer presents it, complete with sales pitch.

"We spend more time selling each other than we do selling the customers," Bro says.

When Elaine Breuers persented her long-legged panty girdle before the all-male jury, for example, it was on the prettiest girl she could find. Elaine lingered long over her demonstration, showing how the girdle enhanced each portion of the girl's anatomy, including, with great attention to detail, the derriere. (Shades of Sewell Avery! He wouldn't permit foundation garments to be shown on mannequins, much less people.) Elaine got her Excellence Award. But then, so did such less sexy items as the new radial tire and three-door refrigerator.

Sears and Penney have similar awards, probably granted only after equally rigorous examination. With such demanding specifications set on each item, the catalog chains have done most of the work before the customer enters the store or opens the catalog.

The contention that the catalog chains and their suppliers produce the best items of merchandise across the board will be contested by many, and with reason. In the matter of refrigerators alone, Wards negotiated with Westinghouse, General Electric, Philco-Ford and others before settling on Frigidaire. Westinghouse did not want to expand its facilities in order to take care of the increasing Ward demands. GE decided against marketing its products under private labels. Negotiations with Philco-Ford got all the way up to Henry Ford II before the bilateral decision was made to terminate the discussions. Surely these companies, and many others, produce serviceable merchandise and have their loyal followers.

Nor does Consumers Union consistently give the highest ratings to either the catalog chains or their suppliers. What Consumers Union does provide consistently is irritation to the people at Wards. When CU gives a Best Buy rating to a Montgomery Ward product, the members of that department do everything but dance in the streets. But when CU gives a medium or low rating to a Ward item, everybody says those crazy people don't know what they're talking about. In a way they're both right. A CU Best Buy classification can make sales skyrocket. But CU can also make mistakes, of omission and commission.

When I brought up *Consumer Reports* in a conversation with Tom Brooker, it turned out that both of us had been reading the magazine since it was founded. I had accepted it as the bible of consumerism. Brooker also enjoys reading it and heartily endorses its basic purpose of advising the consumer on the quality and price of products. But he says flatly that CU's testing facilities are not as adequate as those of the big manufacturers, or of Wards, that it does not test enough samples of each product to present a thoroughly reliable judgment and that of the samples it does test, many, because they are bought off the shelf, are already obsolete.

These two positions — that every consumer study the magazine but that it is not thoroughly reliable — are not at all contradictory in Brooker's thinking. He's all in favor of the consumer's getting all the advice he can and using it to protect himself. As a merchant he likes to deal with well-informed customers who have a wide choice of merchandise. What bugs him is any attempt on the part of government to restrict their choice. He's an outspoken champion of free enterprise and the nongovernmental advisory role of CU fits right into his thinking. He just wishes it did a more complete job.

One of the criticisms Ward people have of Consumers Union is that it frequently omits major lines. The hosiery department at Wards was most upset over CU's evaluation of panty hose, for example. It awarded a Best Buy classification to a Penny and a Sears line of panty hose. The survey, however, though it covered many brands of panty hose, did not include the major selling line of either Wards, Sears or Penneys—Sears Clingalon, Ward's Brent-Lon or Penney's nude heel Agilon. And the people in the hosiery department were rather amused by the high rating given Ward's No. 5766 ($1.97, plus shipping costs), the low rating of Round-the-Clock 69 ($3), a national brand. The two were identical.

While the hosiery people were amused, Ed Lennox was infuriated by an adverse criticism of the Hawthorne spin casting reel in the same issue. This reel was personally designed by Lloyd Johnson of Johnson Reels Company. He is almost totally blind and designed it by feel; it has one of the simplest, most foolproof mechanisms ever put in a fishing reel.

CU rated the Ward Hawthorne 6439 several notches higher than the identical Johnson Commander 150. What bugged Lennox, however, was CU's description of the drags on both reels as rough, and a criticism of the way the drag operates.

"They missed the whole deal on this," Lennox said, mad as hell, "because this is what we call a power drag. No one else has it other than Johnson and Hawthorne. Whoever tested it didn't know what this thing was for. They just didn't understand it. I do understand it. There's an 18-pound northern pike right there on the wall I caught with a 12-pound line, and that drag worked beautifully."

Perhaps of more crucial interest to a larger number of consumers was the report on automobile tires in *Consumer Reports*

Ed Lennox shows 18 pounds of proof that the rod and reel he buys for Ward customers is as good as he says it is.

of August 1971. Ward's Riverside HST tire, though rated acceptable, was pretty far down the list with a tread life rated "well below average," or about 15,000 miles under average driving conditions. This resulted in a cost-mileage factor much higher than the Michelin X and Sears radial tires, which are the same, rated one and three, respectively, on the list.

John Sebastian, the Ward tire man, says that this is an example of comparing apples with oranges. Wards, too, carries a radial tire; it is completely modern, manufactured by Firestone, bears the Excellence Award, and features a 40,000-mile tread wear expectancy. It also costs a lot more than the trusty old HST, which was designed in 1964 for 1964 cars running on 1964 highways. The HST was outstanding for the job for which it was intended. Tires have been steadily improved since then — bias-belted polyester — and Wards carries these modern tires, but CU ignored them. As for the 15,000 miles tread life, in Ward's experience, and it has sold tens of thousands of HSTs and still continues to sell as many as any other line, most customers will get 20,000 to 25,000 miles of service under present driving conditions.

"We don't recommend them for the type of driver who drives constantly on turnpikes at high speeds," Sebastian says. "Even then, only the most abusive get only 15,000 miles as CU reported."

For a family like ours, which makes the ordinary trips around town, to the airport, tennis court and the river, and whose official tire buyer, me, doesn't like to spend money, this is a plenty good tire. If you are required or have the inclination to drive long distances at high speeds your tire salesman will recommend a more expensive tire in line with your driving.

In spite of these criticisms of Consumers Union the people at Wards, and I assume elsewhere, realize that they have to live with it. As John Sebastian said at the end of a four-page bitter letter, "We feel our best solution is to try to do better the next time around." In the meantime you can't help but learn something from *Consumer Reports,* and the more you learn, whether from it or the major catalogs, the better consumer you'll be.

Suppose you do make a thorough study of whatever it is you intend to buy, arrive at a value-judgment decision, buy it from a reliable retailer at a favorable price—and then the thing breaks down. What then?

Well, first of all, it's not your fault; you did the best you could. Next, although of course you can lay the blame squarely on the retailer, who is supposed to know what he's selling, and the manufacturer, the chances are they feel even worse about it than you do. They have to repair or replace the item, and in the case of replacement, that's not just doubling the cost of the replacement, but all the other costs, too, including transportation.

But before getting into that, why oh why do things break down at all? Why won't my car, manufactured in Sweden, start on cold mornings in Virginia? Why did Jim Lutz's new Cadillac rattle? (Someone left a cigarette lighter in the frame.) Why did Bonnie's $75 dress shrink after being dry-cleaned? Why did you have so much trouble with your _____? (If you can't think of anything to fill in that blank, you're one in a million.)

The imperfection of inanimate objects is nothing new. As long as humans have been making things, they've been making some of them wrong. Swords broke in Biblical times. I've found sloppily made arrowheads. George Washington had a chariot built to his exact specifications in England in 1768; he hadn't used it two months before the panels fell off. (He probably said, "They don't make 'em the way they used to.")

Disturbed over the performance, or lack of it, of a couple of items I got from Wards, I made a special trip to Chicago to discuss the problem with John Marchese and Jim Tielke. Neither beat around the bush.

"We buy a billion and a half dollars worth of merchandise

from 7,000 plants," Jim said. "On major lines we work from the inception of the product, beginning with a design which will perform the use for which the product is intended. We maintain a personal contact with each supplier, hold seminars on quality control. With any supplier furnishing over a million dollars worth of goods our people personally walk through the plant with a check list. We have monthly reports, periodic inspections. Further, no badly designed products are being manufactured by *any* company in the country today. No manufacturer deliberately builds a bad product.

"But still bad products are being built."

"By and large we do a good job," John Marchese said. "Why don't we do a 100 per cent good job? Two reasons. One is employee carelessness, both on our end and on the manufacturer's end. The other is the cost of absolute quality control. The nation put billions into the missile program, and tests and retests every component. We can't put that much in your shirt. We reject a lot of merchandise. The faulty items leak through the system by human error, not design."

Another reason is the sheer amount of merchandise being manufactured for modern demand. Shakespeare did all right with a quill pen; I've got three electric typewriters, two dictating machines and three tape recorders. We cut with electric knives, mix with electric beaters and blenders, cool and heat our houses with machinery of one kind or another, wash and dry dishes and clothes in more contraptions, shave and dry our hair with gadgets, cut the grass and hedge with power tools—we can't even open a can by hand. People never had so much, and the more of anything we have, the more can go wrong.

Nor do we customarily wait for things to wear out before dashing out and buying a replacement. Rabid consumerists accuse industry of manufacturing for obsolescence. If that were true, it would actually be a great compliment to modern technology. Figuring out how to make something stop working the day after the guarantee expires would require more expertise than we've got in the twentieth century. Often things last longer than the manufacturers expect. In the early days of TV, for example, electronics experts honestly believed the maximum life of the picture tube to be a year at best. Most lasted for many years.

Industry doesn't manufacture for obsolescence, but for change. Practically everything is being improved all the time, if only in appearance. How many white refrigerators have been discarded simply because the lady of the house wanted one in harvest gold or avocado? Was your black and white TV really beyond repair, or did you just want Living Color? As for clothes, how many perfectly good dresses or suits hang unworn and forlorn in your closet, simply because somebody you don't even know started a new trend?

All this does not apply to merchandise that is cheap and shoddy. You can buy it, but it is manufactured for the person who can least afford it, not the well-informed consumer. What we are concerned with here are the items of reasonable cost, made by good manufacturers, which still do not function the way they're supposed to, or maybe not at all. The ones which Marchese says leak through.

The enthusiasm, the delight in accomplishment, that you see in the white-collar buyers of merchandise and their counterparts in the manufacturing companies do not extend down to the workers on the assembly lines, the packers and shippers and receivers. Let's face it—the working lives of millions of Americans today amount to drudgery. Sure, they never had it so good in comparison to the long hard hours people worked in this very century. But the fact that somebody's grandfather worked fourteen hours in a mine doesn't make his own eight hours stamping widgets any less monotonous. He has a television set; unlike his hard-working grandfather he can see how the other half lives.

The industrial worker today has the sensitivity to get bored, and the freedom to do something about it. He can quit; turnover among the young workers in some plants runs

150 per cent a year. (That means a constant infusion of new people to make the same old mistakes.) He can just decide to take the day off. That day is usually either Friday, to start the weekend, or Monday, to get over it. Consumers familiar with the automobile industry have long believed that cars built on Friday and Monday are the lemons, cars built on Wednesday the best. The theory can be extended to nearly any product.

Tracing a malfunction back to the original cause is often fascinating detective work. Years ago some refrigerators sold by Wards and other retail outlets of the supplier at that time began breaking down. The problem in determining the cause was that there was no pattern to the malfunctions. Some compressors burned out; some from the same shipment did not. The manufacturer had had labor problems, and it was finally decided that the malfunctions stemmed from a clever method of sabotage. One of the steps in refrigerator manufacturing is to squirt a specific amount of lubricating oil into each sealed unit. The worker assigned to this duty carries the exact amount of oil for the number of units to be lubricated in a tank on his back, and at the end of the line an inspector checks the tank to make sure it is empty. The only logical explanation was that the scheming fellow put twice the amount of oil in half the units, none at all in the others.

One winter several Ward customers took home snow-throwers to find, on opening the carton, that they had been packed with no handle. The next to the last process on the assembly line is to inspect the package and put in the handle. It's natural to assume that the man in charge of that detail didn't get back from the coffee break before a half dozen had gone through to the sealer.

Until humans become as perfect as they expect their machines to be, these things are bound to happen. Which one of us achieves perfection in our jobs every day? In the affluent society, in which the assembly line worker is also a consumer, the individual who gripes about the workmanship on the product he bought yesterday may well goof up on the product somebody else is going to buy tomorrow.

What is really more newsworthy than the number of objects which malfunction is the number of products which do give good service. I was present at an Excellence Award committee meeting at which the refrigerator buyer, Fred Helmholz, was trying to win the award for not one, but two refrigerators. He made his sales pitch, and responded to precise and searching questions from Jim Lutz and John Marchese. Finally Jim leveled a Teutonic look at him and demanded brusquely, "If you can't have both, which one do you want?"

Marchese laughed sympathetically. "Which of your children will you kill?"

Helmholz looked from one to the other of his children. He sighed and pointed to one of them. "This one is made for us by Frigidaire," he said, naming the specific plant. "I'd have to put it first. It has had less than one half of 1 per cent returns."

That was the refrigerator that got the Excellence Award, but what sticks in my mind is that rate of return. Of every 200 sold, complete with automatic defroster, freezer, ice maker, third-door compartment, decorator colors, the whole works, only one is returned—and that could be because the lady who bought it decided she didn't like the color after all.

This rate of return, of course, is unusually low. For some products, particularly those representing new fads, the rate is unusually high; they pay the cost of pioneering. Wards has taken opposite positions on various new products. When permanently pressed garments first came out, Penney, Ward's major competitor in soft lines, stocked them. Ward buyers wanted to plunge in, too, but Marchese held back. His argument was that the process was not yet perfected, and that the company stood to lose more in dissatisfied customers than to gain in keeping up with the Joneses. When the process was perfected to his satisfaction—with other retailers' customers serving as guinea pigs—he gave the go-ahead.

On the other hand, when the mini-bike craze hit the nation,

and manufacturers who were barely qualified to turn out bottle tops began churning out pieces of junk called mini-bikes, Wards had to go along.

"At least while we were selling them we were learning how to design better ones," Marchese said. "Now we have the best one on the market."

The odds are strong that the next major appliance you buy will give good service. But how can the intelligent consumer make those odds even higher? One way is to narrow the selection down to those items which have been preselected by experts. I learned this the hard way. A few years ago I received an offer in the mail from an oil company. It said that because I was a loyal customer the company was going to permit me to buy the most wonderful portable radio ever made, with all kinds of yummy features for next to nothing. I bought the radio, and it was terrible. When I sent it back for repair to the address given—totally different from that of the oil company—it just disappeared. I got mad and wrote the president of the company. (Always complain to the president of the company.) Long-distance calls, letters and radios purporting to be personally tested by junior executives poured in. They were all lousy, but what the hell. I kept one, gave it to Sue to listen to rock and roll with and chalked the money up to experience. What does an oil company, or for that matter, a drugstore or a variety store, know about buying radios in Japan?

By contrast, Ward's buyers and executives go to Japan and Taiwan, finance manufacturers if necessary, work with them on design, manufacture and quality control, and even inspect the packing and shipping. In oriental factories Jim Lutz has personally held radios and portable TVs packed for shipping at arms length and let them drop to the floor, then checked them for damage. Some lemons may still get through, but this type of attention must certainly reduce the odds.

All the foregoing has in pragmatic reality been unnecessary reading to the consumer who wants advice, not explanations. The empirical test of any product is not the on-site inspection by the buyer, the tests made in the research lab, or Jim Lutz's dropping it on a concrete floor, but what to do when you buy it, take it home and discover that it doesn't work. Aaron Montgomery Ward gave the complete and final answer to consumerism in 1875 on the inside cover of his catalog: We Guarantee All of Our Goods. If his customers did not find what they bought satisfactory, they could send the merchandise back and get a full refund plus shipping expenses. A lot of customers, even though actually satisfied with the goods, sent them back to see if Ward really meant it. He did.

For the beginning of the Second Century of Montgomery Ward this guarantee was stated and printed in one of the simplest yet most comprehensive guarantees ever given by any company. It takes up a page in the catalog, and is qualified to a certain extent by a paragraph on special guarantees. The meat of the statement is contained in two paragraphs:

> If when you receive your purchase, you find that it is not completely satisfactory, return it. We will gladly exchange it for something that is just right or refund the price and transportation charges you paid.
>
> If, after you have used your purchase, you find that it is not satisfactory to you and is not covered by one of our Special Guarantees, simply return it to us and explain what is wrong. We will make an adjustment in cash, credit, merchandise or repair completely satisfactory to you.

Though it probably says it best, Wards is certainly not the only company in the country to guarantee its merchandise. Further, some people in the selling end of the business, being the hunters of the tribe, and therefore born adversaries, may not happily replace or give a total refund for any battered old item that you may bring in. All I can say is that I, like some of the skeptics in 1875, have made my own tests, one of which could well be considered taking advantage of a good thing. After I'd used a tennis racket for over a year, and lent it to a dozen friends, the frame broke. The break occurred during normal usage, not when I threw it down after missing a shot, but nevertheless that racket had taken an awful lot of punishment. And it was more than a year old.

I still took it in to Ernie Duggins, the manager of our local catalog store; I hadn't even bought it through him. He said he'd see what he could do. Next time I went in he handed me a brand new racket.

Though you may consider this an abuse of the satisfaction guaranteed principle, the consumer should feel no compunction about returning an article with which he is dissatisfied. Keeping something you don't like and grousing about it to your wife and friends does nobody any good. Wards, and other major companies, enter into an arrangement with their suppliers by which it is the supplier, not the retailer, which replaces the unsatisfactory article or refunds the money for it — plus freight. Considering paper work and transportation, the cost of replacing the item is far more than the cost of the item itself. It's a form of punishment, and if you're so mad you want revenge, this is the way to get it. What's unfair is that you're retaliating against the honorable merchandiser and manufacturer. You can't punish the schlock house that ignores your complaint.

The concerned consumer is more desirous of improving quality for himself and all consumers. He can perform this function best by calling the attention of responsible retailers and manufacturers to faulty merchandise. (I'm not speaking here of the consumerist, either professional or amateur, who studies products and trade practices and reports on them to whoever will read or listen.)

Nobody has any way of knowing the fault of a product, much less how to rectify it, unless you speak up. I learned the importance of customer complaints through personal experience. For Christmas last year Santa Claus brought me a unicycle. It was a 20-inch model, and when I tried to ride it my feet wouldn't fit on the pedals. Annoyed, I called the manufacturer direct. In the course of the conversation I mentioned that I weigh 200 pounds. I was told that this model was designed for kids weighing at most 150 pounds. I then suggested to Santa Claus that I be given an adult, 24-inch unicycle. But I never got to ride that one either, because I could not tighten the seat securely.

So now I began to feel pretty silly. What was I, a grown man in my fifties, doing with a unicycle anyway? It sat on the side porch, and I sulked. Finally I got mad enough to tell Marchese and Tielke about my two unicycles. They were happy to investigate both.

In the case of the 20-inch unicycle, they checked the Sears and Penney catalogs and found that one specified an age limit, the other a weight limit. Ward's catalog did neither. Now it specifies that this unicycle is for youngsters. Future adult customers will know better than to buy it.

In the case of the adult unicycle, Tielke and his assistants found that they could not secure the seat, either. The thing was downright dangerous. Every one was taken out of stock. I've given up on unicycles, but it's safe to assume that those Wards now stocks have seats that can be secured. Marchese and Tielke assured me that I had done the company a service by calling my silly unicycles to their attention. They feel the same way about *your* complaints. And surely everybody connected with the manufacturing or merchandising industries would like to know when you are *pleased* with what you buy.

At a national meeting of Better Business Bureaus, Bob Guelich, vice president of Wards, was told by the man sitting next to him, another representative of a major industry, that a Ward automotive shop had damaged the coil of his car. He had written the manager a furious letter and sent a carbon to his senator. Though there was some question as to how the shop could possibly have damaged the coil, the manager nevertheless replaced it gratis.

"Of course you then sent your senator a letter telling him that you had received fair treatment," Bob observed blandly.

"Huh?" the industrial delegate to the Better Business Bureau said.

Consumerism is not a one-way street. It takes two to consume. Wards grants that the consumer has rights, and because the consumer is its bread and butter, the company faces these rights realistically. In a speech to the Merchandising Executives Club of Chicago Jim Lutz cited those first proposed by President John F. Kennedy. They are:

> The right to be safe.
> The right to choose.
> The right to be fully informed.
> The right to be heard.

"Even the most nervous hunter of the boogey man would have a difficult time finding diabolical motives behind these four rights," he commented. "In fact, they should stir our competitive spirit to instant action."

But, as Rita Perna pointed out to the press, with these rights come responsibilities:

> The right to information has the responsibility to use it.
>
> The right to selection has the responsibility to buy wisely.
>
> The right to performance has the responsibility to follow care recommended.
>
> The right to safety has the responsibility to guard against carelessness.
>
> The right to recourse means responsibility to let legitimate dissatisfactions be known.

Virginia Knauer, in charge of consumer affairs for the White House, agreed with Miss Perna, but in a private interview added another responsibility. "All consumers should push for legislation," she said. "When they are fleeced, or at a disadvantage, they should complain to the proper governmental authorities, first on the local level, then, if they get no satisfaction, on the state and federal levels."

Though some executives of Wards reflect the businessmen's aversion to governmental controls, they go along with the setting of minimum standards for quality and safety. Jim Lutz looks upon consumer organizations in both the public and private sectors as "an ever-growing number of people who are frantically volunteering their assistance to help us do more. This includes more than four hundred government agencies administering a thousand consumer programs. . . . Thousands of politicians have jumped on the bandwagon of consumer discontent and dissent. And Ralph Nader.

"I suggest that we welcome this great resource of man and woman power. We should recruit their services with consumer oriented programs geared to today's problems and attitudes."

As for the government's clamping down on dishonest tradesmen, Ward's executives feel that, inasmuch as Montgomery Ward is a reputable and honest concern, such controls can be of benefit to both the company and its customers.

In the private sector, Wards supports the Better Business Bureau and other such organizations on a national basis, and local managers work with local groups.

One of the most heartwarming of the company's activities is its 50-year relationship with the National 4-H Clubs. If the 1,500 boys and girls who attend the National 4-H Congress each year are representative of the total enrollment of some three million, this is one group of American kids we don't have to worry about.

Of the forty-plus companies supporting 4-H programs, it is interesting to note that Montgomery Ward sponsors the consumer education county, state and national award programs, in which more than a million members participate. Winners from all the states and Puerto Rico are brought into the National Congress each year. Wards gives them a banquet with the top executives and their wives as hosts and presents scholarships to the six finalists. I've never met a nicer group of girls—poised, alert, earnest, well dressed and shining clean. Their accomplishments proved the value of the consumer education program.

I naturally sought out the finalist from Virginia, an attrac-

Leo Schoenhofen, left, serves as chairman of student seminar on consumerism with Ralph Nader as a principal speaker.

tive, outgoing girl named Symerdar Capehart, who also happened to be the only black finalist. Symerdar joined the 4-H club when she was 10 years old in order to learn to cook. She obviously learned quickly, because the same year she took over all the household duties for her working parents. Setting herself a strict budget, making the best use of credit, she was able to save enough to send herself to Virginia Tech, where she is studying biochemistry. During those years she also found the time to give demonstrations to others interested in consumerism.

Cathy Marie Siess, of New Jersey, another finalist, is the girl Ralph Nader of the junk mail racket. Cathy observed that teenagers receive a lot of direct mail solicitations offering so-called discount prices, as well as being the target of magazine and TV advertising offering special deals. Personally exploring many of the offers, she found that a large number promised far more than they could or would deliver. She spent her own money on postage, including that for returning merchandise bought on trial. At the age of 17, she was already planning to write a book on consumer education geared to her own age group.

Rita Rowland of Ohio, with two other girls, tested red, yellow and blue dye on ten different types of fabric, then prepared a complete report on color-fastness. One interesting finding: everything faded when touched by detergents plus enzymes. She also researched ten brands of hair spray. Janet Seppa, of California, in addition to helping her parents grow and can fruits and vegetables, found time to put out a newsletter for 35 clubs, lead drives for newspaper recycling, compare prices and effectiveness of appliances, and investigate and turn over to the Better Business Bureau misleading advertisements. One offered spare-time money for addressing envelopes. It turned out to be a racket—the fee paid was far more than the money received. Through Janet's newsletter, thousands of girls in California now know better than to fall for that gimmick. Janet also worked for a veterinarian, where

4-H national scholarship winners with Ed Donnell.

she investigated brands of dog food and determined—and reported—that some contained as much as 65 per cent water.

As these girls and their accomplishments represent only the annual cream of the entire 4-H Club-Montgomery Ward program, you can see that merchandisers of the future had better be on their toes when these girls become full-time consumers. Although Wards has an altruistic motivation in helping these young people—Bob Guelich, a onetime 4-Her himself, is on the national board—the company believes that it will benefit by encouraging consumer education. It's just confident enough to think that knowledgeable consumers will buy Montgomery Ward products.

In light of this philosophy Wards runs several company programs with consumer education features. In sewing and interior decorator courses given in several cities qualified instructors give lectures and demonstrations on how to achieve the ultimate in home decoration without calling in professionals. People taking the course can develop finer taste on lower budgets. Sometimes the company knocks itself out of a potential sale this way. One woman, of a low-income status, had been planning to replace some of her furniture. In the home-decoration course she learned how to re-cover it instead, and tie in the colors with home-made draperies to brighten up her home at a resonable cost.

Wards gives sewing and cooking classes, too, in which people learn how to dress better and eat better economically.

The Wendy Ward program also has consumer education features. Many a short, plump woman has bought a colorful blouse with wide horizontal stripes, a skirt of a bright contrasting color, and a wide belt, taken them home, observed herself with horror in a full-length mirror, then charged back to the store to raise hell. Or a tall, slim woman may buy a dark-color, sheath-type dress to find that she looks like a bean pole. While still in their early teens two million Wendy Ward girls have learned how to select colors, style and fabrics to bring out their best features, hide their worst.

Some Ward managers go far beyond the established company programs to work with customers. I was somewhat surprised one day, in the office of Wayne Matschullat, then manager of the Washington, D.C., metro district, to see a leaflet bearing the symbol of a clenched black fist clutching a green dollar bill. Called "Buyer Beware," the leaflet was put out by the Neighborhood Consumer Information Center, a tough consumer organization. I kidded Matschullat about it and he glowered at me and growled, "Hell, if I was black I would be right there with them."

It turned out that in a large sense he *was* right there with them. Father of a bright young man who worked with indigent groups at Stanford Law School, Matschullat absorbed many of the facts of life of minority groups at his own dinner table. Two other lawyers, Joseph F. Smith and Thomas L. Jones, working with NCIC in Washington, added to his information.

"They told me about somebody buying a sofa from a ghetto merchant. It broke down the next day. The store refused to give the money back—the people had signed a contract not with the store, but with a savings and loan company. No recourse at all."

As chairman of a committee of the Metropolitan Board of Trade he sought both to do something to help the people at the mercy of the ghetto merchant, and to improve conditions at the big legitimate stores.

"Wayne Matschullat has helped us tremendously in setting up procedures in the big stores so that we'll know who to get to, which button to push," Joe Smith, executive director of the center, told me. "He's helped get merchants to recognize the necessity of improving internally on a long-range basis, rather than just answering complaints. In the meantime we've learned the mechanism so that when people come to us we know how to help them get satisfaction. Working out this formula was a beautiful challenge."

Obviously the top management of Wards approved Matschullat's activities. He was promoted to vice president of the north central region and elected to the board of directors.

Readers of this book are surely more sophisticated than the ghetto residents who need help from NCIC in handling consumer complaints, but nevertheless a few words of advice on the best way of handling a bad situation, returning faulty merchandise, may be in order. An experience of mine is illustrative of the process. I needed a new rug for my study, but the cost of anything I could live with seemed high. Just as the dilemma was becoming unbearable here came a letter from good old Sears telling me that because I'm such a fine fellow, and incidentally because I had been paying my bills on time, I could have 10 per cent off on anything in the store. Within a few hours after opening the envelope I had gone in, picked up several cartons of colorful carpet tile, put them down as per directions, and went back to work in much brighter, more stimulating surroundings. (Bonnie made and hung matching draperies while I crawled around on my hands and knees sticking down the tile.)

That was on April 15. As the weeks went by, the tiles kept coming unstuck. I'd replace them, stamp on them, but up they'd come again. I finally realized something was wrong, and on September 13 I went in the store to tell somebody my troubles. The salesman wasn't there, but someone else took my name and said that someone would call. Nobody did, and on October 6, I called the store and got the assistant manager. He apologized and promised to look into it. The next day the manager of the rug department did call, listened to my story and said that he would give me a gallon of cement. I could then take up each tile, smear it with the free cement, and stick it back down again. I'm sure he really meant to be helpful. Some people like to do things like that. I don't.

So now Bonnie, who is more experienced at this sort of thing, and tougher, than I am, called the store. She insisted on speaking to the manager. "You say you guarantee satisfaction," she told him. "Well, we're not satisfied." The next day a man came out, looked at the unstuck tiles and promised to put them down to my satisfaction.

On October 21, the men arrived. They said the reason the tiles hadn't stuck was because the adhesive was absorbed into the grain of the wood. Inasmuch as the floors had been covered with carpet, and consequently not varnished or waxed for some 90 years, that made sense. However, the description of the tiles said that they could be laid on "any surface that is clean, dry and smooth." I pointed it out to them. They shrugged.

"We don't care what it says," one of them said. "The boss said to put these tiles down so you're satisfied." And they did.

I think the whole procedure is typical of retailer-customer relations, and satisfactory to both stockholder and customer. The first fellow I talked to might have simply forgotten, or he may have thought that I would dry up and blow away, thereby saving the store his time and money. The next man made a sincere effort but it wasn't good enough. When the manager himself was convinced that a customer was seriously and justifiably dissatisfied, he authorized whatever was necessary. Okay.

It isn't necessary to go through this routine on every purchase. But in dealing with any retailer, no matter how reliable and reputable, it is wise to remember both that the retailer is a hunter, and that the reputable retailer who recognizes the value of a regular customer also wants to keep that customer satisfied so he can keep hunting him. He may put up a struggle at the beginning, but if you're in the right, and stand your ground, he'll treat you right at the end.

In short, you've got to hang in there. How strongly you do battle depends on the nature of the complaint and the nature of your antagonist. If your merchandise is obviously faulty, there will be little or no battle with a reputable organization. If it's a borderline case, such as a telephone report that a tile won't stick, then the duration, intensity and outcome of the battle may well depend upon the personalities involved. An operations-minded manager will resist more strongly than the sales-minded manager.

Whether taking an item back to the store or reporting in by telephone or mail, it is simply common sense to have all the documents with you—sales slip, description, number and price of merchandise, and date of purchase. In responding to mail complaints alone, Wards spends tens of thousands of dollars annually (one inquiry on a complaint costs about $3 to process) asking the customer just what it is she's complaining about. In the meantime, of course, you are doing without the use of the item you want replaced or the money you want refunded, and you're getting madder and madder.

It is wise, also, to go through the proper channels. Begin with the complaint department in the large store, the salesman who handled the transaction in the first place, the lady who answers the phone in the catalog store or agency or, in the case of direct mail, the man whose picture is in the catalog. Keep the story short and simple; your experiences with other stores, or what happened in the case of your next door neighbor, or how bad your headache is, really don't make much difference. In most cases the person you're talking to has been trained properly in how to deal with you, and is going to do the job properly. Because most complaints are simply matters of exchanging something for another color or size, the matter is going to be settled with surprising ease.

But suppose it isn't. The person you're complaining to may have a headache, or be new on the job. Before proceeding further, it might be well to review the bidding. Are you sure that the stain on that dress you say you never wore didn't result from dropping the strawberry cheese cake in your lap? Did you really wash it according to instructions? Did you really buy it in August of this year, or maybe wasn't it August a year ago? If you're sure you're right, then go to the store manager. Be firm, but don't lose your cool. Again, you're probably going to get that satisfaction.

But if you don't get results, go to the top. You'd be surprised at the attention that the highest officers of the company pay to complaints. I was in the office of Jim Lutz, executive vice president of Montgomery Ward, when a call came in from a man whose wife was upset over the lack of attention paid to a faulty washer. Jim dropped everything, investigated the background of the complaint, determined that the lady did have reason to be upset and saw to it that she was taken care of.

One day Leo Schoenhofen, president of Marcor, Ward's parent company, and not himself a retailer, received an electric knife addressed to him personally. Although certainly no expert on appliances, he looked at it closely and observed with a grin that it sure had picked up a lot of grease for a knife that wouldn't work. Then he sent it through proper channels for action with a note requesting that he be informed of the disposition.

In modern consumerism the old adage that the squeaking

wheel gets the grease still holds true. Some years ago a lady in Chicago had a Ward air conditioning unit connected to her forced-air heating system. The installation crew recommended that the old ducts be replaced with new and larger ones to accommodate the new unit. She refused to have her house torn up and insisted that the new unit be installed anyway.

Sure enough, the heater didn't work properly, and did she holler. In the ensuing battle both Tom Brooker, the chairman of the board, and Ed Donnell, president of the company, talked to her on the phone several times, and some company executives went personally to the lady's house to look at her ducts and attempt to reach some satisfactory settlement. They got nowhere. She made such a fuss that her husband got tired of hearing about it and left home, and her lawyer washed his hands of the matter, and her. At last reports she was still screaming, but the point of the story is that even though she was wrong to begin with she received personal attention, and the offer of a reasonable settlement, from both the chairman of the board and the president of the company.

Finally, of course, you have recourse to agencies like the Better Business Bureau or more militant outfits like Washington's NCIC, to governmental agencies on the local, state and federal levels, and to people like Mrs. Knauer, the President's Assistant for Consumer Affairs. If it is necessary to go to these extremes you may have a case, but the odds are strong that you yourself committed the original sin when you first made the purchase. Because you were almost certainly dealing with an unreliable company.

Credit

On the assumption that you now feel a bit more secure in your purchase of merchandise, the question follows: How are you going to buy it? The answer: charge it, even if you've got the money in the bank.

I can hear the enraged screams of the consumer activists. They have many arguments against credit. Some are:

The usual monthly service charge of 1½ percent totals 18 per cent a year—too much.

Stores use credit to entice you to buy things you don't need, and to buy more expensive versions of what you do need.

Credit should be curtailed rather than recommended: Americans already owe $127 billion for consumer goods. People are in over their heads.

If they don't pay, creditors do terrible things.

If you can't pay cash, do without.

People who pay their bills on time pay extra for those who don't.

Each of these statements has a varying degree of truth. But even if all were 100 per cent true, the informed money manager would still use credit to buy consumer goods from the national catalog-retail chains.

The reason is simply that they give you the use of the merchandise, plus the use of the money it would take to buy it, absolutely free for a certain period of time—conceivably close to two months.

The three major catalog-chains, Sears, Wards and Penneys, all assess no finance charge during the first billing period, provided you start out with a clean slate. After that terms vary according to the different policies of the companies and to the laws of the individual states. But with Montgomery Ward, and in nearly all states, as long as you pay for your purchase in full before the *second* billing date, you pay no service charge whatever. You have money free for that period of time.

Your billing date is determined by your last initial. Being about a third of the way through the alphabet, my initial, H, has a billing date to match, the 12th of the month. It's printed on my monthly statement. Suppose that on March 13, the day after my billing date, I buy, on credit, $1,000 worth of merchandise from Montgomery Ward. It cannot be entered on the statement printed the day before—even computers aren't that efficient—so it will not appear on my statement until April 12. If I pay it in full before the next billing date I'm home free. To play it safe I'd better pay it the day before the billing date so that the computer will pick it up—that's May 11. That amounts to 60 days I have had both the merchandise and the money I would have paid for it, with no finance charge whatever.

This is what economists call *tenure of ownership.* Naturally, the longer my tenure, the more I can do with the money. Sixty days constitute a short tenure and my use of the money is therefore limited. I could not invest it in a savings account at my bank, for example, because the bank will not pay interest until 90 days have elapsed. If I were certain that a stock, or a parcel of real estate, was going to appreciate in value in that period of time, over and above the brokerage fees for buying and selling it, I could use the money for that type of speculation— but of course I don't know it. However, providing I have an existing account in a savings and loan association which pays 5 percent interest on a daily basis, I can get $4.20 a month on that thousand dollars, or a total of about $8.40. And I've had the merchandise all along.

Now of course this is a pretty far fetched proposition. I don't even have an account in a savings and loan company. Nor could I get away with it if I lived in a few other states, Maryland for one, where state legislation on credit has forced Wards to use another method of assessing finance charges. (The three methods used by retailers are based on the *average daily balance,* the *previous balance* or the *adjusted balance.* The differences appear to be simple but, like all computations, can be complex. The wise money manager would do well to find out which method is used by the company with which he does business in the state in which he lives, and make his own determination based on good financial advice—ask your credit manager—as to what time of the month to buy, what time to pay.)

But it is a perfectly valid example of the way sophisticated money managers work. It is a standard technique. Money-wise individuals, institutions and corporations all delay payment of their bills as long as possible in order to use the other fellow's money.

The example also demonstrates one reason why 1½ per cent a month does not equal 18 per cent a year. The first month, at least, equals zero per cent. One fifth of all Ward's credit customers pay their bills before the service charge comes due. Although the average account runs around $200, in some states large purchasers—building materials, for example—pay only 1 per cent over $500. Most purchasers make regular payments, which reduce the amount on which the service charge is based. A few states have legal limits of 1 per cent on all purchases. On the average Wards actually receives about 15 per cent in gross service charges.

This is not net profit. In 1970 the company collected $168,-858,000 from service charges on credit sales of $1,146,850,000. It paid out interest of $59.4 million—Wards has to borrow money too. Other expenses and taxes ate up more money. The company wound up with a net surplus over expenses on its credit operations of $3.7 million—less than one half of 1 per cent. In that year, incidentally, Sears made $26 million, or .08 per cent, and Penneys, which operates on a system slightly more generous to the credit buyer, lost $23 million. With figures like these, you can hardly blame credit managers for being sensitive to accusations that they are gouging their customers.

They are also sensitive to the word *interest*. You may have noticed that I have not used that no-no, but instead the terms *finance charge* or *service charge*. The difference is more than semantics, it's money. To the retailer, interest is what he pays the bank for the use of the money he needs to buy more merchandise while he's waiting for the customers to pay him for what they bought on credit—and sometimes it's a long wait.

To the interest the retailer pays the bank, add all the costs of administering the credit system—computers, salaries, space, postage, deadbeats, and a lot more—and you get what he charges you. That's why credit people climb the walls when you refer to a finance charge as interest—it ain't the same thing.

Even the apparent rate of 18 per cent is cheaper than borrowing money from most other sources. Bank rates are lower, but banks don't usually make small loans for clothes, TV sets or refrigerators—a $300 loan costs as much administratively as a $30,000 loan—and if they do, interest begins when you sign your name to the note. I asked my friendly banker what it would cost me to borrow a thousand dollars for one minute, and he answered immediately, "Five bucks."

Incidentally, retailers who say "no finance charge if paid in 30 days" don't really mean it in most cases. If the purchase is added to an existing balance, the charges begin immediately in the accounting methods used by most firms. If the purchase is made when your balance is zero, you still have to pay the amount in full to get the free period; if you don't the free period covers only the time between purchase and billing date. It could be *one* day.

Small loan companies, which lend smaller amounts than banks, and to people who couldn't get the money from banks anyway, can legally charge as much as 3½ percent in some states—that's 42 per cent a year. In Louisiana there is no legal limit whatever on loans over $300.

By contrast, 1½ per cent per month doesn't look so bad. Indeed, one of our great social problems in America today is not the cost charged for credit by reputable establishments, but that so many decent honest people who pay their bills can't get it. The real abuses of the credit system, the ones that make your flesh crawl, are perpetrated by the lenders of last resort. But let's go into that later after we finish with credit as administered by the people you and I do business with.

Many people, including some who are in the money business themselves, feel that too many people owe too much. "My advice is, don't charge, period," a lady banker told me. "People owe so much money now it's frightening."

There is no question but that millions of Americans are over their heads in debt. Some people seem to be acquisition drunk; they buy things when they can't afford what they already have. They welsh on their debts, give false information to obtain more credit from other sources, go bankrupt, skip town. Probably the elimination of the credit system would make it more difficult for these people to get themselves in financial trouble, but that would be an awful price for the rest of us to pay. Those of us who can pay cash for everything we buy are either rich or easily satisfied.

The nation itself, the gross national product, couldn't stand a strictly-cash basis. Thirty-five per cent of all consumer goods are purchased on credit, and that represents an even greater proportion of the products of manufacturers; most cash purchases are made for foodstuffs and small items.

About half of all Ward's sales are made on credit, and just look what this one company contributes to the national economy. In order to provide merchandise to its customers, it purchases $1.5 billion worth of goods from suppliers all over the world, but predominantly in the United States. This keeps a lot of people on the job, collecting pay checks, paying taxes. One out of every 1,000 dollars collected in taxes by federal, state and local governments passes through the company.

As Wards does not blanket the country it consequently does not contribute on a large scale to national television, but it spends big money for newspaper advertising in communities where it does business. Along with just about every member of Congress, not to mention the White House and the judiciary, I begin the day with *The Washington Post*, whose news coverage is surely enhanced by the $1,290,000 a year Montgomery Ward spends there in advertising.

Aside from its national, impersonal benefits, credit enables us to use and enjoy the products of industry. Few of us have the cash on hand for a replacement when one of our major appliances breaks down; we use our credit. Credit enables us to get our kids off to school in the fall in what they consider presentable clothing, and to buy the carloads of bicycles, toys and noise-making instruments like stereos at Christmas.

Our grandparents called thrift a virtue, and it's still a good quality to have. But people today don't want to scrimp and save until they are too old to enjoy what they can buy today on credit. Young homemakers no longer start out cooking on beat-up old stoves and washing dishes and clothes by hand; they grew up in kitchens equipped with every appliance known to woman. They want what Mama had and, with credit, they can get it. This does not necessarily mean going over their depth in debt, but only that they can stretch out their purchasing power. They can look at television and pay for it at the same time.

Of course credit enables merchants both to make sales and to trade up—talk a customer into buying a better and more expensive grade of product. The most valid criticism of credit in my opinion is that it enables the merchant to have it both ways. Ward managers admit that credit is "sales supportive." That means it's much easier to sell you something when you can hand the cashier a credit card instead of hard cash. Joe Brannon, manager of the Phoenix metro district, places tremendous emphasis on credit in his courtesy shopper program. A salesclerk can knock himself out in every other way, but if he doesn't push credit he doesn't win a prize.

If credit is this important to merchandising, is it fair to the customer to make money on him all over again on credit?

Some businesses don't give a damn whether it's fair or not; they're out to get all they can any way they can. I hope you don't want to know what I think, because after running back and forth between credit people for months they've got me so confused I don't know what I think. Credit people, always on the defensive about their operations, have developed a talent for using the same figures to answer different arguments, or different figures to answer the same arguments. But one solution to the problem would be for retailers to absorb the cost of credit as just another one of the costs of doing business.

Few consumers, to take one of those costs, would question the 5 per cent Wards spends in advertising, yet most people don't even see it and of those who do, the percentage which actually purchases the item advertised is certainly small. That's millions of dollars thrown into the wind, but nobody lets out a peep. By contrast credit goes into effect only after the company has actually made the sale; it is certainly a more productive cost of doing business. Why should I pay more for it?

But the idea of treating credit as a routine expense is a wild-eyed dream and I withdraw it. The policy of singling out credit as the one cost of business on which a separate charge is made has become inextricably interwoven with both business and consumerism, and we're all stuck with it.

On the question of making an additional profit on credit

Concerned about credit? Ashley DeShazor would like you to hear his side of the story.

operations, Ashley D. DeShazor, the earnest, red-headed vice president-credit of Wards, presents a reasonable case. He points out that the company has a separate investment in accounts receivable, or money owed by credit customers. This is the largest single asset the company has.

"We have to raise that money through medium and long range planning so that we're covered completely, for now and in the future," he said. "Don't you think that apart from the sale of merchandise some modest return is due a company on the money it has borrowed in order to provide customers with this billion dollar investment? Isn't that only reasonable?"

It is also only fair to point out that Ward's net earnings on credit, one half of 1 per cent, isn't that big a deal. If you owned stock in a company making a half a cent on a dollar, you'd holler.

It would hardly be consistent with either good business practice or a phobia against credit to expect the company to *lose* money on its credit operations. Breaking even seems fair, but here the human element comes in. Breaking even is like a tie ball game, which in turn, as athletes say, is like kissing your sister. Credit people want to run their own profit centers, too, just like the hunters in merchandising. They want to get a bonus, win trophies. They want to do a job.

The opportunity to do that job was a major factor in bringing to Wards one of its key executives, Gordon R. Worley, financial vice president. From a village in Nebraska, where he trapped skunks, muskrats and badgers and sold the skins to Montgomery Ward ("We'd get a dollar for a skunk!") Gordon came to the big city with an old car and $40. A bigger asset was his wife, Geneva, whom he'd met at college. Jobs were hard to get, and Geneva landed one before her husband— with an employment agency. When an opening came in for an accountant at Alden's, a smaller mail order house, Geneva called Gordon. He was the first applicant, and he got the job. Over the years, with only grudging consent from the president

Gordon Worley joined Wards in 1967 as financial vice president.

of the company at the beginning, he built up Alden's credit business to more than 70 per cent of the total. What prodded him was the opportunity to be the manager of a profit center, a chance that rarely comes to staff personnel.

As Alden's credit prospered, and Worley with it, he'd occasionally get together with the people at Sears and talk about what was happening at Wards. "Sometimes the only conceivable explanation was that the people at Wards had absolutely lost their minds," he said of the period in the late fifties.

During the Avery years the company reflected the aversion of the old man to anything but cash on the barrelhead. A better credit system was set up when he left, but then, in the mid-sixties, Montgomery Ward and its boss, Tom Brooker, got caught in a real credit crunch. Its financial vice president, Andrew Lamb, had joined the company as an analyst and

221

became vice president through attrition. There's a lot of close rapport in the financial world and the big bankers, like just about everybody else, like to deal with friendly people who keep the lines of communication open. As an analyst, Lamb had more affinity with figures than with people.

In 1966, with a national credit squeeze and Wards losing money hand over fist in Chicago and Los Angeles, the company found itself in trouble. Tom Brooker made the tough decision to cut the length of time a customer had to pay for his purchases from 20 months to 14. The rate of collection went up, but so important is the credit operation to retailing that the six months' curtailment lost customers. In published accounts of Ward's problems that year Brooker has taken full responsibility. But what made his action necessary was the inability of the Ward financial management to get long-term money from the big bankers. Those friendly lines of communication had not been kept open.

When Lamb went into the investment business Brooker needed a new financial man; he got in touch with Gordon Worley. They had several meetings over the weekend and the beginning of the week. Worley could see a great opportunity at Wards, but he wanted to be convinced that he would be permitted to pursue that opportunity aggressively. He had made his reputation through pushing credit as a tool to increase sales. Would he find at Wards the environment to push on to greater heights? He was in the driver's seat; Brooker had come to him. He asked searching questions, including several pertaining to the cutback in the credit plan.

Brooker explained the situation in detail. He assured Worley that nothing would please him more than to get back into the credit business in an aggressive way. But, he warned, first the new financial vice president would have to get his house in order. Gordon had no doubts of his ability to do that. He knew bankers all over the country.

On Tom Brooker's personal commitment, Gordon Worley gave his own. Oddly enough, though Gordon was coming in to take a job handling billions of dollars, his own personal compensation was no factor in the decision. He was far more concerned with the title and the opportunity. "I know I'm going to have all the money I can ever use, or all that my family can use," he explained to me later. "So, you know, what's the big deal."

Gordon is the only executive I know with a salary of well over $100,000 and several times that in stock and options whose checks bounce regularly. He and Geneva have three or four checkbooks and both like to use them. "I'm supposed to keep the books in order," Geneva says, "but with a system like that it's hopeless. Every now and then I get a phone call and an unctuous voice says, 'Mrs. Worley, I believe your account is overdrawn again.'"

But although Gordon doesn't pay much attention to his personal finances, he works hard on the company's. Within a month after joining Wards, thanks to his friendly lines of communications, he raised $150 million in long-term financing. With that backing Wards could return, under his overall direction, to an aggressive credit policy, and credit sales have shown a substantial increase. Probably if credit costs to the consumer were reduced, sales would increase at a higher ratio, but the company states flatly that such cost reductions cannot be expected. If reductions are forced by law, the difference must be made up in increased prices, to cash customers as well as credit customers.

The credit people in a reputable retail establishment walk a fine line as it is. If they extend too much credit to people of moderate incomes, they may cost the company money when the customer can't pay, and actually do the customer a disservice by overloading him with debt for something he can't afford. But if they draw the line so tightly that they curtail sales, their merchandisers are going to scream. The disappointed would-be customer would probably walk across the street and buy what she wants from a less conscientious merchant anyway.

One day Ash DeShazor was visiting the Ward store in Colorado Springs when a young couple came in and wanted to buy the works—dishwasher, stove, refrigerator, washing machine, drier. They were nice young people with a fairly good income, and they were both used to living with that type of equipment. DeShazor, who believes in both credit and people, was sympathetic. But through his personal work with the National Foundation for Consumer Credit, he knew that young people can easily overextend themselves. The foundation, and he personally, have worked with many young people who were considering taking bankruptcy and convinced them that this is not the way out. Through counseling them on management of their personal finances, and getting creditors to cooperate, the foundation has helped many people across the country get off to a fresh start without the black mark of bankruptcy.

With this background, then, it would have been difficult for him not to get involved in the discussion.

"We'd love to sell all this to you," he told the young couple, as the commission salesman restrained himself from wringing DeShazor's neck, "but why don't you just buy the stove and the refrigerator and put off buying the rest for a while? It would really be to your advantage if you waited until you could more easily pay for the additional things. We'll be here then, and we'll work with you."

The young people took his advice, bought only what he suggested and promised to come back for the additional items after they were more firmly established. "We could have been greedy and put the whole thing on the books," DeShazor said later, "but I think that we in industry have an obligation to counsel these people who are inexperienced even up to the point of losing the sale. Now they may have gone somewhere else and bought the other appliances, but I really think that they appreciated our advice and will come back when they are ready, just as they promised they would.

"I'd like to underscore this. We hear a lot about the unrest in regard to credit, and accept the fact that there is some cause for it. But it is not necessarily in the cost of credit as much as it is the practice of some retailers of pushing a customer into buying more than he can pay for. No one has unlimited ability to pay for everything. I don't, and I don't think anyone else does. We like to keep our customers within their indicated ability to pay. That's been the basic policy of the company as long as I've been here, and in the last five years we've executed this policy increasingly in the direction of facing up to the concerns expressed by consumer groups."

We've all heard the horrendous tales of innocent people suffering extreme hardship through the abuses of credit. Joe Brannon recently recounted two extreme cases in one issue of the Phoenix Planner. In one example a man bought about $400 worth of power tools from Joe's friendly competitor, paid until he had reduced the balance to $200, then decided that he didn't like them. He called the store and told them to come and pick up the tools; he wasn't going to pay the balance. They didn't and he didn't.

Several letters were ignored. The case was then turned over to a lawyer who got authority to hold a sheriff's sale on the irate gentleman's real estate; it was worth about $200,000. The man chose to ignore the sale and his $200,000 property went for $450. He still could have gotten back his land through legal means, but he continued to ignore the whole thing. Once worth at least $200,000, at last reports he was working as a carry-out boy, and still mad.

In the other case, a semi-educated immigrant bought a car, paid 25 per cent down and signed a note for the balance. A secured note is worth money, and the dealer sold it to the bank. After a few days the purchaser of the car realized he had a lemon, returned it, told the dealer to keep the money he had already received, and left thinking that was the end of the matter. But it wasn't, because the bank still held the note.

It demanded payment. The immigrant refused to pay another nickel—he had taken the car back. The only thing he had worth money was a mobile home, in which he lived with his wife and children. The bank got a court order and sent two deputy sheriffs out to claim it.

The man resisted, with a gun. In the shoot-out all three were killed.

The two stories prove two different points. The first was a tragedy of errors involving what must have been the world's most stubborn dissatisfied customer and a reputable firm which surely, if only in retrospect, could have handled the matter better. A succession of human errors messed up a common, everyday, ethical transaction.

The second case illustrates the potential venality of the third-party transaction, in what is known as the selling of paper. This practice, too, happens everyday, and the cost of three lives is rare, but it's still the type of deal the well-informed consumer stays away from.

Unfortunately, too many consumers are not well informed. Millions make third-party purchases everyday. The first major drawback is that, in spite of the truth-in-lending laws, the unscrupulous seller can gimmick up the sale so that he receives not only a high price for the merchandise, but a high rate of interest. The second drawback is that, should anything go wrong, and we have seen that many things can go wrong, the purchaser has little recourse. The third party—the bank, finance company or even an individual—doesn't want a used car, television set, refrigerator or whatever, particularly since it was probably low-end merchandise to begin with. As for the original seller, he has now sold the paper as well as the merchandise. He can disclaim responsibility for either or both.

Typical of this type of vendor is the schlock house, and the ghetto merchant. And typical of his customer is the person who cannot get credit, or is afraid to try, from the reputable merchant who stands back of his merchandise. The person who can least afford to get stung, gets stung the worst.

Granted that many of the people who purchase goods in this way have themselves burned up their credit with reputable firms and shouldn't make the purchase in the first place. But there are others, financially and morally capable of paying their just bills, who still fall into the trap through ignorance or circumstances largely beyond their own control. These are the people I feel for.

Ironically, it is the very consumer activist groups which honestly have their welfare at heart who contribute to the increase in their number.

As we have seen, of the three major catalog chains, all of which charge a maximum of 1½ per cent per month interest —oops, service charge—two show a net profit on credit operations of less than 1 per cent, and the third loses money. What happens when well-intentioned consumer groups and responsive politicians legislate lower maximum rates? One result is that the retailer, in order to avoid a loss, raises prices on merchandise to cash and credit customers alike. In the state of Washington, where the maximum finance charge for purchases of goods is 1 per cent per month, the price of a given item of merchandise is higher than that which people across the state line pay for the identical item. Those who can afford the higher prices go on and pay them. But what concerns, or should concern, bleeding heart liberals like me is the effect the lowering of interest rates has on people who can least afford to pay. When credit managers have to pare their costs, one of the first steps is to make credit harder to get for people who could conceivably be risky prospects.

Credit is awarded to applicants on a point system. When you fill out an application for a credit account with Montgomery Ward, you give your name and address, of course, age, name of wife, occupation, employer and how long you've been there, how long you've lived at your present address and whether you own or rent, your phone number, your bank (checking or savings account) and two other credit references. Strangely enough, what you put down as your annual income is of least interest to the tabulators. You can, after all, put down anything. Your age is more important; people under 25 are higher credit risks. So are unmarried people; that's why the application asks for the name of your wife—to see if you've got one. She's worth points.

Your occupation or profession is carefully considered; some occupations have poor reputations. Credit people don't like to designate which ones, but, because they are no longer on the doubtful list, it is safe to say that at one time painters and barbers had a poor reputation for paying their bills.

It's obvious that the length of time you have been with your employer has a bearing on credit, as does whether you own or rent your home, and in the latter case, how long you've lived there. If you have been there a long time, you've obviously been keeping up with the rent or mortgage payments. But why does the company want to know your telephone number? Well, if you have a telephone number you must have a telephone, and for a telephone you get points. As for other credit references, if you don't have any, no points. If you do it means that somebody else has trusted you, and of course your credit will be easier to check.

Credit applications which rate a high score on the information given may not be checked at all. Others may be checked with varying degrees of thoroughness before credit is granted and, without the applicant's knowing it, a limit set on the amount he can carry. An application from a young unmarried person, unemployed, living at a rented place for a short time, with no phone, no bank account and no credit references, would be turned down automatically.

In some areas of the country, too, an application might be accepted while in others it would not. A marginal applicant living in Iowa, for example, would have a better chance than in Minnesota. In both states people have a proven record of paying their bills, but because in Minnesota the finance charge is limited by law to 1 per cent, the company has to be more cautious. It must be more restrictive in high-delinquency areas. In Washington, D.C., for one, the situation is terrible.

Here the horrendous examples of the abuses of credit are on the other side. Wards has records of married couples, both working with good salaries, who just simply refuse to pay their bills. After trying every reasonable means of collection, the company hired an off-duty policeman and sent him into the neighborhood where several people with long-overdue accounts lived. The people in the neighborhood, including several who weren't even on his list, got together, beat him up and chased him away.

Robert Freeman, Ward's credit manager for the eastern region, is naturally distressed over the situation, but his concern goes beyond the loss of revenue to the company. He blames much of it on the decrease of morality in the country today.

"I've been in this business for 30 years," he said, "and it didn't use to be this way. People used to be embarrassed when they couldn't pay their bills. Now they laugh at you. A lot of it comes about through couples divorcing or separating. 'What about that money you owe us?' I say. Back comes the answer, 'My wife bought all that. Get lost.' People skip town, just disappear. No morality."

Wards does not use the harsh collection methods of the high risk small-loan company, but it doesn't give up easily, either. "We follow you to the grave," Freeman said grimly. By the time the normal routine of letters and telephone calls have been exhausted, the company sends collectors out at times when the delinquent is most apt to be at home—seven in the morning, nine at night. (A small loan company collector might well make *his* call at midnight, and scream "Why don't you pay what you owe, you deadbeat?" loud enough for everybody in the block to hear.)

If the goods are worth repossessing, the company tries to do so—although the men may find all the tires flat when they come back to the truck. Long before the time comes to seek legal garnishment of the delinquent's wages, the local credit manager might write his employer a letter. It will not mention anything like a bad debt, heaven forbid, but rather suggest that the credit manager would like to see Mr. X on a matter he has knowledge of. The message is there.

If at any time during all this the man or woman who owes the money makes a sincere promise to work things out, he will usually find the credit manager willing to go along. For all their tough talk, credit managers are patsies for sincerity— and they know it when they see it. It's not only good business to work with a delinquent account in order to retain a customer, but the credit manager sees so many rotten eggs that he's delighted to find a good one.

Some of the tricks people use to beat the retailer are most imaginative. One ploy is for your wife to take my Ward card, my wife to take your Sears card, and go shopping. Each can then say she didn't make the purchase, and indeed she did not sign *her* name to the credit form. But it's still stealing, plus forgery, and if they're caught we'll have to visit them in jail.

An obvious way to get a credit card is to steal it. A credit-card thief can simply knock somebody over the head and take his wallet, or follow the mailman around and lift anything that looks or feels promising out of the mailbox. One credit-card collector in Washington had 600 when he was arrested; 27 were from Wards.

Stores stop credit as soon as the theft of the card is reported, of course, but people even take advantage of that. One day a woman called in to say that her card had been stolen. A couple of hours later a person was caught making purchases with that card. She turned out to be the person to whom the card was issued. She had called in first, then went out to make the purchases. She obviously didn't have much faith in Ward's efficiency in getting the word out.

But can every credit card be checked by every salesperson or cashier? One time, making a relatively small purchase in a Montgomery Ward store in Washington, I was kept waiting for several minutes. It turned out later that every credit sale of over $5 made in that department of that store that day had to be verified by the computer center in Baltimore. Every purchase of over $50 is verified routinely, but that day I happened to pick the department where a spot check was being made. Departments are chosen in a random pattern so that nobody knows what's going to be checked when. Sometimes you don't even know it when it is made. Under perfect conditions the call goes through in a matter of seconds to an employee who has the credit card numbers on a computer print-out in front of her. She can okay the number in a few more seconds.

It doesn't always work that smoothly, and some customers get understandably annoyed by the delay, but you'd be surprised how many stolen credit cards turn up.

Because of the beating Wards takes in credit in these areas, it has to be overly choosy about extending it. Here is where the innocent pay for the guilty. At the Neighborhood Consumer Information Center in Washington Joe Smith decried the point system in general, the tightening up in particular.

"It's based on a status situation which just doesn't apply to many of our people," he said. "In some ways it's an outright discrimination against black people. A lot of us couldn't conceivably own our own home, or give credit references. Many black people are uncomfortable in banks. Some don't want telephones. Those are the white man's status symbols. But that doesn't mean we're bad money managers. We're good managers; we've got to be. My parents never made

$10,000 a year together in their lives, but they sent six children through college and they always paid their bills. That would be the worst thing in the world, not paying your bills. So where do you go when you need money? The bank? Are you kidding? You go to the finance company and pay an arm and a leg.

"You can't get credit in the big stores so you go where you can get it, and that's the ghetto merchant. He drags you off the street to give you credit. So you buy furniture that falls to pieces before you pay for it. We looked into a case the other day where a family bought a whole suite of furniture and all the legs fell off. Off of everything.

"Clothes? Well, I'll tell you. There's nothing in those stores that *you're* going to buy. Look, these stores don't have good merchandise, they've got lousy merchandise. What they have is credit and that's what they sell."

Though the ghetto merchant charges all the interest the law allows, and maybe more if he thinks he can get away with it, the big profit is not in usury as much as it is in the inflated prices of the shoddy merchandise. He doesn't mail out bills and receive checks in the mail. His customers don't have bank accounts. They come in personally on their assigned day to make their weekly payment. This way he not only gets his money, but he gets them back in the store. And when they're in the store he turns on the pressure and sells them more junk. They may not even know it's junk; all their neighbors have the same type of goods. And all are in hock, forever, to the ghetto merchant.

If we can make any apology for the ghetto merchant, it's that he, too, is a hunter, doing his thing. He's in the jungle, and he doesn't believe in protecting his prey.

Nor is it fair to blame all small-loan companies for all their operations. This type of company provides a vital service to millions of people. One of the major reasons persons go to finance companies is to pay their medical bills. The health industry wants its money, too, and its members do not extend credit to everybody who walks or is carried in.

Even the best money managers in the low-income brackets cannot put aside enough money to take care of major medical expenses. If the doctor, dentist or hospital won't extend credit, some member of the family of the sick person has to get up the cash. Should we criticize the finance company for lending money at 30 per cent, or the eventual recipient of the money, the doctor or hospital, who demands it, sometimes in advance? My local finance company tells me that it frequently lends money to people for false teeth. Some dentists won't even take the impression, much less deliver the teeth, until they have the money in their hands.

One of the most disgusting side effects of credit practices among low-income groups is that they tend to rub off on the supposedly reputable retailer who crawls down in the gutter with the ghetto merchant. The food chain which we prefer in my home town also has a big outlet in the inner city of Washington. It raises its prices, even on staples like rice and black-eyed peas, on the first of the month and keeps them there for a week or so. That's when the relief checks, the pension checks, the disabled veterans' checks come in. The people go to the store to cash them, and the store socks it to them.

Before Wayne Matschullat was promoted from Washington metro manager to vice president of the company, he was endeavoring with the Neighborhood Center to reach some equitable way of distinguishing the high credit risk from the decent, hard-working person who would welcome the opportunity to pay bills on time for good merchandise at reasonable prices. In the meantime, at the company's headquarters in Chicago, Montgomery Ward had become involved in one of the most far-out experiments in consumer history — credit for people on welfare.

One day Ash DeShazor got a call from George Wiley,

director of the National Welfare Rights Organization, who wanted to talk about credit for his members. DeShazor didn't know it at the time, but Wiley had already been turned down by both Sears and Penneys. Wards was third choice, but it was a good one, for when he discussed the matter with Gordon Worley, DeShazor was encouraged to explore the proposition further.

"Let's see if we can use this opportunity to learn something about granting credit to the poor," Gordon said. "It could be an opportunity to get solid scientific data with which we may be able to modify our point system. Both our industry and society as a whole could benefit from it."

As a credit manager, DeShazor appreciated the fact that while it may be low, the income of people on relief is steady. As a humanitarian, he realized that if anybody needs good merchandise at a good price, it is the welfare recipient. After preliminary discussions with Wiley, and further encouragement from his financial vice president, DeShazor and other interested officers of the company met with Wiley and members of his organization in other cities. At a meeting in New York the discussion was halted temporarily while one of the members of the NWRO board put her crying baby down on the conference table and changed his diapers.

Though the NWRO is considered a militant organization and it came in with strong demands, DeShazor found Wiley and its other representatives reasonable and flexible in conference. Though the NWRO may have considered DeShazor a conservative establishmentarian, they found him equally flexible. For DeShazor began looking in the stores where welfare recipients are forced to trade—frequently being the only white man in the block, much less the store—and was shocked at the merchandise and the prices.

"If business doesn't find ways to live with social problems we may live to regret it," Ash told me.

Eventually a system was worked out by which $100 worth of credit, repayable at $5 per month with a service charge of

1½ per cent, would be extended to members recommended by the organization in seven metropolitan areas, Chicago, Baltimore, Washington, Los Angeles and Oakland, Kansas City, Detroit and Dallas–Fort Worth. Local NWRO committees screened all applicants and the company accepted most of those recommended.

I went to see Dr. Wiley to find out how the program was going along. National NWRO headquarters is in an old loft in the ghetto section of Washington, and I sat for a long time in a messy corner waiting for the director. Suddenly a large woman in a full length, Indian-style dress rushed up and cried, "George is in jail!" He had been walking in a picket line somewhere. However, Jim Evans, chief of staff of the organization, wearing a dashiki, told me about the program.

"Even poor people don't have cash," he said. "But they do have expenses. Their kids go back to school just like all other kids. And when it's winter and it's cold out there the kid needs a coat. It costs $15 but his Mama ain't got it. We'd like to have more than a $100 limit, but when you haven't got any credit at all, except at the ghetto merchant, that $100 looks pretty good."

As important as credit to the welfare family is the combination of the catalog and feeling secure enough to walk into a store where good merchandise is displayed. The catalog itself is a major tool in consumer education. People on relief can read and look at pictures and they can examine better goods at lower prices than what the ghetto merchant unloads on them. The altruistic benefits of providing consumer education to the people who need it most have been very satisfying to the officers responsible for the program. DeShazor has studied hundreds of accounts and concluded that the money is being spent for the same things other people buy, mostly clothing, then bedding and furniture.

Announcement of the program in the press brought in some static. One customer wrote: "This country is going to the dogs and people like yourself are helping to speed its de-

To victims of the ghetto merchant, the catalog—available through a special credit arrangement—is an eye-opening consumer price guide.

mise. . . . If you extend credit to these loafers and prolific breeders you must extend credit to *any* who apply for an account . . . I shall not patronize Montgomery Ward any more. . . ."

The program, unfortunately, had only a limited success in its first years of operation. The company expected 3,000 new customers; it got only half that number. The delinquency rate was above average. No significant new data on point scoring showed up.

"I'm still glad we did it," Gordon Worley said. "I only wish we'd had more applications so we could have developed some standards. . . ."

But from this one small sampling, including kids with warm clothing, a case can be made that what the country needs is not a restriction on credit, but a means to extend credit to the people who need it most, the ones who don't have cash.

Credit is one of the most complex and confusing aspects of consumerism, and pressure activity from both consumer groups and financial interests make it more so. The adversaries are locked into their viewpoints and justify them with vehemence. For all his active participation in social responsibility in the credit area, Ashley DeShazor would personally prefer to administer a credit system that is even more favorable to the company.

"Personally," he told me, "I'm against any free period." He would begin service charges from the first day of purchase, based on the average amount owed each day, and at the monthly rate of 1½ per cent. It would definitely cost you more.

His adversaries the consumer groups militate for a lower rate plus other features advantageous to the credit-using consumer, even though this would result in low-cost credit's being unavailable to the groups which need it most.

If you are interested in getting into the battle, one avenue is through the Uniform Consumer Credit Code as proposed by the National Conference of Commissioners on Uniform

State Laws. One of these commissioners, appointed by the governor of Illinois, is Fred Zeni, general attorney for Montgomery Ward in charge of consumer credit practices, who has devoted much time and expertise to the conference.

The code, adopted unanimously by the conference, was threshed out in many lengthy sessions of representatives from both industry and the public as well as professional experts. Open hearings were held in many states. You could have stood up and spoken your piece; practically everybody else did. Finally, after both sides had given in a little—some would probably say a lot—the commissioners came up with a consumer credit code which they believe is fair. Legislatures of a half dozen states have agreed, and adopted it as law.

Insofar as rates are concerned, the code does not fix them, but sets maximum ceilings. In the revolving credit field, the ceiling would be 2 per cent per month up to $500; 1.5 over that. This doesn't mean that's what you'd have to pay; the actual rates would be determined by free and open competition among the companies with which you do business. (In Illinois, for example, which has not at this writing adopted the code, the legal rate is 1.8 but the competitive rate is 1.5.) But the 2 per cent rate would make it possible for retailers to extend credit to groups they cannot now take a chance on.

This is great for the industry. What does the consumer get out of it? The second basic premise of the code is protection against the abuses of credit—balloon payments, repossession of merchandise without fair credit for payments made, being held to sales agreements which you realize next day you were hypnotized into signing, being fired when garnished.

No matter what the actual provisions of the code, its enactment by all states would at least relieve the immense confusion suffered by members of our mobile society who move from state to state to find themselves in a whole new ball game, and the enormous difficulties encountered by companies doing business in several or all states. The code would repeal all state laws covering consumer credit, which constitute hodgepodges of complexity, and replace them with one code applicable to all companies and all individuals in all states.

For those who'd like to get into the subject in detail, information is available from the National Conference of Commissioners of Uniform State Laws, 1155 East 60th Street, Chicago, Illinois 60657. This is a free country and anyone can criticize credit as it is administered in America today, but for the criticism to have relevance to the problem it should be based on facts, not political propaganda.

Service

Whether you buy merchandise for cash or with credit, you want it to do what you bought it to do. You want your TV to bring you the Superbowl and your refrigerator to keep the beer cold while you watch it. You want your washer to wash and your drier to dry.

When these appliances break down, you want them fixed. And this leads us to another area of consumerism: repair service.

Here again Montgomery Ward offers a laboratory for study of a much discussed subject. At the beginning of its ninth decade, Ward's service department was small and antiquated. Within ten years it was number three in the industry (Sears and RCA are bigger) with some 5,000 trained service personnel working out of hundreds of up-to-date facilities; no other service system is in the same league. During this period the sale of appliances at Wards increased from 6 to 15 per cent of total sales; good service obviously appeals to customers. How the service department grew, and what its managers have learned watching and making it grow, could be of interest, if not help, to any consumer with questions on service. Why do they charge you a fortune for a few minutes' work? Why doesn't it stay fixed? Why do they ask you silly questions when you call in to report something wrong?

While we're on the subject of questions it might interest you to know that frequently the person taking the call is secretly wondering what in the world is the matter with you. Because more than a third of the calls Ward's service department receives shouldn't have to be made in the first place.

Repair people, from apprentice to executive, are a separate breed entirely. Neither hunters nor toolmakers, they are a mechanically oriented refinement of both. Their greatest happiness comes from hunting for ways to second-guess the toolmaker. They get enormous satisfaction out of patching up other people's mistakes, and gleefully reporting what was wrong. They service not only equipment but, through fixing and calling attention to its weaknesses, provide a vital service to their fellow consumers.

Dean R. Lewis, vice president of customer service for Wards, works on his own automobile, does all the repairs around the house. "I have a Golden Contract which covers everything I own, but I still make all the repairs myself." He worked his way through high school and college repairing automobiles. He built a television set way back in 1939. When he went to work for Sears after the war he was encouraged to go into management and received several promotions up the line, but he missed that toolbox.

"The farther up I got, the more I realized the fantastic potential of service; frankly, the excitement of service. We're involved in everything."

Lewis is the type of man who wants to be involved in everything. He can't sit still. When he joined Wards in 1963, he was like a kid with a dozen different toys on Christmas morning, all of them needing fixing. He was ecstatic. After looking over the situation he reported in to Tom Brooker, who listened to him for a few minutes, then held up his hands and said,

"Dean, you and I agree on everything. Go." So Dean went and started fixing the fixit department.

Wards had several problems, problems that your local repairman may still have. One was its facilities. They were hidden away out of sight as though the company were ashamed of them, as indeed it should have been. In Chicago the service department was located on the ninth floor of the catalog house across the street from headquarters—"you had to have an Indian guide to even get to it." It was neither large enough nor efficient enough to stock all the parts necessary to make repairs.

Another huge problem was in the turnover of its personnel. About the time anybody learned anything, he'd leave. The reason could be traced back to the contract an earlier administration had signed with the union, which provided for comparatively low wages. Lewis found himself in the peculiar management position of pleading with the union to accept a wage increase for its technicians so that they would stay with the company. In exchange the company got the right to insist on top performance based on a fair appraisal plan.

Wards had particular need for continuity of experienced repairmen. Take a washing machine. Sears has had the same supplier for 40 years. Wards, under the previous procurement policy and through trial-and-error search for one dependable supplier, has had a half-dozen different sources in 15 years. It takes an experienced man to be able to work with that many different machines.

To train the company repairmen Lewis set up schools over the country. That didn't work out too well, because when a man was attending school he was away from the job, and the calls piled up even more. So Lewis invented a mobile training center, had several built in trailers, and hauled them around from location to location. In two days of training in the mobile center repairmen get up-to-date instruction in fixing the entire line of merchandise. Home-study courses, done on the technician's own time, add to knowledge. The individuals who go into this type of work are hungry for information. They love it. And of course the more they know the quicker and higher they are upgraded, which means more money.

The education of a service technician includes far more than replacing a tube, gasket, or switch. Indeed, one of the major concerns of both consumer and industry today is that too often the serviceman fixes something that really doesn't need fixing and leaves the real problem unsolved. Lewis says that developing what he calls the think process is the crucial part of training. Fixing is easy; diagnosing what to fix is the most difficult and time-consuming part of the operation. When your television set goes on the blink, the technician usually spends twice as much time diagnosing the cause as effecting the remedy. This may not be so surprising in the case of a color TV, but as more and more of our household appliances are improved by modern technology they too become complicated. We tend to think of our stove as a stove, but an over-and-under self-cleaning electric range has just as complicated circuitry as a TV set. The technician must not only keep up with all the technical manuals, but must also develop his own analytical skills. He's got to think.

Training clerical workers, especially the women who take the calls, is fully as important in a sense as training the technician. About 40 per cent of all requests for service are in effect unnecessary. It's not the equipment that's at fault, but the person trying to run the equipment. In these cases the problem can sometimes be determined over the telephone. Taking service calls is pretty much a thankless job—they usually begin with an angry customer screaming—and one of the ways to keep from going crazy is to play a sort of game. If the woman answering the phone can elicit enough information to diagnose the problem herself she considers herself the winner. As this frequently satisfies the customer who was berating her just a moment ago, both win.

No matter how well trained the repair personnel, they are

helpless if they do not have the replacement part for whatever is wrong. Keeping those parts in stock is a major headache of any repair department. Many Ward customers have appliances that are 20 years old or more, manufactured by companies which passed out of the supply picture long ago. Before Lewis took over the service department, the unwritten policy at Wards was to take care of the items still in warranty first, then, if convenient, get around to those on which the warranty had expired. Many companies still feel this way, which is why you may have to wait for your local repairman to get around to you.

Lewis has an entirely different viewpoint. He considers one of the most important functions of the service department to satisfy the customer, and keep that customer coming back to the store. If this means taking care of a 20-year-old appliance manufactured by some long-gone supplier in its proper turn, well, that's part of the job.

As a result, most service centers in the metropolitan areas stock some 22,000 parts. The big new facility in Chicago, located near O'Hare Airport, carries an even larger supply. Parts requisitioned by teletype during the day go out by air freight that night, and may possibly be installed in the customer's appliance the next day. Part of Lewis's job is also looking ahead into the future. When the buyers in the merchandise department come up with either a fantastic new gizmo or just another appliance, he sees to it that they also arrange for parts to be available over the next seven to ten years.

After talking with Lewis, I went to the Washington, D.C., service facility to see the application of his dreams in the field. The service facility in the Baltimore metropolitan area is a handsome new building. Pat F. Cosentini, the manager, was a management trainee who went into the service department when it was just getting started. He started with three people; now he has 135 employees. Cosentini operates on the assumption that every complaint received is a legitimate one, and that it should be taken care of immediately.

From the national distribution center, parts for an ailing appliance can be flown out overnight. Dean Lewis was so proud of it that he got Harold Dysart, executive vice president, and two other VPs to come check it out. Left to right, Herman Nater, Lewis, William J. Harbeck, and Dysart.

His biggest problem is the recruitment and development of personnel. His recruits range from 20-year men retiring from the military service, who go through a transition program of six months before final discharge, to distributive education majors in the nearby high schools. Technicians start at $120 a week, go to $170. A high school graduate with a greater aptitude for repair than for intellectual pursuits can be making almost $9,000 a year before he would be in his senior year in college.

Cosentini is well aware of the public's skepticism of technicians. "It's natural to be suspicious when these intricate technical gadgets are involved," he said. "It's not like wearing out a pair of pants."

Wards makes many efforts to allay the customers' suspicions. The company itself controls its technicians by an individual work order for each job. Whether it's the replacement of a

244

television tube or a belt on a drier, the job carries a definite cost printed on the authorized price list. The technician carries it with him and shows it to the customer. He gets no commission, no extra compensation for additional time. If he's an inexperienced worker and takes twice as long to do the job, the price to you is the same. If he replaces a TV tube, he must bring back the old one in the box the new one came out of. The box is torn up and the tube is crushed.

"We just have to hope that the customer believes us," Cosentini said. "We do all we can to justify his belief in us. That goes for most people in this business. I know that there are some shysters around, but most repair men are honest. Take the neighborhood TV shop. The only asset that fellow has is neighborhood goodwill. He'd be silly to jeopardize it."

Cosentini also handles small appliances brought into the stores for repair. Many times they are simply junked and replaced. It's cheaper to do that than to spend the time looking for the trouble and repairing it.

One of the features retailers harp on, and of which I've always been skeptical, is the service contract. If nothing goes wrong with the appliance after the warranty, why then, you certainly don't need the service contract. You may also figure, as I do, that if something's going to hold up for a year it's probably going to hold up for another year. Finally, the company wouldn't be selling the service contract if it weren't profitable.

Cosentini explains it as simply an extension of the warranty. For the fact remains that things do go wrong, on the 366th day as well as on the 364th, and when they do the service contract is a good deal for the consumer. It's insurance. The service contract in Washington for a color TV set is $29.95 if you bring it into the shop yourself, $49.95 for home service. (The technician isn't contributing a thing to the company while he's driving to your house, and the truck he's using wasn't free.) If a $135 picture tube burns out you're obviously ahead with a service contract. Other tubes average out at about $5, and the cost of the call is $6.95. "You just couldn't get away for less than $25," Cosentini said.

A major consumer complaint is that the technician arrives at the house, fools around with the appliance a while, then takes it to the shop and keeps it there for days. Cosentini's answer is that his technicians make every effort to do the repair work in the home. Over the years the department has built up a knowledge of what is most likely to go wrong. When it leaves the center in the morning each truck assigned to TV service carries three sizes of picture tubes and a complete stock of smaller tubes.

Others carry parts for different household articles. The driers built for Wards by Norge a few years ago came equipped with a belt not strong enough for the job. Every laundry-service truck carries a supply of heavy-duty belts to replace the original, and a technician can install it in a few minutes. (This experience also exemplifies another important role of the service department, feedback to the buying office and from there to the supplier. Later model driers, whether sold under the Ward or the Norge label, come with stronger belts.) In short, service-center personnel call on past experience to anticipate the trouble they'll find, and are frequently ready for it. But they can't be prepared for everything.

When the technicians go out in the morning, they carry with them both the work orders for the job and the parts they think will be needed. Here is where Dean Lewis's emphasis on training the women who answer the phone, and their supervisors, pays off. If the person taking the call has been able to get sufficient information, she, the supervisor on examining the service order, or the technician, may be able to diagnose the problem. The technician may have just exactly the right replacement in his hand when he knocks on the door. But this is not always so easy to do.

"We've got three strikes on us when we pick up the phone," Cosentini said. "People start cussing out the girls before they say a word."

The irate housewife calling in to say that her television set has suddenly gone bad just when she wanted to watch the afternoon soap opera may get even madder when the voice at the other end of the line asks if she has small children. What's that got to do with it? Well, small children crawl on floors and knock plugs out of receptacles. Many a woman has done a complete flipflop, from hollering harridan to an embarrassed but much relieved and appreciative person, on discovering that the set was indeed unplugged. She may have done it herself when she vacuumed the floors.

Another complaint is that the icemaker in the refrigerator isn't working. The woman taking the call asks if the arm is

Many an impatient housewife calling for service wonders why in the world Ward telephone girls ask if she has small children. That question could save you the money for a service call, for frequently the reason something won't work is as simple as a child's pulling out a plug.

jammed against the basket. It frequently is, and another customer has been saved the expense of a house call. Others call to report that there is water on the floor under the automatic-defrosting refrigerator. Question: Is the pan under the hose? Sometimes freezers have ice on the bottom. This is usually caused by a small piece of food getting stuck in the drain tube. It's easy to poke it out. The way it got there in the first place is that, when the housewife cleaned out the freezer, she took out the screen over the tube and forgot to replace it.

All of these, and many more, save the customer money by obviating the house call entirely. Other questions can save the company time, therefore the customer money, in determining what the problem is before starting out to fix it. A frequent complaint is that the television set has ghosts on the screen. Are they on every channel, or just one? In the latter case, the fault is with the antenna, not the set.

The largest single category of calls does not involve the fault of the article in question, but that of the owner. It may be as simple a matter as not plugging in the appliance, not cutting on the water, trying to run something on manual when it's set on automatic. Frequently it's a blown fuse or a tripped circuit breaker.

The second major cause of complaint is simply not reading the instructions. Lewis, commenting on this, said, "I defy any woman, certainly my own wife, or for that matter, any man, including myself or even a technician, to get a new range, or washer or drier or dishwasher, probably with eight push buttons on it for everything you could possibly think of—I'll defy that person to remember what every control is for without referring to the instruction book for a long period of time. About a fourth of all our calls are made simply because somebody pushed the wrong button or did something the instruction book said plainly not to do."

It will cost you less to take small appliances that don't work back to the store yourself. For big items, whether calling Wards or anybody else to complain about something that doesn't work, follow these steps:

1. Make sure the appliance is plugged in, that the water is cut on, that the fuse isn't burned out or the circuit breaker tripped.

2. Read the instruction book and make sure you are attempting to run the appliance properly. These things can be complicated.

3. Before calling in check the date of purchase, in order to determine whether the appliance is still in warranty, and most important of all, look on the appliance itself, find the model number and write it down so that you can repeat it over the phone. Every article is keyed to a model number. There are so many numbers, designating equipment running back so many years and built by so many suppliers, that the service center keeps them on microfilm. By checking the model number before he starts for your house, the technician has a good idea of what he's getting into and may be able to cope with it more quickly.

4. Cool down. Think about what the trouble is, and be prepared to describe it. The person who receives your call may be able to help you on the telephone. If not, her notes on the service order will be of value to the technician assigned to the job. And when the technician arrives, your simple description in nontechnical language may provide an additional clue. Remember that diagnosing the problem is the most difficult and time-consuming part of his job.

5. Determine when you want the technician to come. If your refrigerator isn't running and your food is spoiling, of course you want immediate service. But Wards has discovered that a good percentage of customers on being questioned suddenly remember that they have to go out this afternoon and as a matter of fact it would be inconvenient for the serviceman to come tomorrow, too. Prodded into consulting their calendar, they find that next Tuesday is really the best day.

If you think about this in advance it will save time and make it more convenient for everyone, including yourself.

And finally, all of this leads to still another observation in favor of the mass merchandiser. Only a company as big as Wards can afford a Dean Lewis, his ideas and the implementation of them. The smaller operation can't afford to train the person who takes the call, much less stock 22,000 parts and fly the rest in overnight. It would be great for the purchaser of merchandise from other stores if they could avail themselves of Ward's service facilities across the board, from can openers to outboard motors, but, sadly, they can't. Wards, and the other mass merchandisers, are hard pressed to take care of their own. The wise consumer, therefore, before purchasing any item which can break down, finds out who's going to fix it if it does. If the store doesn't have its own service department—caveat emptor.

Shoplifting

Though you probably never thought of working out the percentages, you surely are aware that the money you spend for consumer goods goes to pay for the actual cost of the merchandise plus several other expenses such as salaries, rent, taxes and contributions to fund drives. But did you ever stop to think that a portion of it also helps support your local thieves?

According to the National Retail Merchants Association, $8 million a day goes to what retailers call shrinkage, which includes thefts by employees and shoplifters. The percentage of shrinkage varies in different locations and from merchant to merchant, but nevertheless it's you, the consumer, who pay for it. And if the current situation continues, in which 75 per cent of all shoplifters get off without being prosecuted, you're going to pay more.

In 1969 Montgomery Ward apprehended 22,533 shoplifters; there were 29,590 in 1970, 29,055 in 1971. They included people of all ages, from all walks of life—junkies, housewives, teenagers or kids even younger, professionals. Harry E. Stirmell, who has headed the protection department of Wards since 1944 and has talked to thousands of apprehended shoplifters, says that they all have one thing in common—they want something for nothing. He impatiently brushes aside the suggestion that people steal for emotional or psychotic reasons.

"I've heard every excuse in the book," he said. "The clerk didn't wait on them. They're suffering from some kind of frustration. They're depressed—that's what a lot of pregnant women we pick up say. But it doesn't make any difference what they say, they're just plain thieves. As for kleptomaniacs, people who are really sick, they're about one out of every 500,000. The thing about kleptomaniacs is that they steal for no gain, no use. We caught a woman who had $8,000 worth of dresses in her apartment. She'd never worn one. Most were long out of style. You may read about people like that but you rarely see them. Shoplifters aren't sick, they're thieves. They steal things of value for their own gain."

Even Stirmell is surprised at some of the people his men pick up. Men with good incomes, kids from good families, wives of prominent and well-to-to community leaders. In a midwestern city a woman was caught red-handed. Her husband was the president of the local chamber of commerce who was that very week organizing a city-wide campaign against shoplifting.

Teenagers comprise the largest group of shoplifters. In 1971 in Ward's western region, 4,866 shoplifters were apprehended, and 3,327 were referred to juvenile authorities. Stirmell blames the increase in teenaged shoplifting on three factors: a general looseness in moral fiber and lack of respect for other people's property; a stratification of the age group, in which they band together against establishment and authority and prove their cohesion by doing what the others are doing ("They don't want to be called chicken"); and the need to impress someone with their daring.

My personal spy in the enemy camp, our daughter Sue, says

that she hears much more about shoplifting from girls than from boys, and that the reason is nearly always an effort to impress someone. "I know girls whose parents can afford to buy them anything they want who come to school in the morning and the first thing they say is, 'Guess what I ripped off yesterday.' They'll steal a bracelet, or put on three bathing suits under their dress. In summer the big deal is to walk in barefooted and come out wearing shoes, but it's not because they need shoes. I don't think it's so much a protest, either. Sometimes you'll hear somebody say they're getting back at the evil capitalistic system, but if you ask them about it they really don't know what capitalism is. It all sounds kind of silly to me — but a lot of kids do it."

One of the worst areas in town, incidentally, is not the low-income section but the shopping center across the street from one of the most exclusive girls' boarding schools in the east which also has a large proportion of local day students. One merchant estimated that the rich girls get him for hundreds of dollars worth of cosmetics and other little items every weekend. But he'd rather take the loss — and pass it on to me — than nab the girls themselves. It wouldn't be worth the repercussions he'd get from school and parents.

The proportion of teenaged shoplifters may be large, but the items they steal are not necessarily expensive. It's the professional thieves who cost the retail industry the most money. They wear bulky overcoats and somehow manage to put on layers of clothing underneath them. They have specially constructed pockets in which to conceal small, expensive items like jewelry, watches, even transistor radios. They carry tools of the trade, suction cups with which to slide open the glass fronts of display cases, skeleton keys for both locked cases and cash registers.

In the State Street store in downtown Chicago, small boys have been caught stealing from display cases which can be opened only by unlocking them from the rear. They lie down in the narrow space between the case and the floor, hidden from both clerks and customers, reach up with one hand and open the locks with skeleton keys. Though still of grammar school age, they're proficient at their trade.

A store detective nabbed a 10-year-old boy with a large shopping bag full of items, and a hand-written list. The boy's mother had carefully prepared a shopping list of the merchandise she sent him out to steal.

The store detective leads an exciting life. A young man I talked to, William Stewart, became a sales trainee after graduating from Michigan State, then volunteered for the security program. The Detroit store to which he was assigned was built before the days of protection devices, and the only vantage points from which he could survey the store were the ventilation grills in the ceiling. To reach them he had to crawl through the vents, bucking the blast of hot air in winter, cold in summer.

When he saw a suspect, he'd have to crawl back through the vent, then hurry to the exit in time to apprehend the thief coming out. It's routine to wait until the shoplifter has left the store with the merchandise, otherwise he could always say he intended to pay for the item he had tucked away. Often people would make a run for it; Stewart chased them wherever they went, through backyards and into other stores. "I never had any get away," he said quietly.

Like other members of the protection detail, he carried no weapons, nor was he trained in special techniques to overcome people physically. "If the other guy is armed, or fights back, we let him go," he said. "The company goes on the principle that being killed or injured isn't worth the money we might recover."

In nearly all cases, the shoplifter does not resist in the first place. The professional knows it would only make matters worse. The teenager who's just picking something up for kicks may make a break for it but whether he's caught at the end of a chase, or at the door before he gets a chance to run, he's too scared to do anything. Female shoplifters, whether teenaged girls, the woman next door who picked up something on impulse, or even professionals, may protest their innocence, bluster or cry, but rarely run or physically resist. The dangerous shoplifter is the dope addict. He's desperate and he's got nothing to lose. But he doesn't hit the suburban store as much as the stores in the rundown downtown areas which he frequents.

Whoever the shoplifter may be, Stewart walks him or her back through the store to an office, calls the police and in the meantime tries to get him or her to write out, by hand, a statement. Stewart's only means of persuasion is his suggestion that the statement will make the guilty person look a little better in court. Because, in spite of the tears, protests or threats, he finally gets the point across that the shoplifter is definitely going to court.

I met Stewart at the opening of the big new store in Rockford, Illinois, where, on the strength of his good record in Detroit, he was in charge of store security. He'd come to Rockford well in advance of the opening, talked with people in other stores and established a rapport with the police. To get personnel he had run a want ad in the paper.

"About 80 or 90 responded," he said, "and boy, a lot of them were right out of the bottom of the barrel. I eliminated the tough guys and the dumb ones right away. Women are the hardest to find. They've got to be forceful but tactful and polite, not lose their temper, keep cool and be smart enough to handle the situation."

The Rockford store is of a new design. In the center of the store is a fitting room, and over it a small space. Behind a curtain the carpenters had built a tiny ladder against the wall, leading up to a small aperture in the ceiling. It was a tight squeeze; I just could get through. The space above was carpeted, so that someone trying on a suit below wouldn't hear anyone moving around above. One-way glass portholes looked out over the store. It was no coincidence that from one side you could look down directly on the shoe department. Wearing an old pair in and a new pair out is an old trick.

"I hope I can make ten arrests right away," Stewart said, wistfully. "I'd like to establish a reputation right off the bat. Once they learn we prosecute, the amateurs will stay away."

And Wards does prosecute. As far back as Harry Stirmell can remember, the company has had only one policy in regard to thieves. "It's one sentence," he said, "and it's very clear. *Report all instances of crime to the proper prosecuting authorities as dictated by public duty.* We pursue that policy in any case regardless of any unpleasant publicity that may result. I don't think you'll find that policy in any other company in the United States. We don't fear unpleasant publicity because we don't think it is unpleasant. We think that prosecuting criminals is a real public duty, and that no honest person will stop trading with us as a result of it. We've never been elected as judges to make a determination of which shoplifter we should turn loose, which one should get 30 days, which one gets a year. That judgment is up to the courts, regardless of any unusual or exceptional circumstances.

"The only reason we don't prosecute a case is because we don't have sufficient evidence. An example of that is when

Surveillance saves the honest consumer money. A security guard spots a shoplifter and alerts his partner by phone.

one person steals something, then slips it to someone else on leaving the store. That kind of case is sticky—one of them has it but didn't steal it, the other one stole it but doesn't have it in his possession. In some communities the prosecuting attorney won't accept the complaint if it's under, say, $10. It's too much trouble, and too many cases increase the crime rate and he doesn't look so good. We're not too pleased when legal authorities won't let us help them do their job.

"But in every case, when we have the evidence and are permitted to present it, we prosecute."

Often people bring tremendous pressure on Wards to drop the case. A doctor threatened to have the company boycotted by the state medical association. The company went ahead; there was no boycott. The son of a stockholder was apprehended; the father threatened to sell his stock if the company prosecuted. It did and he did.

It won't even do any good to go to the top. Tom Brooker, Ed Donnell and other officers of the company occasionally receive letters from people saying their wives (or sons or daughters) had never done such a thing before and this has taught them a lesson and how terrible it will be if the news got out, and won't they please drop the charges. Such letters are automatically turned over to Harry Stirmell, and by now it should be obvious what he does with them.

Few companies are this determined to leave the disposition of the case up to the courts. According to Stirmell, 75 per cent of the shoplifters apprehended are released. Some may have learned their lesson, but others may well try again, and get away with it.

Curious about this, I asked a friend of mine who manages a large local store, part of a regional chain, what his policy was. "We prosecute," he told me firmly.

"Look," I said, "You mean that if Bonnie walks out with a purse and I come to you as a personal friend and say I'll make it good and remind you of the good she has done in the community and what the repercussions would be you'd still file a complaint with the police?"

"Well," he said, "I guess we'd have to make an exception in that case."

Wards leaves the exceptions up to the courts.

In the light of the fact that you, the consumer, pay the bill for shoplifting (you can bet that the retailer passes it on to you), what can you do about it?

First, if you see someone slipping an item into her handbag, tell the nearest clerk. He or she has been told what to do. Do not, Stirmell advises, take any direct action yourself. You are not trained to handle the matter and you may be the one who gets in trouble. If the shoplifter is a professional, or a junkie, it could even be dangerous.

"Yeah," I said to Harry, "but suppose I see a kid half my size stealing something. He's not going to stick a knife in me."

"No," Harry said, "but his parents might sue the hell out of you. *Stay out of it.* Tell the clerk."

A more important involvement Stirmell recommends is to work as a citizen and taxpayer to support the enforcement of the law. "I'm not talking about law and order in the sense of depriving people of their rights or discouraging dissent," he said. "I mean supporting and encouraging the law enforcement agencies and the courts in doing their duty to uphold the law. And stealing is against the law."

Though Stirmell calls shoplifting "a cancerous situation," he believes that it is exaggerated. "I'll make a statement now that will get me in trouble," he said, "and that is that there are too many companies, especially the smaller ones, which are too quick to identify every shortage as shoplifting. The whole thing boils down to inventory shortage at the end of the year. The auditing procedures could be atrocious — just plain poor paper work. It's easy to blame the losses on shoplifters. Some companies refuse to admit the possibility that they have a silent partner in their midst, that nice kid who's somebody's wife's cousin. We know better. We had a receiving clerk in a small town who took us for $100,000. But we didn't write it off as shoplifting. We knew something was wrong, and we caught him."

One way to avoid supporting thieves, whether they are shoplifters from the outside or pilferers from the inside, is to deal with a company which keeps a close rein on its inventory. Retailers use the work *shrinkage* to describe the difference between what comes in and what goes out in sales accounted for. Stirmell said he knew of a company which accepted a shrinkage of 5 per cent. In other words, as long as no more than 5 per cent of its goods remained unaccounted for, it was content. This figure, remember, represents the cost of the goods to the company, not to the consumer. The loss of five cents on the dollar on inventory means the loss of perhaps eight cents on sales—eight cents which the company has to pass on to you in order to catch up.

Checking around town, I found one local company which also estimated its shrinkage as high as 5 per cent. Other figures ranged from 1½ up. Several managers said their shrinkage figure was confidential. A couple of small local stores didn't know what I was talking about. And one manager of a large store of a regional chain said, "Frankly, I have absolutely no idea."

With these figures, or lack of them, in mind, let's look at the shrinkage of Montgomery Ward. It is .3 per cent, one third of a cent on a dollar. The figure is kept that low through a rigid accounting system, further auditing of the basic system, and security.

"Those are the three tangible factors," Stirmell said, "but perhaps most important of all is the total involvement of all personnel. From the manager down to the guy on the loading dock, we're motivated. We work at it."

"Okay, so your shrinkage is three tenths of 1 per cent," I said. "But what about that protection. You've got to pay the people in your department."

"It averages between twenty-two and twenty-five hundredths of 1 per cent," he said. "We have a few stores in rough locations —Richmond, California, Baltimore, State Street in Chicago— where it might go up to four tenths. That means a store doing ten million a year would have a protection payroll of $40,000. The average store of that size has a payroll of only $22–25,000. Only 125 stores have protection personnel. In all the rest it's handled by the manager and his assistants."

Thus the cost of shrinkage plus protection comes out to a little more than half a cent on a dollar. This half a cent protects Wards and its customers against the additional costs of shoplifting, items lost and broken, and the thieving employee. With a leakproof audit system and an alert manager, the pilfering employee is sooner or later going to be dectected. When Sean Lee took over the store in Staunton, Virginia, he knew from the numbers that something was wrong. One department was way off. The Staunton store is one of those which has no protection staff and Lee called in the trained agents from the regional office. They quietly and efficiently went to work. They used a tested method far more efficient than the third degree; it's based on the simple premise that there is no honor among thieves. Ninety-nine times out of a hundred, show me a man who steals and I'll show you a man who squeals. Every man in that department implicated every other man, and, by golly, what they said was true: everybody in the department except the manager was stealing.

Another indication of pilferage was harder to isolate. Cash registers would turn up short at the end of the day but the shortage occurred sporadically, with no pattern. Lee and one of his assistants used all the time-honored methods of catching the thief without success. Then one day a customer who had given the store a bad check came in to make it good. The cashier remembered him, and the crumpled $20 bill he gave her. A few minutes later Lee's assistant made his routine check of the cash register, and when the cashier looked back in it, the crumpled $20 bill was gone. The man assigned to catch the thief was the thief.

In another city an agent assigned to investigate the strange disappearance of small items about the store came in early one morning. From his hideout he watched in amazement as the manager, a well-paid and successful operator, went to the record department, selected two albums, then proceeded to the Christmas display and picked up a couple of ornaments. He took them to his office, then home, without paying.

An authorized search of the manager's home proved it to be filled with merchandise acquired in a similar manner. Though a truck was required to haul the loot away, no single item was of great value. For that he had ruined his career. Why? Nobody knows.

The good folk at Montgomery Ward probably will not appreciate this revelation to the public that there have been thieves in their midst, but the point is not that they exist, but that they are caught. And if they can continue as long as they do in a company with the intensive and sophisticated protection of Montgomery Ward, then how many more are dipping into tills in less well-audited companies throughout the nation? Nobody knows, but we do know that they are costing us money. They cost us less in the carefully audited, efficiently protected retail organization.

The Ward protection department walks a fine line in carrying out its function. For all of his tough talk about lawbreakers, Stirmell administers a most liberal policy in one area of retail internal security. For generations, the retailing industry has had a phobia about the possible immorality of its managers. It's tradition in retailing, dating back to the days when the two key people in the typical small store were the manager and the bookkeeper, who was nearly always a woman, that the worst thing that could happen would be for the manager to have an affair with the bookkeeper.

Before auditing techniques were perfected, this combination could drain the profits out of any store. An unwritten regulation developed which prohibited intimate relations between managers and their female employees, particularly if either or both were married to someone else. (Many an above-board courtship has begun in a retail store, of course, but that's another matter.) To prevent any possible occurrence of illicit liaisons, internal security sections operated on gestapo-like techniques. Any whispered rumor would be grounds to tail a suspect around the clock. Agents pried into private lives, and reported what they found regardless of whether it had anything to do with a person's capability to do his job.

When John D. Foster was brought in from the New York Port Authority as vice president–personnel, Stirmell made a routine get-acquainted visit to his office. In the course of the conversation Foster asked Stirmell what he could do to help him. It set Stirmell back on his heels—"That was a question that had never been asked of me before by anyone."

Out of the resulting discussion grew a completely new policy in the protection department. Stirmell had long maintained that, even if investigation proved an intimate relationship between a manager and a lady friend, chances were everybody had known it all along anyway. It was not a protection problem, but a personnel problem. The question was not one of the individual's morals, but whether his actions affected the performance of his official duties. Further, the gumshoe activities of the protection department, spying on its fellow employees, could only result in prejudice against its operatives instead of the cooperation so frequently necessary.

Though some other executives objected to this reasoning, Foster backed it. On reports of immorality within the company today the people involved are approached directly and openly and told of the rumors. That's all. No efforts are made to catch them in the act. If the actions of the people involved reduce their effectiveness on the job, or reflect on the image of Montgomery Ward in the community—and indeed an organization which deals directly with the public must be overly careful about its image—that's a matter for the personnel department.

Neither department sets itself up as a big brother to dictate the social conduct of its employees. As long as you're discreet about it, get your job done, and do not damage the image of a company which is dependent upon the public, you can do anything you damn please.

7

Past, Present, Future

We have seen how the products which we consumers
desire and need are procured for us and sold to us.
Together they form the concept, integration of products and
sales, or mass merchandising.

The concept is like a river drainage system. Products like
bedspreads and three-door refrigerators flow from the tribu-
taries into the main channel of the river from 7,000 different
sources. But then they branch out again, into the retail and
catalog outlets. If they aren't sold—and they won't be sold for
long unless they're sold at a profit—they dam up the river all the
way back to the headwaters. Mass manufacturing depends
upon mass merchandising, and when the two work together
better goods flow into your house and mine. The flow makes
possible the system by which people who can't afford to buy
what they need when they need it can use somebody else's
money—credit. And when something breaks down, as even
the best of merchandise and people do sometimes, the flow
makes possible the facilities through which you can get somebody to fix it with reasonable promptness and efficiency—
service.

Since the dawn of civilization mankind has been working

more or less steadily toward the twin goals of better production and more efficient distribution. Attempts have been
constantly made to put the two together, in isolated cases
with success. But the highest form of its development to date
had its beginnings during World War I when a multimillionaire
retailer found himself working for a former Spanish teacher.

Robert Thorne, the businessman, was one of the five neph-
ews of Aaron Montgomery Ward. Back in 1872 Uncle Aaron
had single-handedly created the most significant breakthrough
in the history of trade: he had made it possible for people
over a wide area to buy a variety of goods at fixed prices,
without haggling. He brought his brother-in-law, George
Thorne, in to help, and a grateful public made them both
rich. By 1912 his 1,665 shares in Montgomery Ward, and
the 5,000 shares passed on to George Thorne's five sons,
had increased from a par value of $100 to a book value of
$2,500 and paid a dividend of 100 per cent. The next year
the stock was split 58 for one.

When America went to war in 1917, Robert Thorne, president of the company, could afford to serve on the Quarter-
master General's staff for a dollar a year. His boss was an
Army career officer, Robert E. Wood, who had served in the
Philippines and Panama and taught Spanish at West Point.
Thorne liked Wood's ideas for mass procurement of merchandise and the energetic way he went about implementing them.
When the war ended Thorne brought the General into Montgomery Ward.

At that time the company did a big business in grocery
staples, and in a burst of confidence it cornered the sugar
market at 20 cents a pound. In the post-war depression its
5,000 tons of sugar dropped to a nickel a pound. Prices on
practically everything Wards sold—and which as a big mail
order house it had procured far in advance—also dropped.
New York banks had to bail out the company and sent in their
own man to replace Thorne. The new man didn't like the ex-
Army vice president's ideas.

Wood foresaw what the automobile would do to American

demography, and proposed setting up retail stores to serve customers who could now drive to town. He also saw the advantage of buying into large suppliers, thus becoming in effect their partners and assuring a steady flow of merchandise. He had no compunction against buying stock in these favored suppliers himself; the General was not averse to making a buck on the side. Ward's management opposed, and still does, the ownership on the part of its executives of stock in companies with which it does business. Wood returned from a hunting trip in Alaska one day to find that he had been fired.

A friend of his, knowing that Julius Rosenwald, chairman of the board of Sears, was looking for a new president, got the two together. Sears, Roebuck and Company had started when Richard W. Sears, who got in the mail order business selling watches, joined forces with A. C. Roebuck in Chicago. In 1895 Roebuck sold his interest to Rosenwald. At the time Wards was doing close to $4 million gross, Sears less than a fourth of that, but Rosenwald brought the company up fast. By the early twenties his managerial ability and personal fortune had built Sears into a larger and more profitable company than the original mail order house, Montgomery Ward and Company.

But Rosenwald, who was Jewish, was aware that prejudice existed in America, especially in the twenties when the Ku Klux Klan was almost respectable, and he wanted a vice president who was both capable and Christian. General Wood met the specifications. As vice president, president and eventually chairman of the board of Sears, he used his managerial expertise to develop loyal sources of products and to build retail facilities to merchandise them. Sears was already a huge enterprise; the General made it bigger.

In keeping with his willingness to put borrowed money into new enterprises, General Wood liked to play bridge for a cent a point. He kept on the lookout for good bridge players, and on toward the end of World War II he discovered he had just hired one, Tom Brooker.

The presence of General Wood and Tom Brooker at the

bridge table together was less unlikely than their presence in merchandising. One had started out as an Army officer, the other as an engineer. When I asked Tom how he happened to go into merchandising it almost startled him for a moment. We talked about something else for a few minutes and then he brought the conversation back around to it. "You know I never thought about that until you asked me," he said.

In his first years with Southern California Edison Company Tom was on the company basketball team, softball team, and tennis team. He was elected vice president for athletics of the company social club, then president. In that capacity, though he was only in his mid-twenties, he frequently saw the top executives of the company in order to put the bite on them for social functions and established a good rapport. Management began assigning him to broader duties. One of his first projects was to look into the purchases of medical supplies for the company's clinics and hospitals. The doctor in charge resisted the lay meddling. The young club president had done his homework — Tom Brooker has always done his homework. He had the figures to prove that by consolidating the procurement of medical supplies and buying them in large numbers — mass merchandising! — the company would save a lot of money. With his clout with management he was able to get his recommendation for mass purchases to the top. The chief of the medical department threatened to resign; the president said he'd hate to accept his resignation, but. . . . There was no resignation, and Brooker's purchasing program was adopted.

By the time he was 27 he was making $200 a month plus $150 on the side selling stock in the company to suppliers. As the depression deepened, the company stopped selling stock, and there went that additional income. That's when he went to Firestone.

Brooker has often looked back at that move and wondered what would have happened if he had stayed on at the utility company. "I'd have probably done all right," he told me, "but the progress would have been slow." At the time, the shift in careers which led to his becoming one of the world's leading figures in merchandising was simply a matter of immediate expediency. He was married; he needed more money.

Nor did he realize at the time that he was embracing the concept which he would later ride to prominence. General Wood, first at Wards, then at Sears, had put the two mail order houses into the tire business. The competition hurt Firestone. The company decided to open retail stores across the country; if the stores only broke even their sales would still provide augmentation of production at the factory. And that's where the profit was.

Brooker stayed with Firestone for ten years, covering the entire west, but with World War II travel became miserable. He decided to quit and settle down in Santa Rosa, running a tire store and retreading operation. He had an interest in a company manufacturing automobile accessories, and he could see possibilities in real estate. Life would be rosy in Santa Rosa.

At the same time Sears, usually three deep in executives, found itself in the embarrassing situation of having no replacement for the supervisor of the tire department, a position similar to the president of a major company. A manufacturer who sold to both Sears and Firestone recommended Brooker. With visions of spending seven days a week at home in Santa Rosa, Tom said he wasn't interested. Nothing increases a man's value as much as being hard to get, and Sears insisted that he come to Chicago where he was interviewed by everybody from General Wood down. He was asked how much he intended to invest in Santa Rosa. Sixty thousand dollars, Brooker said proudly. How much did he think he'd make? Tom told them.

"You can make that much here without putting up a nickel."

Brooker went to work for Sears. He quietly and confidently got things done, and played bridge with the General. On a trip to Venezuela in the company plane Wood needed a fourth and took Brooker along. Stopping over in Miami, the General told Brooker he had a new job for him.

"That's fine, sir," Tom said, immediately seeing himself in Venezuela

"Don't you want to know what it is?" the General said.

"No, General, you've always been fair with me. You tell me what it is and I'll take it."

The new job was vice president of factories. For the next several years Brooker dealt directly with the manufacturing concerns Sears owned outright, with those in which it owned a part interest, and with those with which it had major contracts. He acquired factories, merged them, moved them, created them. Edward Gudeman was vice president of merchandising and the two men worked closely together, dovetailing production with sales. During this period, the fifties, the many complex pieces of the simple-sounding concept, integration of production and merchandising, came together. Sears had sources, the outlets, and the technostructure. In General Wood's third of a century at Sears the company's sales grew from $200 million to $8 billion.

Montgomery Ward's pattern was far more erratic. In the mid-twenties the company embarked on an expansion program that was almost frantic. It put in hundreds of new stores, nearly all in the downtown sections of small cities. Stock went up to $450 per share. Then came the depression. Again the banks took over. Sewell Avery, a law school graduate from a wealthy family who'd become president of U.S. Gypsum Company in 1905 when he was 32, had brought Gypsum through the post World War I depression in good shape. Though he had no retail experience whatever, on the basis of his track record with U.S. Gypsum he was talked into taking over Montgomery Ward.

Avery ran the company well, and as the country came out of the depression Wards began another period of expansion.

It continued to build its new stores in the downtown areas but the company prospered because Avery insisted on quality merchandise, frequently testing it himself, and because Ward personnel and customers were loyal. The company operated on sound business principles which were plenty good enough for the thirties and forties. With a couple of anachronistic exceptions, it had no factories of its own, no participation in others. Avery had no Tom Brookers running around meddling in manufacturing. His buyers shopped around for the best quality at the best price, and left the manufacturing up to the manufacturers. It was a perfectly good way of running a big retail operation then, and it's a perfectly good way of running a department store now.

During the war, however, with consumer merchandise in short supply, Wards, like other retailers without financial interests in their suppliers, found goods harder to obtain. What was so tragically unique in the situation of Montgomery Ward, its stockholders, personnel and customers was the obsession of its absolute ruler, Sewell Avery. He believed, he was positively convinced, that a depression would follow the war. It always had and it always would. He had an elaborate chart, in color, depicting the fall of the economy following every war since Napoleon. Revolutionary War, Civil War, World War I, you name it, and he could point his finger to the dip on the chart immediately following. He projected a depression following World War II on his chart and he could point to that too.

And he was preparing for it. The last Ward store was built in 1941, and just about the last coat of paint was applied to any Ward wall at that time, too. Store managers have told me, their voices breaking with frustration even after all the years, of pleading in vain for authorization to slap on a coat of paint on their dingy walls. General Wood's decision to expand Sears retail operations to new locations after the war only increased Avery's determination to hoard money for the depression plainly marked on his chart. When it came Sears would collapse and he would step in and buy his competitor out. He was stashing away the cash to do it with.

Tom Brooker, an overly patient man, gets an edge in his voice when he talks of Avery's banking money during the period of the excess profits tax. Put into capital improvements at that time, each of those hundreds of millions of dollars would have gained value. In terms of modern corporate finance Avery was paying money to save it.

It's ironic that the general public's pejorative memories of Avery are concerned less with his financial errors than with his battle with the War Labor Board. I'm constantly amazed at the people who bring up the famous picture of Avery being carried out of the building by soldiers. Some weren't even alive in April 1944, but they have seen the picture.

Actually, arranging to be carried out of Wards was a pretty clever legal maneuver. Though the matter is legally complex, the issue was simple. At that time Avery was a generous employer. He insisted on good merchandise and he paid for it; he insisted on good people and he paid for them. (Although he did not believe in pension plans and similar fringe benefits; he contended that his people would be better off planning for their own future.)

Nor was Avery opposed to unions. He dealt with the unions in Wards fairly, in his way. In one strike, begun over the banning of a local business agent from Ward's property, the business agent, who was not an employee, offered to sign a secret paper that he would not set foot on the property if Wards would only cooperate in ending the strike. Avery answered that he had no right to be on the property anyway, and the strike continued until it petered out.

Ward's war with the War Labor Board involved compulsory union membership. Avery didn't believe in it. When he refused to comply, an order to seize the property was issued by the President of the United States. (It didn't help matters that the President was Franklin D. Roosevelt; Avery was a charter member of the Hate FDR club.)

Stuart Ball, then president of the company and an attorney, advised Avery that Wards had no recourse to the order. It had to have some overt act to get its day in court. And so Avery goaded the government into committing that overt act. As he was being carried out, he looked at Stuart Ball, winked, and said, "Is this what you want, Stu?"

The Army remained in possession of the property, but Wards was now able to get into court. The case went up to the Supreme Court and back again, but by that time the war was over and the Army decamped.

While running the store the Army paid out $300,000 more than it took in, and Wards never did pay out a million dollars in retroactive pay increases ordered by the War Labor Board. Avery won his point and saved Wards a lot of money.

In 1950 Avery nearly died with pneumonia, and suffered

Sewell Avery was actually more pleased than he appeared when carried out of his office in 1944. The action enabled him to take his case to court.

a severe stroke. He was 77 years old, and his brush with death brought on a psychopathic fear of being old. He had seen his father retire and wither away with nothing to do, and he now lived in terror of the senility which had already seized him. He refused to retire. He stubbornly continued to stash away the decreasing profits in banks. Martinets emerged to toady to him and made life miserable for others. One got the brilliant idea of firing successful, well-paid managers and replacing them with younger, unproven men who'd work for less. During the first half of the fifties hundreds of managers were either fired, or quit to find opportunity elsewhere. But Avery stayed on.

In 1955 Montgomery Ward was a dying operation—with $360 million cash in the bank and that much more in real estate. It was fair game for a corporate raider, and Louis Wolfson, a former Georgia tackle who had gone far in finance, organized the hunting party. It became one of the great proxy fights in financial history. Presiding over the stockholders' meeting, Avery, badgered by Wolfson and his lieutenants, cracked up and became incoherent. It was a pitiful sight. John Barr, a vice president, quickly stepped up and smoothly conducted the remainder of the meeting. Wolfson did not gain control, but even the moribund board of directors— one of whom had been an interim president of the company 35 years before and who regularly slept through meetings— saw that Avery could not continue. There was no one left but John Barr, and he became chairman of the board.

Barr frankly admitted he didn't know how to run this massive operation. But where could he go for help? There was no one left at Wards even remotely qualified. The board would not permit him to approach Sears, even if there'd been any hope that any Sears executive would take on the job. Barr had to bring in department store people, and they didn't work out. Five years after he took over, although sales were way up, earnings were way down, and the dividend was cut in half. This time the board let him go to Sears.

When Sewell Avery, left, faltered at the famous stockholder proxy battle, of 1955, John Barr quickly moved in to maintain control of the meeting. Later, he was elected chairman, a post he held for 10 years.

Even then Barr didn't see the current management, but a former chairman of the board, Theodore B. Houser, who'd been fired from Wards along with General Wood many years before. (Ward old-timers take delight in pointing out that four of Sears' board chairmen—Wood, Houser, Arthur S. Barrows and Austin T. Cushman—were fired from Wards.) Nor did Houser recommend any current Sears people, but two who were no longer with the company, Eddie Gudeman and Tom Brooker.

I've been told by several responsible people, including financial reporters, that the reason Brooker was no longer with Sears was because General Wood fired him. Another story has the General saying, "I would have fired him but the son of a bitch got away." Actually Brooker stayed on the Sears board of directors a year after he left.

Whatever the story, all sources give the same reason for the Wood-Brooker break-up: Brooker had the General's son,

273

Bob, Jr., fired from one of Sears' suppliers. All also agree that Brooker probably had cause. "Bob was a pleasant fellow but he was the kind of guy who gets on the green in two strokes and then can't sink a six-inch putt," Joe Brannon says.

Inasmuch as the General died in 1969, at the age of 90, and is consequently not around to give his account, we have to get the answer from Tom Brooker. When I asked him, he grinned. Brooker likes to talk about high-level intrigue even when he's the victim of it. "Well, first of all," he said, "I didn't fire Bob Wood. I sympathized with him. He had enormous pressures—it isn't easy to be another Robert E. Wood. Anyway, the first I heard of his resignation was when he posted it on the bulletin board. He later told me that he was afraid he may have given his father the wrong impression, but the General never discussed the matter with me."

Although General Wood had told Brooker in the presence of others that some day he'd be president of Sears, that wrong impression obviously changed the climate. Nor was Wood pleased with one of Brooker's contributions in putting Whirlpool together.

"To get wholesale distribution," Brooker explained, "I wanted to bring RCA into it—it was necessary to bring RCA in. That meant dealing with General David Sarnoff, the head of RCA, and the General didn't like Jews. But he saw that he had to go along, and he did.

"If I'd stayed with Sears I might have waited out the General and eventually become president, but I'm not sure. It was hard to leave Sears, and I'd of course be honored to be chief executive of the largest retail operation in the world, but I have no regrets. I made the decision to go to Whirlpool. It wasn't a lot more money in compensation, but *much* more in stock options."

As a director of the companies involved in the Whirlpool merger, he had already had great influence in establishing sound principles of management with capable personnel.

As president, his greatest contribution was setting up a long-range program for the company's future growth, profitability, and executive development. He was so successful that he rendered himself, at least by his own demanding standards, unessential.

Elisha "Bud" Gray II, who had been with the parent organization and remained chairman of the board, was also a highly capable executive. A giant corporation made overtures to them, hoping to obtain their management skills in addition to the company, and in their frank discussions on whether to accept they concluded that either one could run the business. Brooker could have gone along placidly, piling up millions, traveling, building his beautiful home, being involved in worthwhile causes, playing golf and fishing, and working moderately hard. This life would satisfy some 56-year-old millionaires, but it wasn't enough for Tom Brooker.

When John Barr came to him with one of the great industrial challenges of the century — Tom refers to it, of course, as an opportunity — the decision was an easy one to make —

John Barr, left, welcomes new president Tom Brooker in 1961.

provided he would be in control. His primary condition on accepting the job was that he would have a board of directors which would support him. With that guaranteed he didn't care whether or not he would be chief executive officer in title, because he knew he would be in fact. He came in as president and, with his purchase of a million dollars' worth of stock, the largest individual stockholder.

A statement of policy was circulated which attempted to explain the duties of the chairman of the board and the president, but they didn't fool Harold F. Dysart, the man in the next office. It takes one to know one, and Dysart, a tough, hard-driving Texan, saw Brooker come in, start tearing his office to pieces, and he knew that Tom Brooker was The Boss.

Brooker, looking around in desperation for someone, anyone, who could give him solid information on the company's personnel, discovered that he had his man on the other side of the wall. Dysart became Brooker's native guide in the jungle of Montgomery Ward. He quickly found things were going to be different, beginning with Harold Dysart. "I'd always been in the habit of planning the day's work the night before," Dysart said. "But Tom and I began coming in on the same train together every morning and by the time we got to the office he'd rearranged my whole damn day."

Ask Dysart a question and you get an answer. He knew the strengths and weaknesses in every merchandising department. Brooker did not have the time either to determine for himself the character of each of hundreds of individuals, or to coax the information out of insecure, pussy-footing hangers-on. Dysart told him what he wanted to know—or what he didn't want to know—straight out, *bam!*

Brooker's first blow on taking over Montgomery Ward was finding out that the company was $50 million poorer than he thought. Some say the figure could have been in the hundreds of millions. It was represented by outdated merchandise which store managers had been stuffing away in basements and lofts for years and carrying as full inventory. The company was in a precarious enough situation as it was without announcing that it was $50 million poorer, and Tom had to arrange to unload the merchandise and take the loss over a period of time. More important, and this was a massive undertaking which required months of planning under Dysart's direction, an internal audit had to be set up so that the situation could not repeat itself.

Another blow was the discovery of just how weak the company was in personnel. For many years the company had been ruled by fear. Then had come the regime of the department store people whom Barr had brought in because he couldn't get anybody else, and whose only predictable quality was that they were going to change their minds tomorrow.

John L. Kistler, a department manager hired by Brooker from the outside, once told me that the company was a desert, devoid of executive life. Chuck Higgins, however, commented that there was plenty of life, it just didn't know which way to grow. "Brooker was dealing with a bunch of rubber bands," he said. "We'd stretch any way we were told to stretch. Trouble was, it was never the same way."

Brooker knew only one direction, only one mercantile policy, and he admitted it. He was throughly familiar with the workings of the most successful retailing operation in the world, and that was the policy he was determined to establish at Wards. He had no doubts, no fears that this was the only policy.

One time, musing about the situation he had found, he commented that his predecessor as president had intelligence, but lacked know-how and courage. "You've got to have one or the other," he said.

"Which one do you have?" I asked.

Tom grinned. "Well, at least I had courage," he said.

In putting together a management team, he demonstrated his courage by giving both the men he brought in from Sears and those he gathered around him at Wards his personal commitment that with their help he would establish a profitable operation at Wards. This personal commitment was what tipped the scales in the decision that was made by the Donnells, Lutzes, Veaches, Worleys, Abbotts and others to join the company, and the rededication of the McKnights, Dysarts, Wagners, Mungers and others who were already with it. With the middle management, both in the merchandise department and retail operation, he showed his courage in the steady, unwavering presentation of a stable, deliberate policy. It was a frustratingly slow process.

"He did it through the regular meetings, in Chicago and across the country," Dysart said.

"After the introductory meetings we set up budget reviews every six months. At these meetings Tom would review the performances of the past six months, establish the goals to be met in the next six months. Here is where we could see the man's image, his total plan. He was patient—too patient sometimes, I thought—but he was always going in the same direction. He presented a stable policy that you could lean on. The way he works with people was deceptive at first. We were used to being yelled at, criticized, fired. All Tom would do was ask a question. If a fellow presented a budget that was out of sight, Tom would just say quietly "You know that's too high, don't you?" That guy would think about it, and get himself involved. Imagination is worse than criticism."

As for the resentment of the influx of the Sears mafia, Dysart dismissed it. "There were people here who loved this company," he said. "The big ones could see the value of the Sears imports, and worked with them both to improve the company and their own position in it. Not one important person had any resentment—*and I would know.*"

Along with setting up a stable policy, Brooker established motivation. He did it with money—bonuses, stock options, opportunity for advancement. A look at the proxy statement of 1970, the year before Brooker retired as chairman of the board, gives an idea of the remuneration of the men at the top: Brooker received a salary of $219,890, retirement benefits of $33,639, deferred compensation of $75,000; Donnell $199,568, $48,747 and $15,000; Worley $117,741, $20,263 and $15,000; Lutz $139,363, $28,172 and $40,000. All are also loaded with stock and options. At the opposite extreme, Wards was bringing in trainees at $7,500 to $8,500, perhaps more in special cases. In between, the remuneration of the members of the Executive Roll, particularly those hired away from Sears, is confidential, but some are happy and proud to let the world know how they're doing.

Sidney N. Doolittle, for example, a manager of a $25 million department in his early thirties, told me his salary was $27,000 (an improvement over his starting wage of $38.50 a week) plus $10,000 bonus. Among his fringe benefits are a $100,000 life insurance policy and a disability plan which would pay him one-half of his salary for life. He'd had options on 1,000 shares of stock at 16; the dividends pay the interest on the money borrowed to exercise them and the value has nearly doubled.

An additional cost-of-living benefit is the 10 per cent employee discount, plus special sales of merchandise. Every Christmas, for example, I have to leave $5 for the postman and milkman and all the rest; Doolittle distributes $5 Montgomery Ward fruitcakes which he buys in his departmental clearance sale for two bucks. I don't know what I'm going to get for Christmas next year, but we all know what Sid Doolittle's milkman's gonna get.

I also know that Sid had better not sell his stock. For though Brooker has an intense money orientation, he does not look upon the dollar as an entity in itself, but as a symbol of recognition. This is particularly true in the case of stock and options. They are glorious things to have, but they represent merit badges, not cash. "Sell one share and you get a phone call," an executive observed.

On the subject of stock and stockholders, Brooker has a

positive philosophy on the relationship of shareholders to management. "Seldom," wrote John McDonald in *Fortune,* "has the treaty between stockholders and management been more explicitly expressed than in Montgomery Ward. Seldom has the influence of the values of management had more explicit effect on the fate of a corporation than it has on Wards during Brooker's administration."

Of course shareholders want the stock to grow in value and to pay high dividends, and management wants the same thing—under its control. By making more stock available to members of the management team, and by having more directors to represent management, both can have it both ways—if the enterprise is profitable. To make it profitable management is motivated to work, plan, contribute, which is where we got on in the first place.

Financial motivation extends down through the ranks in the Ward profit-sharing plan. In former days Ward employees, as in the case of most people working in all industry today, drew their paycheck and that was it. Through profit sharing everybody can gain a little more through extra effort. And with everybody putting in extra effort the entire company shows extra results. The circle goes around again.

Harry Stirmell, manager of Ward's protection service which also oversees safety, tossed off an example of financial motivation one day which should be made required reading for every management team in the free-enterprise world.

Montgomery Ward is not in the class of heavy industry, with its constant dangers to production workers, but it still has areas in which people can get hurt. In the tire-battery-accessory stores, for example, a worker inflating a truck tire might let his mind wander, and blow the tire and himself right up through the roof.

Since profit-sharing has gone into effect, this and other classifications of accidents have shown a sharp decrease. In other words, the incentive of a share in the profits discourages people from accidentally killing themselves.

Motivation is inspired not only by reward for accomplishment but by an environment inducive to accomplishment. A flophouse has the image of a flophouse, and its residents reflect it. When Ed Donnell first set about establishing the handsome image of prototype stores throughout the country, Chicago headquarters were a disgrace. Set in a slum neighborhood, the eight-story building was itself a slum. Air conditioning consisted of opening up the windows and letting in the soot. From their headquarters in the greasy-spoon cafeteria on the fourth floor, the cockroaches spread out to make it an insect megalopolis. It took some years, working floor by floor, but the building was gradually completely renovated. The pleasant cafeteria and the handsome executive dining room were completed first. The eighth floor, where the big shots' offices are located on mahogany row, was last.

The only complainant was Chuck Higgins, the company's official observer of minutiae. "The old building used to have a kind of pleasant nonconformity," Chuck said, "particularly in the plumbing fixtures. They must have been picked up in some rummage sale, because they were all different sizes and shapes, hung on different walls. You'd face different directions on different floors. Now in every men's room, on every floor, you pee to the south."

As for the immediate surroundings of the building, when Brooker first joined the company he looked out on one of the world's ugliest buildings. A grubby restaurant and bar was on the first floor, with three or four stories of dingy brick and blank dirty windows piled on top of it. Brooker, human proof of the territorial imperative, couldn't stand it. He asked John Barr about buying it.

"Do you know how much that fellow wants for that building?" Barr asked. "$350,000."

"Why that thing can't be worth more than $70,000 or $80,-000," Brooker said.

"We've had people over there negotiating with him time and time again," Barr said, "and every time he pushes his price up."

"Well, I'll take care of that," Brooker said. He called in Edwin Pehrson, the Ward real estate man, told him to go to the treasurer and get a blank check, then go across the street and buy the building. An hour later Pehrson came back and said he had bought it. Brooker asked how much.

"Eighty-one thousand dollars," Pehrson said.

"You got stuck, didn't you?" Brooker asked.

"Well, no," Pehrson said. "He was asking $350,000."

"Okay, good job," Brooker said. That was just about what he had expected. For years the company had been making appointments with the owner, getting a price and then sitting on it for months. He had gotten fed up with the indecision and kept raising the price out of sheer annoyance. But when somebody walked in with a blank check he wasn't going to let him walk out with it.

Brooker bought up several square blocks of old warehouses in front of the building in the same way (it backs up on the Chicago River) and today the area is composed of well-lit parking lots for Ward employees. Posts with basketball nets and backboards stick up all over the area, and on the long summer evenings the area is a playground for the kids in the neighborhood.

A good executive is interested not only in the environment his people work in, but the environment in which they live. That includes the physical condition of their bodies. In the corporate grind, a man has got to be in shape.

In his early days with Montgomery Ward, in which he exposed his policy and his own leadership to all the Ward people throughout the country, Brooker held continuous rounds of meetings with different groups in different locations. Harold Dysart remembers one grueling period in which he accompanied Brooker to a two-day series of meetings on the east coast and another two-day series on the west coast. They returned to Chicago at the end of the fourth day, slept at the airport and left next morning for another series in Kansas City.

"At the end of that last meeting I was so tired I couldn't hold up my head," Dysart said. "We'd been up since six. Tom looked like he was just starting out. As we walked out of the meeting I asked him, 'Aren't you tired?' He strode along, smiling, looking fresh as a daisy, and said to me out of the side of his mouth, 'I'm so tired I'm about to drop.'"

Brooker does indeed have a high energy level, just as do all his executives who have made it to the top rungs of the corporate ladder. Fred Veach, who likes to quote his wife Peggy's put-downs, says that she told him one time "You people aren't any more intelligent than anybody else, you just have more energy."

When he told me this Fred and I were riding to the station; he was taking a train to a meeting near Chicago. I hadn't seen him for months and this 10-minute ride was the only chance to visit. He'd been going hard all day as usual, and still had work to do. But he couldn't even sit still in the back seat of the company car, bouncing and gesticulating with his teeth flashing like a heliograph. At the station he jumped out and ran for his train, leaving me exhausted. I asked the driver if he was always like that.

"Yes, sir," he said, "Mr. Veach don't *never* run down."

But Fred only flaunts what all the others less flamboyantly possess. One night Ed and Rose Donnell took Bonnie and me to dinner. First we looked at their house, with its chronographic layers representing Ed's career. An electric organ dated back to the Sears period; a new microwave oven was the latest Ward acquisition.

It was curling night at the club, and after dinner Rose, Bonnie and I watched Ed, in his tam, perform on the ice. In curling each member of the team bowls heavy stones as his teammates frantically sweep the ice in front of it to help it along. There was the chief executive officer of Montgomery Ward, long and lean, sweeping away with enthusiasm of a happy little kid.

Who would have guessed the schedule Ed had kept the past few days? For two mornings in a row he'd gotten up at five in order to attend seven o'clock breakfasts in downtown Chicago.

He'd made the keynote speech at the luncheon kick-off of the YMCA finance campaign. He'd done his work at the office. And, because Ed has a guilty feeling about reading on the job, he'd brought his reports home and pored over them at night. He should have been a walking zombie, but he was the most zestful curler on the ice. This guy is superhuman—which, of course, is one of the reasons he's where he is.

Good physical condition, Tom Brooker told me once in a discussion of personnel, is number one. He repeated it, *number one.* The man who is not in top shape can't take this life. You can't carry on the long days of conferences, encouraging assistants or criticizing them constructively, and being actively involved in community affairs with an ache or a pain. When you're hurting somewhere you might snap at someone, and that's not the way to get people to work for you. Of slightly more serious consequence is dropping dead. A company has an investment in its men and in their future performance. One of Ward's most serious problems stemmed from a key man dying of a heart attack on the golf course. At that time the company did not have sufficient depth for an executive to die.

For most of his working life Brooker participated in vigorous racket sports, but on opening up the can of worms at Wards he found he had time only for weekend golf. But he still got his exercise just as always, in the morning on arising and at night before going to bed. During the years he was on the road for weeks at a time for Firestone, the first thing that went into his bag was his jumping rope—15 minutes, twice a day. Later he got a tape recording of a series of calisthenics, and though he has played it so many times he knows it by heart, he still continues to play the tape and follow its instructions in cadence, to keep from going too fast.

Though Ward executives are not expected to skip rope in the morning, they have semiannual physical examinations, and they are complete. Even Dick Abbott, the Christian Scientist, undergoes his checkup; he has to set the example for the New York office. In Chicago all executives are examined periodical-

ly by Doctor Charles E. Thompson and Associates, whose work
is restricted to examining executives of the Chicago community.
Curious as to what it takes to be a top executive, I had the
examination myself. It began with a dose of castor oil the night
before, a self-administered enema in the morning, and ended
with a written report telling me that I am a well-developed,
well-nourished, overweight individual who smokes too much.
I showed it, and the $255 bill (including breakfast) to my
doctor at home. He whistled. "I'd have told you that for five
dollars and a quarter," he said.

Talking with Dr. Thompson on executives in general, I received a professional reaffirmation of what I was already beginning to conclude: Successful corporate executives do not
conform to the pill-happy stereotype set forth in popular novels.
First of all, Dr. Thompson said, the one thing that he has noticed is that the number one man is always the healthiest guy
in the group.

"I once thought, like everybody else, that the head of a major
corporation forges to the top through political pull or some
other happenstance," he said, "but by now I'm convinced that
health and ability play the most important roles."

Dr. Thompson has been examining Tom Brooker since he
was fifty, and he could tell then that he was not only an excellent physical specimen, but a man on the way up. Of more
than ten thousand executives he has examined, Dr. Thompson
would put Brooker in the top dozen men of super-intelligence.
He has worked closely with Brooker, because in the early days
at Wards, when Brooker was desperate for manpower, he could
not entrust the growth of the company to men who couldn't
take it physically. Thompson is only in a narrow sense a medical
hatchet man, fingering the unfit. More important, he diagnoses
and prescribes in order to provide some assurance that the
individual's contribution to the company will continue and the
company's investment in him will pay off.

These men live with tension, but they should not be afraid
of it. Tension is a part of life, and the higher the individual

goes, the more opportunity he has to experience it. The man in excellent physical condition can experience tension better, use it to greater advantage. Again Dr. Thompson pointed to Tom Brooker as the perfect example; even in the sea of problems into which he had plunged, he never lost his cool, was never affected physically by the strain. Tom Brooker was never about to get ulcers.

On executives in general, Dr. Thompson, on the basis of his close experience with so many, says that regardless of what the executive's company may do or how much money he makes, his major motivation is serving people—"unless he has it, he's a miserable bastard."

The most difficult task executives have, and the one which brings on the most tension, is firing somebody. They're miserable for a month before they can bring themselves to do it, frequently bringing the physical problems of the strain to Dr. Thompson, and then question themselves for a month after the deed is done.

And to destroy two other commonly held opinions of big businessmen, they are neither drunks nor oversexed. Ninety-nine per cent of the more than ten thousand executives he has examined drink, but he has encountered exactly three with a drinking problem. And though the executive usually has a healthy sex life, instead of taking his frustrations out on the office couch with his secretary, he is much more apt in periods of stress to lose his interest in sex.

Dr. Thompson and his staff clamp down hard on cholesterol and overweight; Brooker, like so many people who control their diet, is a nut on it. Six feet two, he never gets over 183 pounds. A look of disgust comes over his face when he talks about fat people. One of the conditions under which Charlie Wagner was made a vice president of the company was that he would take off a big chunk of his 280 pounds. Charlie agreed, but the pounds didn't come off. He said it didn't matter; he was the active type of fat man. Brooker had an audit run on Wagner's visits to the field and concluded that he was not getting around as much as he said.

The conflict was finally resolved by a mild heart attack. When I saw Charlie he was starving himself to death, drinking pots of black coffee with saccharin, walking six miles a day and weighing himself every other minute. He was the only over-weight executive at Montgomery Ward, and he was knocking himself out to overcome that singularity.

Over the years, under the prevailing atmosphere of suspicion, distrust, and not infrequently a knife in the back, there had been little communication among top people after hours. Brooker changed that, too. He had himself been a guest at the home of General Wood when several steps on the ladder separated them and he began inviting Ward executives and their wives to dinner parties at his home, along with other prominent members of the Chicago community.

"He would mix us," Dysart said. "We'd get to know what we were like outside of the office. It was wonderful for all of us. All the women wanted to see his house, of course. They'd have sold tickets to get in."

Brooker also brought into Wards a modest beginning of wife identification and involvement. Unlike the popular stereotype of the corporation wife, who moves her husband up the ladder by cooking the boss's steak the way he likes it, the lady of the house in Wards had never played too big a role. Though there are exceptions, executives have gotten to the upper echelon at Wards with wives who didn't know when to quit drinking, much less how to set a graceful table. Social graces of the wife have never become a substitute for the talents of the husband, but nevertheless some social phenomena were noted by close observers. One of the Ward old-timers whose wife demon-strated the synergy of a big mouth and booze showed up at the Brooker's house just once, and no more.

At the opposite extreme, Charlie Wagner, though he does not think it was by any means a deciding factor in his elevation to corporate officer, nevertheless looked upon his wife with both pride and gratitude after she had staged a perfect dinner for the top brass.

Some years ago Brooker had to choose one of several highly qualified applicants for an important and sensitive job with the company. One seemed to be outstanding, but Brooker postponed his decision. One night he just happened to be at a concert also attended by the applicant and his wife. Brooker, in his quiet way, just happened to engage the young lady in conversation at intermission. Handsome and gallant, he has the gift of making the lady with whom he is talking feel that he is interested in her every word. In their 15-minute chat, Brooker learned more about her than she probably knew herself.

Next morning he told Dysart, "She has a very good mind and she'll fit in well." Her husband was hired immediately.

A good wife may not be a necessity, but she's icing on the cake. Although Jim Lutz could hardly hope for more prestige and respect than he had from his peers as an unmarried executive, Brooker expressed both personal and corporate pleasure when he got married. "Florence is vivacious and attractive," Tom commented on the new Mrs. Lutz, "and her good taste and graciousness will be big assets to Jim."

The only person I ever heard make any protest about her role as a corporate wife was Wendy Hoffman, but, as Wendy explained, "I've got a big mouth." A voluptuous young woman with beauty and brains, Wendy married Glenn H. Hoffman after he had already become established as one of the young phenomenons of the company. Glenn had gotten his master's degree from the University of Chicago at the age of 20, and had intended to go into the academic world, but got sidetracked in the excitement of Wards and couldn't leave it. He became research director of the company, an important position with income to match, when barely 30. And then he and Wendy got married.

Not for Wendy the role of sitting in the parlor after dinner talking with the women about baby sitters and clothes while the men are in the kitchen talking business and sports. A life master at bridge, a sports enthusiast and a woman interested in the world around her, Wendy wants to be in on everything. Nor does she like anything that smacks of a pecking order.

"I got into an argument with one of the men on Glenn's staff," Wendy said, "and on the way home Glenn told me I shouldn't have been so controversial. I didn't speak to him for two days. I was so mad! And then, to make it worse, the man I had the argument with called and apologized. It was so phony. If he didn't believe what he said he shouldn't have said it in the first place. He only called because Glenn's his boss."

Wendy was getting warmed up now, and her dark eyes were flashing. "What about the time we were going to go on vacation and you canceled it just because your secretary quit?" she asked Glenn. "But that didn't stop you from going off with Mr. Donnell in the company plane and flying all over the country and there I am sitting at home. I want to go places, too."

Women can be very contradictory creatures, and the next thing I knew Wendy was telling me about some of the trips she had taken with Glenn, and what fun they had. Then she told me how she buys just about everything she can use from Wards, tells all her friends to do the same, goes out of her way to Wards to have the car serviced and has been in Ward stores all over the country. When the family drives past a Sears store the kids stick out their tongues at it.

"I'm emotional about Montgomery Ward," she said. "Glenn has had a meteoric rise and a good life and I know he's happy there and if he's happy I'm happy, too. But just because I love him doesn't mean that I can't hate him, too."

It's fairly safe to say that even the fiercest woman liberationist need have no qualms over her husband starting out with Wards. On the trainee and junior level, little if anything is expected of the wife. As her husband rises to the eminence at which she will be expected to contribute to his career, the chances are 99 out of 100 that his paycheck will more than make up for any sacrifices she might make in the way of independence—and all that's expected of her in the first place is to be a reasonably pleasant person. If she wants to wave the women's lib banner nobody is going to take it away from her. However, in conversations with the wives of the top executives, Bonnie and I couldn't help but notice that all were what Glenn had told Wendy to be— noncontroversial.

As for the wife's meddling in her husband's business, even that can cut both ways. Jack Adelson, Baltimore metro manager, told me of a young man whose wife needled him into quitting because he wasn't progressing fast enough. He had already been ticketed for a good promotion. Adelson was hoping that he'd be man enough to come back.

On the other hand, Charlie Wagner was standing at the door of one of his stores at quitting time one night and overheard a young woman who had come in to pick up her husband complain to another young wife that he didn't seem to be getting anywhere. Curious, Charlie looked into the personnel records, found that her husband was indeed overdue for a promotion. Her remark, overheard by chance, resulted in the promotion coming through—and the personnel department getting chewed out for the oversight.

As for the future of women themselves in retail, the outlook is brighter than it used to be. Ward's little bundle of energy, Rita Perna, became the first female corporate officer of any retail chain. Many department managers, sometimes assistant store managers, are women, but the rise to store manager requires long hours and frequent transfers from city to city, two features of retailing which do not appeal to women. In the New York and Los Angeles buying offices, which are almost entirely devoted to soft goods, many women hold responsible positions—but even in the intimate apparel department, men outnumber women.

The only woman buyer in Chicago, where all departments but soft goods are located, is a young lady named Ruth Weber, and to get that job was a major operation. A psychology major, she started out in personnel, but got bored. She wanted to go into merchandising, because that's where the action is and Ruth is a girl of action. She was offered an opportunity in New York, but she said she didn't want to be a rag peddler.

She checked over all the departments in her mind and decided to make her pitch to the paint department, not because she was particularly interested in paint, but because its manager, Chuck Higgins, had a reputation for being progressive. She plotted her approach carefully: not too hard sell, lest he think her too unfeminine, but not too soft, lest he think her too weak. The approach must have worked, because Chuck took her on.

A buyer trainee has to go through the rigorous steps of retail first, beginning with receiving the merchandise at the store. The other trainees moved the heavy cartons of paint around for her. She put in 12 hours a day as a salesperson, and discovered that a woman is an asset to a paint department. One customer came in and wanted to paint the living room over the weekend, but without any idea how to go about it. Ruth helped her in all details from selection of colors to how to apply the paint. The next week the customer came in again, reported the living room a success, and said, "Now let's get going on the bedroom." Ruth was delighted—a repeat customer!

Finally she was brought back to the merchandise office as assistant paint buyer for the aerosol line and craft paint. She played an important role in the determination that the aerosol line could be improved, and the consequent selection of a new manufacturer.

As Brooker's management team developed confidence in themselves and each other, he could now begin to fit them together into his personnel jigsaw puzzle. It was the acceptance of Donnell by his peers which enabled Brooker first to bring him into headquarters, then to knight him president. Dick Abbott's contribution at headquarters made it possible for him to take over soft lines procurement in New York, with Fred Giersch eventually and happily emerging in the important Los Angeles buying office. Marty Munger, who had been traumatically demoted by the previous administration, came back so strong that he could replace Donnell in the eastern region. Loyal Sid McKnight, who couldn't possibly have an enemy in the company, was perfect for the job of liaison between headquarters and the field, and Charlie Wagner was ready to replace him as vice president in the Kansas City office. Thanks to Jim Lutz's willingness to take two giant steps backward and prove himself all over again, the key position of executive vice president in charge of merchandise could be filled by the man Brooker had in mind for it all along.

As Brooker stabilized his policy and members of the management team knew where they were going, the new attitude extended out into the field. Two isolated examples demonstrate it.

In Grand Rapids, Michigan, Robert O. Bergman, manager of the existing store there, went over to the other side of town one day to look for a location for a new catalog store. All he wanted was a 150-by-100-foot lot. He found, instead, a 55-acre tract. Acting entirely on his own initiative, Bergman took an option on the entire acreage. "I'd never thought of it under the old regime, much less dared to do it," Bergman said. On the site rose a big new shopping mall, with Wards holding down one end.

In New York, Steve Van Leer, an ultramod young man in his early twenties, was so eager for Wards to get groovy and so confident of his own ability that he proposed a program for mod-style clothes and himself to head it. He didn't buck it up through channels, but sent it straight to Dick Abbott. Instead of tossing the fresh kid out on his long locks, as earlier Ward potentates would have done, Abbott bought both the program and its originator.

Jim Lutz likes to quote a slogan: "Behold the turtle; he makes progress only when his neck is out." In headquarters, and all over the country, men and women began sticking their necks out to receive a bonus instead of decapitation. Under such conditions work becomes fun, and though not every crazy idea was accepted, some were—and paid off.

Some did *not* pay off. Did you ever hear of the Hoop-a-Lariat? It was going to be bigger than the Hula Hoop. If you want a few million I know where you can get them cheap. But the unhappy fellow who bought them, along with the chap who swung the big Italian motorcycle deal, is still on the payroll. A little subdued, maybe—but wait'll next year.

In such an atmosphere shrinking violets burst into blazing chrysanthemums. Take Phillip Lifschultz, vice president in charge of taxes. Short of stature, with a short bob and an end curl, Lifschultz has the defensive appearance of a CPA and tax law specialist, which he is, thrown into an Irish barroom on Saturday night. But no one at Wards, or most other places, can express well-thought-out and provocative philosophies ranging over the broad field of the humanities more lucidly. He is the house articulate intellectual. He is also the only tax attorney I ever knew who writes poetry, creditable poetry. The subject of one of his poems is Tom Brooker—who told me he had never seen it. It is an allegorical encomium in free verse.

To buttress his description of Brooker as "bold and courageous" Phil gave me an example in which Brooker made a monumental decision in less than 10 minutes' time. Only after he had explained the extremely complicated background did

I realize, without his ever saying so, that the bold and courageous decision of Tom Brooker was made on the bold and
courageous recommendation of Phil Lifschultz.

Brooker has said that he doesn't spend the majority of his
time making decisions, but does spend it in the groundwork
of selecting and encouraging personnel to make recommendations on which to base decisions. Lifschultz exemplifies
that groundwork. For years, even when he was with Arthur
Andersen and Company, working on the Ward account
before joining the company, he had pondered a change in
the tax structure of Wards. As nothing is duller than taxes
I won't go into the infinite detail, but first, it involved changing
from a method under which Wards paid taxes on the profit
earned the year it made the sale to paying taxes when it
collected the money. In credit sales this could be the next
year, two years, or not at all.

Second, it involved a choice of three forms, one a consolidated return of all the company's subsidiaries. Consent
from the Internal Revenue Service to consider this method
was delayed until two weeks before the return was due — a
Monday in October. Tax and financial experts worked frantically during those two weeks preparing the returns in three
separate ways. Meetings were held over the weekend. Sunday
afternoon additional advice was needed from one of the outside accountants working with the firm, and a rush call went
out to him. He was in the act of putting on his long underwear to go to a Chicago Bears football game when the call
came, and he didn't even have time to give away his tickets.

Late Sunday night the returns were completed. Andrew
Lamb, the financial vice president, signed them. When he
signed the consolidated return, the one Lifschultz had recommended and fought for, but which even its proponent admitted
was most controversial, his hand trembled and his face was
white.

The three returns, each complete and representing a massive
undertaking, were presented to Brooker on Monday morning.

Lifschultz, though fully aware of the repercussions that could possibly evolve and not minimizing them in his presentation, recommended the consolidated form. Brooker asked a few pertinent questions and then, after no more than 10 minutes, pointed to the consolidated form. It was rushed to the Chicago office of the Internal Revenue Service.

On Thursday checks representing refunds of $50 million including 6 per cent interest on taxes paid over the past three years was delivered to Montgomery Ward. A total deduction of $320 million was generated over the nine-year span covered by the change in tax structure. The method will continue to have positive effects on Ward's operations in the future. And though it was reviewed on every level of the IRS and by a joint congressional committee, there were no repercussions.

The tax deferral was a factor in a Brooker coup heralded by financial pages the country over. In business, even success brings problems. To the smart-money manipulators, as early as Ward's temporary setback in the mid-sixties, it was becoming obvious that the sleeping giant was on the verge of awakening in a burst of rapid growth. The base was there on which to build incremental volume. The price of its stock did not represent its true earning potential. The company represented a golden opportunity for a corporate raid. There were indications that people were thinking about it. In New York Dick Abbott was approached by a man representing himself as a member of a syndicate considering making an effort to take over Montgomery Ward. If Dick cooperated and the raid were successful, he could become president. The approach was made to the wrong man; Dick turned the proposition down cold.

It would almost certainly have been turned down by any other major Ward executive. Having made his own personal commitment to some three score executives with the company, Brooker exacted theirs. They had agreed that, if the company should be acquired by a syndicate such as that put together by Louis Wolfson a dozen years before, they would quit the company cold. Though it would surely have caused some emotional distress, none would have been financially affected to an extreme degree. All were capable men who wouldn't be unemployed long, and most were men of means who wouldn't have to work at all if they didn't want to.

Anyone taking over the company through a successful proxy fight would, therefore, find only a shell, devoid of the executive ability which had made it worth taking over in the first place. Around this strategem Brooker had the law and public relations departments coordinate a complete program designed not to repel raiders as much as to discourage consideration of an attempt. The defense was designed only to thwart any effort to take the company over against the wishes of its stockholders. Should a reputable, acquisition-minded conglomerate have made an open and bona fide offer acceptable to the stockholders, Brooker and his team would of course have discussed the possibility of staying on.

More than the possibility of a raid, another problem concerned Tom Brooker. He thinks five years ahead, and in 1971 he would be 65. He was not going to be another Avery. But who would succeed him? He had a fine group of executives, some with the future potential of running the whole show, but none with the current maturity to provide the overall leadership of this most demanding enterprise. He knew or knew of most of the handful of men in America capable of being chairman of the board of Montgomery Ward, and considered the possibility of bringing someone in from the outside.

Another method of acquiring his own successor would be through merger. By combining forces with another company headed by one of that handful of qualified executives, he could provide the resulting corporation with a two-deep layer at the top, double strength against takeover, and greater advantage of the tax deferral.

A businessman for whom he had great respect was Leo H. Schoenhofen. Brooker had known Schoenhofen since, in 1961 at the age of 46, he had become president of Container Corporation of America. A Chicago-based firm designing and manufacturing containers of all sizes in plants located throughout the United States and overseas, it was an excellent, progressive company with a good earning potential which would be enhanced by Ward's deferred taxes.

Brooker knew Schoenhofen well; they had had a long business and civic relationship, and had frequently attended the biennial meetings of a marketing executive group whose members meet in three-day off-the-record sessions to exchange information and perhaps play a little golf. He could easily have picked up the phone and called Schoenhofen, but that is not his way. This is his way:

The same outside auditor, Arthur Andersen and Company, handled both firms, and one night Leonard Spacek, president of Arthur Andersen, and his wife had dinner with the Brookers. After the meal—which in the Brooker home is only a pleasant preliminary—he took Spacek aside and sounded him out on Schoenhofen and Container. They were in accord; Spacek volunteered to call Schoenhofen. Brooker gently suggested the two might better talk it over in more leisurely detail at lunch. A few days later Spacek and Schoenhofen had lunch together, and a few days after that Brooker and Schoenhofen sat down to talk it over. Gradually the positive advantages began to emerge.

From then on it was a matter of working out the arrangements. Combining two such large corporations always brings up some sticky problems. Members of Container's board of directors quite naturally raised some questions. Brooker patiently explained that, while Wards was indeed interested in management primarily, the merger would be good for both companies. Both had management teams capable of running each company with Schoenhofen as president of the parent corporation. He was then only 52, which would provide plenty of time for his successor, whether from Container or Wards, to develop. Separate auditors served as consultants to each firm, separate financial houses worked out the terms, involving an issue of debentures.

One of the touchiest problems was in whittling down the number of members of each board of directors to make up a combined board of workable size. Eventually, with approval of the FTC and the Department of Justice, the merger went through and the two companies became subsidiaries of Marcor Inc.

All this for the primary purpose of getting one man. I talked with Leo Schoenhofen about two years after the merger went through, and peered at him in vain for a glimpse of a halo of genius floating over his head. A bald, ruddy, round-faced man with pale blue eyes, he looked like he'd be more at home wearing a wool shirt and taking a hook out of a bass's mouth, and it turned out that I was just about right; he's an outdoors man.

Following the formation of Marcor by Montgomery Ward and Container Corporation of America, the press pursued Brooker to report the rationale and objectives of the consolidation.

Though he and Tom Brooker don't look alike or talk alike, it's something of a coincidence that both started out with engineering degrees working for public utilities.

As for being president of a company whose largest subsidiary is a huge retail chain, Schoenhofen didn't appear to be particularly awed by the task. His principal concern at first had been with the people; he hadn't been sure that in only eight years Brooker could have gotten as much talent on base as he had been pleasantly surprised to find. I smiled to myself when, in checking off some of the talent, one of the first persons he discussed was "a boy that heads the tax department here at Wards who is an uncommonly thoughtful and intelligent, philosophical sort of a guy." That was no boy; that was Phil Lifschultz, who had contributed so much to one of the key advantages of the merger.

"As for the rest, the numbers game is simply one of familiarization," he said. "If I see it and ask a few questions then I can finally understand it, so it's no great problem. The application of the important bench marks is different and those are what I had to find out about. If you wade through the statistics that they run on the retail business, you wouldn't come out with anything, so you have to learn how to find the danger point, the sensitive point . . . at least I had the background to ask maybe some of the right questions and I didn't feel strange in discussions."

After that Leo got to talking about the main business of Container, packaging products, and its contribution to forestry, the clean, clear river water below its pulp mills, its recycling of paper which was going on long before the rest of the country could even spell the word ecology. In metropolitan areas, he observed, the city itself is a forest; it provides enormous amounts of wood pulp in the form of waste paper.

But for all of Schoenhofen's personal love for the great outdoors, he remained the pragmatic, conservative businessman when it came to the question of preserving the environment. He has no empathy with those ecologists who want conservation without paying for it. Some of the worst offenders are

The New York Society of Security Analysts enjoyed its largest turnout when

the old, family-owned pulp mills, he pointed out. Thier financial existence is marginal. They can not afford the equipment necessary for pollution-free operations. Will the public pay extra for their products?

I could only infer that, just as only the biggest corporations can afford the technostructure to provide good management, so only the biggest corporations can provide, as does Container, the safeguards against pollution. Conservationists and big business — what an alliance!

One of Schoenhofen's most interesting discoveries on becoming connected with the retail firm was the effect of the Montgomery Ward ENL (employee no limit) credit card and the 10 per cent discount on the Schoenhofen family finances. His wife, Emily, like Leo a friendly, natural type of person, took a great delight in putting the combination to use. Finally, Leo gently explained to her: "Emily, 10 per cent doesn't mean free."

Marcor executives made their presentation at the Waldorf Astoria in 1969.

Some of the corporation watchers—financial editors and securities analysts—called the merger a strange marriage of two companies with nothing in common, others termed it a brilliant business coup. By the beginning of Ward's Second Century, however, ten years after Tom Brooker began the turnaround, Marcor Inc. was fully accepted as a powerful and permanent entity in the national business community. Part of its acceptance was pure performance, part aggressive selling of the Marcor image by people who know how to sell.

At presentations to groups of editors and analysts in New York, Chicago, San Francisco and other cities, leaders of the management team stood up and said where the company was financially, and where it intended to go.

"This isn't like the old Monkey Ward," one analyst told me at a New York meeting. "A year or so ago we had a convention in Chicago and a couple of Ward people made a kind of apologetic appearance and asked us to come around next day and see their operation. Two or three of us showed up, just to be nice. We kind of felt sorry for them. Today they're standing up there full of confidence, telling their story, answering questions straight from the shoulder. This is a pretty brave thing to do, you know. If they don't deliver, every analyst here will chuckle about it in every bar in the financial district — and they know it. They've got guts. They're putting on a damn good show, but just being here makes a good impression."

In the 10 years between the time Tom Brooker took over and the beginning of Century 2, the value of the common stock had risen from 32 to 54 per share, then split and climbed as high as 38⅞. Total assets increased from $742 million to $2.4 billion, and stockholders' equity from $704 million to $900 million. Total sales increased from $1.4 billion to $2.4 billion.

Of greater importance to the analyst specializing in retail stocks, however, one of them told me, was the direction in which the company was going. More than 250 old stores had been closed down, yet total gross space of retail stores increased from 32,176,000 to 45,270,000 square feet. Sales in the new large stores in major marketing areas were producing an ever-increasing percentage of the total, and the company publicly committed itself to an aggressive policy of further penetration of the major markets with big stores.

"It's not your assets as much as what you're doing with them," the analyst said. "Wards is putting its assets to work where the growth potential is largest."

Even with this impressive increase, Wards still ranks third in sales behind Sears and Penneys in this distinctive method of merchandising. As president of Wards, Ed Donnell makes no promises that Wards will ever catch up to the front runners in total sales. His goal is to be first in profitability. The hackles of the consumer may rise at that, but on reflection, Wards can't make more money on us unless we help it; it's got to attract our trade. Again it's the incremental circle — greater earnings make possible better products at competitive prices and more efficient service which attracts more customers who spend more money which provides greater earnings. Everybody wins.

The Postal Service gets thousands of requests for commemorative stamps a year and everybody said Bob Guelich had no chance of getting one for the 100th anniversary of mail order's founding by Montgomery Ward. Well, here it is. Left to right, James R. Holland, assistant postmaster general, Smiling Bob and Robert L. Lambdin, 86-year-old artist.

Donnell has practical dreams of expanding into other geographical areas, perhaps Latin America with which he has close ties, and into other fields related to service—repair, travel, education. . . . "A company that's in such broad lines of merchandise as we are can take any logical extension of any of these lines and pursue them if there's enough growth there."

"You're throwing the world open!" I said.

"Exactly," he said.

"You can send Montgomery Ward to the moon under that premise," I said.

He made a pyramid of his hands under his chin and smiled at me. "Exactly," he said.

Tom Brooker, who despite his retirement as chairman of the board remained typically active as chairman of the executive committee, had a positive program worked out for the future.

"In my opinion," he said, "Wards now has a base which in the next five years will enable us to double the earnings of the company. The real job has been done. We've taken a worn-out machine and replaced it with a good one and now we've got to get the knowledge out of it that you get when it matures. In five years we'll have a system with our new concepts which will enable us to replace all of our older stores at an accelerated rate. Through our new system of central merchandising, removing all of the inventory counting and ordering from the stores, and the predicting of risk taking, in five years this will change the whole complex of Montgomery Ward.

"It will be the most significant thing that has happened in the history of Wards in its hundred years."

He was referring to the computerized, mechanized system of merchandising which the company has been developing. It is far ahead of that of any other retail chain; if it is half as good as Ward data process people say it is, it's better than any system anywhere anytime. By the end of Ward's first century a score of stores utilizing the new techniques had been opened.

Through modular construction methods developed by the Rocky Mountain Prestress Company, a subsidiary, the new stores can be erected in half the construction time at less cost. But the primary secret of success of the 3-G (third generation) stores is the labor-saving, detail-saving method of operation brought about through centralization. In traditional retailing, a large amount of space and time, both clerical and executive, is devoted to the unimaginative tasks of counting and reordering units of merchandise. Under the 3-G system the flow of merchandise is tabulated on tapes at the cash registers. Data from these tapes, the country over, are teletyped to the computer facilities in Merriam, Kansas. The center there does the replenishing.

Working out comprehensive programs for each store, located in different parts of the country, required the expertise of some of Ward's finest merchandisers under the direction of John Lippman, national merchandise manager for modular stores. That isn't all it took; if Lippman wasn't a nervous-looking man before taking on the project, he sure is now. He had to overcome the reluctance of the traditional-thinking managers who believe that they have to see merchandise, feel it, touch it, in order to sell it.

"We're all used to working with the count-and-order system of merchandising," Lippman said, jerking his head as though dodging punches and moving things around on his desk. "In the new program the manager can forget the years bent over the counter, let the computer do the paper work, and get out in the store."

The computer, of course, is only as smart as the interpreters who speak both its language and the language of merchandising. It has to be told that in Minnesota the girls wear large bras, in Texas small, and that it shouldn't ship in a carload of galoshes in July. But once it's told, it remembers.

Scheduling 100,000 items in stores in different climazones may have given the programmers headaches but once the job was done, the computers took it over permanently. Relieved of this onerous detail in the stores, fewer people can do more constructive selling in less space. Operating costs go down; service to the consumer goes up. A conventional store takes two or three years to justify its existence; a 3-G can show a profit in a year.

"We could crack the Indianapolis or Milwaukee market, where we aren't represented at all, in five years with 3-G stores," Lippman said. "With conventional stores in shopping malls it would take *many* years. Nationwide, we can go as fast as they'll let us."

With the tall thin man leading the way ("Exactly") in Tom Brooker's rebuilt machine, that ought to be pretty fast in Century 2.

That's the future of Montgomery Ward and Company, but what about the future of its people? Wards, and undoubtedly other retailers as well, offer an excitement and a constant challenge to young men and women. Living in a university town, in the spring of 1972, I heard moans and groans from young men and women who had put in years obtaining advanced degrees, and could then find absolutely no jobs in the areas in which they had worked so hard so long to become qualified. Industry just wasn't hiring that year.

Times were not too good for Wards, either, but that did not keep the company from successfully recruiting more than 700 college graduates. The reason for the difference was simple: Wards will open 300 new stores during the 70's, and regardless of conditions today, management must be trained for the opportunities and personnel requirements for the future.

(The company restricts its recruiting for management training to college graduates. Its personnel department recognizes the fact that not all brilliant young people go to college, but as it has no trouble getting recruits, it's easier to find them there. Noncollege people are hired every day at Wards, and the doors of advancement are not closed to them. But if you want a rewarding career in retailing, it's wise to get a degree.)

Trainees taken on by Wards include all types of college majors: commerce and business, liberal arts, even fine arts. Personnel directors vary in their preferences from region to region. Some seek graduates with business training; others maintain that business training in college is ineffective; a person should be a well-rounded, well-informed individual and leave the business training up to Wards. One personnel director said he leaned toward people who had had calculus or other forms of mathematics, as they helped develop systematic thinking; others could care less. Some have expressed an interest in sociology and psychology majors; in a period of rapidly changing mores it's good to have people on board who understand and can relate to their changing customers.

As for those with master's degrees in business administration, here again opinions vary. Some say that the advanced degree kicks the young man off to a quicker start, others that the time spent getting that MBA could be better utilized in a training program.

I have one comment to make here, based entirely on personal observation. I've mentioned earlier talking with Vic Sholis, a Harvard MBA who was intensively recruited by several major corporations. In being recruited he learned to be interviewed, and in the company he demonstrated an excellent ability to articulate his thoughts and experiences. He was also involved, with company encouragement, in activities outside the business. He actively participated, for example, in a program to help set up minority businesses.

By contrast I talked with a young man named Douglas Melrose in an old green awning store in Hagerstown, Maryland. The Baltimore personnel office designated him as an up-and-coming young man with a good future in Wards. Rather than being recruited from the Harvard Graduate Business School, Melrose had answered a want ad after graduating from Bethany College with a major in political science. He had moved along up the line to assistant manager of the Hagerstown store, where he was doing an outstanding job under the direction of a veteran manager who was also an excellent trainer.

In his conversation with me, however, Melrose showed the lack of experience in verbal communications. And though earnestly concerned with social problems, he had not had the opportunity of a Harvard MBA to become involved with solving them even if his hours at the green awning store had permitted him to. If it is fair to draw a conclusion with this limited sampling, the MBA has a running start.

Unfortunately for many young men and women who would find an exciting challenge in retailing if they had the opportunity, many of them will not get it. Retailing still has a somewhat plebeian image, with a built-in prejudice against long hours and frequent transfers. As a result Wards does not even bother to recruit in Ivy League and other sophisticated institutions; nobody comes near the University of Virginia. Recruiting for those going into the selling end of the business is done largely by interested managers or assistant managers of stores located in or near college towns. The national office recruits independently, though it, too, goes only to the schools where experience has shown that recruiting will produce results.

In the light of the commonly held idea that humans today are being reduced to numbers and punch cards by computers, it's interesting to note that Wards has developed a system by which these very computers further individual advancement. The computers keep track of every potential vacancy five years in the future, and the potential candidates to fill them. Especially with new stores opening up, new positions are constantly being created which require promotions to fill them, and each advancement leaves a vacancy. Thus the computer printout shows a succession of opportunities in the future, and matches these vacancies with another print-out of some 10,000 personnel in the management program.

Jack Foster showed me, in confidence, sheets on which the step-by-step rise of actual individuals over the next few years is indicated. The computer monitors these steps. If an opening occurs and is not filled, or if a man is eligible for promotion and does not get it, the computer blows the whistle. If there is one thing on which all Ward personnel directors agree, it is that the person with the ambition and taste for challenge that attracted him to this rat race in the first place must be pushed along.

"Leaving people in place too long is a built-in factor for turnover," Foster said. "If you don't give a man more responsibility you're asking him to quit."

And so, though you may be just a number to a computer, you're a number that the computer is not going to forget and is not going to let management forget. In the modern world of this sophisticated corporation, individual advancement for the ambitious and capable is not just controlled, it's guaranteed.

8
Of Conscientious Men

Your municipal library is full of the works of articulate spokesmen for the cause of humanity who have lambasted corporations for their lack of social responsibility. One of the first in this country to champion the individual against materialistic civilization was Henry David Thoreau, who staged a one-man revolution by refusing to pay his poll tax and created a one-man commune when he wandered out to Walden Pond. This century has produced many more corporate critics, from Upton Sinclair through Ralph Nader. In 1972 Robert L. Heilbroner, a highly respected scholar, summed up the anti-corporate stance in his book "In the Name of Profit: Profiles in Corporate Greed."

But do all corporations fit in the mold of greed and irresponsibility? Not according to the pioneer polemicist himself. Over a century ago Thoreau wrote, in "Civil Disobedience": *It is truly enough said that a corporation has no conscience, but a corporation of conscientious men is a corporation with a conscience.*

I would like to qualify Thoreau's statement two steps further. These conscientious men must be permitted and encouraged by their conscientious leaders to exercise that conscience. And to make the real breakthrough, from a corporation which conscientiously attempts merely to observe the rules to a corporation which conscientiously strives to improve the quality of life of its neighbors, its leadership must make the big push of all-out commitment.

Again Montgomery Ward furnishes a fertile field for study. After those halcyon days of malted milk breaks and company picnics, the company, during the Avery years, showed little concern for its own employees, much less for their environment. John D. Foster, vice president-personnel of Wards and subsequently vice president–organization planning and policy of Marcor, observed, with the fresh viewpoint brought in from a completely different milieu, that Sewell Avery's greatest damage to Montgomery Ward was not so much in his merchandising methods or his failure to expand as it was in his autocratic and dictatorial nature of management. "What he really left was a bankrupt organization, socially and spiritually."

In effect Tom Brooker took over that social and spiritual bankruptcy. He had been on the job less than a year when he asked his public relations director, Bob Guelich, to send out a questionnaire regarding the participation of Ward's store managers in community affairs. When he saw the resulting memorandum, Brooker angrily scribbled on the margin: "I am amazed at some comments."

His own people weren't even participating in such elementary activities as civic club luncheons. Brooker realized that in addition to prodding the hesitant and rewarding the producers in their profit and loss performance, he had to apply the same methods in simply getting the people who represented Montgomery Ward to become involved in their own communities.

Though Brooker has involved himself in community affairs wherever he has been, he doesn't like to be considered a crusading altruist. In our conversations he refused to admit that his and Montgomery Ward's activities in the area of social responsibility are anything but good business.

"It's a cost of living in a community to support the under-privileged," he told me once. And another time, "It's sound economic sense to preserve an environment in which we all do our fair share for our community. It's the greatest product in the world to sell."

He made it all sound prosaic and routine, like the markup on merchandise, but one day I caught him in a flank attack. I mentioned that in fund-raising drives in my community I hated the job of actually asking for money, and implied that everybody else did, too.

Suddenly he leaned forward, looked me in the eye, and said, "I *like* to do it, Boo." I'd never heard such intensity in his voice. "I like to ask people to support worthy causes."

Of the many worthy causes Montgomery Ward people have augmented or inaugurated under Brooker's encouragement, some are designed to be of direct benefit to the company itself, and rub off on the community as a by-product. Others are designed to be of benefit to the community (and as such improve the environment in which Wards does business), and rub off on the company. Let's take a look at some examples of each type.

One of Ward's most heartwarming ventures has a sound financial basis. Teenagers spend $15 billion for consumer goods in this country, and Wards wants its share of it. It also wants its share of the even larger market which these teen-agers will provide when they grow up, acquire household goods, have children of their own and start the whole cycle over again. (The company lost a whole generation during its pokey days.) The Wendy Ward program was conceived and set up as one way to expose Ward's merchandise to teenagers and at the same time derive direct income from membership fees.

Wendy Ward, the original retail store charm school, teaches young ladies how to bring out the best in themselves through knowledge of make-up, style and quality of merchandise, courtesy, and how to put it all together to develop poise, confidence and charm. It's a pleasure to talk to Wendy Ward girls. They're living demonstrations that a teenager can be up to the minute, *with it,* and still be pleasantly courteous.

Currently over a half-million girls are taking the Wendy Ward course, and, since its inauguration in 1963, two million have completed it. The course is given not only in some 180 stores, but in at least one public school system — for credit — and in several institutions. The fee — about $15 — pays for six one-and-a-half hour sessions, a make-up kit and a huge, comprehensive manual. Most girls also buy their graduation dresses at Wards. Their parents, dropping them off and picking them up, are exposed to Wards and its wares; one father who had never been in a Ward store before attended his daughter's graduation ceremony and wound up buying a snow plow. Many of the girls, and parents too, remain loyal to Wards.

The program obviously does a lot for Wards. But what does it do for Wendy? Well, first of all, the course emphasizes that one of the ways to be charming is to do things for other people, from helping your mother set the table to being a candy striper at the local hospital. Wendy Ward alumnae have won beauty-contests on every level, from Miss America to Miss Podunk. Many girls have gone into modeling. Cindy Henderson of Los Angeles began making professional appearances on national television shows when she was nine years old.

"I owe it all to Wendy Ward," she said.

Wendy Ward girls are asked to participate in all types of civic affairs, and they usually respond. They are the best advertisement for the program. Many institutions have asked the Wendy Ward directors to give courses. Helen James, national Wendy Ward director, enrolled 34 girls from the Texas State School for the Blind when she was at Austin. For a grand finale the graduates put on a fashion show to raise $500 for a Braille printer. Wards and rival merchants donated merchandise and a rock band made up of blind boys played. The girls paraded out on a narrow runway, pivoted just two feet from the end — they'd carefully counted the steps—then walked back. They weren't nervous but Helen James held her breath each time.

Instead of raising the $500 needed for the Braille equipment, the show netted the school $2,700. Service to the blind has expanded to the point that material in Braille is used in 24 states.

The course has also been given in schools for retarded children and in psychiatric hospitals. One of the most baffling

Everything nice . . . that's what little girls are made of. They're even nicer after learning the basics of charm and grace and thoughtfulness and good grooming in Wendy Ward programs for girls of all ages. Above, a regular class for younger girls; at right, a special free program for inner-city children.

experiences occurred in a correction institute. The course was given to two groups of inmates, one in the morning, one in the afternoon. The girls in the morning class loved the course and responded eagerly. The afternoon girls showed no interest at all. The director later learned the reason for the difference. The girls in the morning class were prostitutes, those in the afternoon class lesbians.

In Chicago in the summer the course has been given free to girls from the neighborhood around Montgomery Ward headquarters. It is a tough, black ghetto, but the poise and grace the girls have developed through patient and understanding instruction have already helped many break the invisible barriers and find a richer life.

In Oakland, California, a pretty black girl named Alecha Newbern enrolled in the course. She went on to become Teen Princess, USA, with a prize of a month's tour in Europe. She was made an honorary member of the Oakland City Council, became interested in politics and planned to become a lawyer.

"If Alecha wants to be president of the United States," her Wendy Ward instructor said, "I think she can make it."

Not too many years ago the neighborhood in which Montgomery Ward headquarters is located, in the near north side of Chicago, had almost been given up by all but the most optimistic social workers. Northeast of the Ward complex, across Chicago Avenue, is the huge high-rise Cabrini-Green public housing development. During the sixties it degenerated into a place of terror. Teenage gangs roamed the area; women were raped in elevators. Two policemen were shot by snipers from upper floors of the high-rise buildings. One evening, as he was leaving work, a bullet shattered the glass of the taxicab in which Jim Lutz, Ward executive vice president, was riding. Wards arranged to have city police patrol the streets at the beginning and end of the working day to protect the people coming to work.

As Wards faced its crises and emerged in the seventies as a successful and growing concern, it was obvious that head-

*Ed Donnell and author. In the background, construction of new
headquarters building in the heart of an inner-city neighborhood.*

quarters needed more space. Now came the decision: Would
the company stay where it was, or move to a safer, more
convenient location? There would be precedent for such a
move; Sears had already announced plans to relocate from
its own similar-type neighborhood to a one-hundred story
building downtown.

But Brooker chose to stay put. Instead of moving to a better
neighborhood, Wards would remain where it was and attempt
to upgrade its own. The decision was, he told me, a pragmatic
one based on the results of an economic study.

"There's still some work we have to do with the community
to give us the right environment," Brooker said. "But we've
made a good start. We've organized the local agencies to

315

where they are effective and we have improved the immediate neighborhood. We're going to get it cleared up to where the entire neighborhood will be good. But I don't want to press that angle of it. People think you're a do-gooder when you talk along those lines. This is sound economics for Montgomery Ward."

Once the decision was made, the Ward leadership went all the way. Minoru Yamasaki, the internationally famous architect who designed such outstanding structures as the World Trade Center in New York City, was commissioned to design the expansion of company headquarters. President Edward S. Donnell, in revealing the artist's rendition of the proposed building, said it demonstrated Ward's intention to perpetuate its historic architectural contributions to the beauty of Chicago. The striking design would enhance the architectural fame of the city and bring greater esthetic beauty to the near north side. Donnell put particular emphasis on the beautiful park planned as part of the campus-like complex. He likes the parks in London; the sheer beauty of the relandscaped area was going to have a profound effect on the entire neighborhood, he said.

Though Tom Brooker may not want people to think he's a do-gooder, at least two prominent Chicagoans do. Mayor Richard J. Daley, at ground-breaking ceremonies, said that Ward's decision to stay and rebuild showed "business not only is interested in its own operation, but what happens to the people in the city and the country."

Emmett Dedmon, vice president of the *Chicago Sun Times* and *Daily News,* told me that Ward's determination to stay was a great social decision.

"Do you really think that it's going to make more than a dent in that neighborhood?" I asked Dedmon.

"It's going to make much more than a dent," he said. "That public housing complex is 30 to 40 per cent empty because people are afraid to live there. Wards is making a major commitment to clear up one of the most explosive areas in

When the decision was made to stay put, Wards went all the way with this striking architectural design and campus-like complex—Minoru Yamasaki's first contribution to the architecture of Chicago.

this city. Those people there now have nothing to lose, but as Wards offers a job market and motivation, they're going to have something to lose and they're going to make sure they don't lose it. They'll have money and TV sets and all the evidences of middle-class materialism and private accomplishment. They'll become functioning citizens. This is the first major decision influencing this area, and it's going to make a big impact. I considered it so important that I had editorials written for both our papers."

Both editorials were laudatory. The *Sun-Times* said: "The project should anchor and stabilize the area not just in the interest of brick and mortar, but in the interest of people. We applaud Ward's foresight."

The *Daily News* concluded with the congratulations to Montgomery Ward "for a new substantial demonstration of faith

317

in our city, and for choosing a role of constructive leadership in making its hometown a better place to live."

To prepare for this sound economic decision, Brooker had been laying the groundwork for years. One of the potential stabilizing forces in the neighborhood is the YMCA. As Ed Donnell pointed out in the kickoff for a finance campaign, the Y has come a long way from the swim and gym days. Through such agencies interested citizens can build bridges. The Y does indeed run dozens of programs of great benefit to the people in the community.

Tom Brooker has told me what an excellent job Curt Ward, manager of the sporting goods department, had done in raising funds for the Y. Curt was proud of his participation. "As recently as 1967," he said, "the Y was a forgotten step-child in this neighborhood. That year contributions from this entire building totaled just $400. In four years we've gotten the total amount raised by Wards up to $100,000 — $25,000 from the sporting goods department alone. It was a challenge, and hard work, but it's rewarding. We can see the good that money does in helping the young people of this neighborhood, and through them, all the people."

Working on the fund drive was purely voluntary; Curt Ward and his helpers raised the money and the Y professionals put it to good use. Other neighborhood programs were created, coordinated, and financed by the company itself. A young native of Chicago named Herbert W. Thompson, who had been active in social causes as a college student and a Jaycee coming with Wards, was assigned to coordinate the operation.

For the first time in Chicago history a business was permitted to use a public school during the summer. Thompson arranged for programs involving music, art, drama, dance and language; the participants even published their own newspaper. Though some people were apprehensive, the neighborhood people put on a music show in the Ward parking lot, with 1,500 people present and applauding. There were no problems.

Wards furnishes furniture and equipment for a day-care program operated by a church, and equipment for the baseball teams in the neighborhood.

The baseball awards banquet was held shortly after two policemen had been shot and again there was apprehension, for some of the baseball coaches were policemen. The fears were groundless, because the kids and the cops had baseball in common and responded to each other. In the warm glow of togetherness some of the neighborhood people confided to Herb Thompson, whom they knew as an understanding friend, that the purported schism between themselves and the cops did not actually exist.

"We want and welcome police protection like anybody else," they said.

In any society there are people who crave learning. In the housing development live some 14,000 minors, many of them members of fatherless family units. The story-book American pattern of children doing their homework around the dining room table under the kind supervision and guidance of their parents rarely exists in the ghetto. Schools are crowded, and children do not receive individual attention.

Out of this combination of factors, and the need to do something about it, grew the Ward's tutoring programs. More than 100 employees signed up to stay on after hours and work on a one-to-one basis with kids from the housing development. The tutoring sessions are held in the cafeteria in the basement, and long before the sessions are scheduled to begin dozens of kids are there waiting. They are enthusiastic and eager to learn—they love any kind of attention. The company had had training sessions for the tutors, distributed kits with simple instructions, and you wouldn't believe how quietly and smoothly the period went. The kids were slicked up, clean and well behaved.

An interesting sidelight is that in this almost completely segregated neighborhood the Montgomery Ward volunteer

Ward employees tutor neighborhood children after working hours.

tutors, most of whom are white, are just about the only white people they've ever talked to. In this relationship whitey didn't turn out to be so bad.

Out of all these activities is growing a community grass roots cohesion, if not an organization, which has never existed before. By helping to arrange activities, taking part in community affairs, the people of the neighborhood, a small city in itself, are for the first time beginning to get a glimmer of what members of much smaller communities take for granted, as sense of organization.

Running back and forth between Tom Brooker and Herb Thompson, I was fascinated by what each said about the other behind his back. "I generally don't agree with him," Brooker commented to me about Herb, "because he tends to be quite liberal in his thinking about some of these things, but he does his job very well."

"I'm constantly being amazed at Mr. Brooker's depth of understanding of social problems," Herb told me. "I expected him to know how to run a business but I was surprised at his knowledge about what's going on in levels that I thought would be so remote from him. He's personally interested in our tutoring program, for example. As a result, I can go direct to him, Mr. Donnell or any other top executive with complete confidence that they'll listen."

Though separated by both many layers of the corporate structure and a wide gulf of social philosophy, the young member of the public relations staff and the top brass can work together in areas affecting Montgomery Ward and its environment.

Even stranger bedfellows in advancing the cause of Montgomery Ward were the moderately conservative majority of executives and Daniel Walker, vice president–law and government affairs, who left the company in 1971 to seek, successfully, the Democratic nomination for Governor of Illinois. Walker was considered a maverick even by some elements of the Democratic party. As member and then president of the Chicago Crime Commission, he was instrumental in publishing and distributing a list of Chicago businesses that had a connection with known members of the crime syndicate. It named both the businesses and the hoodlums involved.

After the Democratic National Convention of 1968, Walker was appointed director of the Chicago Study Team of the National Committee on the Causes and Prevention of Violence by its chairman, Dr. Milton S. Eisenhower. He accepted the job with the full approval of Tom Brooker, even though both knew it was going to be a backbreaking job, and that Walker already had plently of work to do as general counsel of Montgomery Ward. Among other duties, Walker was in charge of the legal aspects of the merger with Container Corporation which resulted in the formation of Marcor Inc.

As director of the Chicago Study Team, Walker and his staff had to examine thousands of transcripts, press and TV coverage, and eye witness reports. He set up a schedule by which he would work on the merger and other Montgomery Ward legal affairs from 7 A.M. until noon, then go to the Study Team Offices in the Federal Building and work there until 7 or 8 P.M. He'd get home for dinner with his wife and seven children a couple of nights a week, then meet with his top staff in the seclusion of a hotel suite until two or three in the morning. He worked with the study team every weekend.

The result was "The Walker Report," which caused almost as many repercussions as the demonstrations themselves. Headline writers picked up the phrase "police riot" from the book and Walker was accused of denigrating all law enforcement agencies. The 362-page report, widely sold in paperback, also contained verbatim reports of obscenities used during the demonstration. This was a particularly difficult decision for Walker to make, as he does not countenance the use of obscene language by his children or in his home. But he finally decided that in order to be completely objective the actual words spoken simply had to be used.

Following the release of "The Walker Report," Dan and his wife received telephone calls and letters which were both threatening and obscene. His children were subjected to abuse in their schools. But before he had undertaken the job Walker had discussed the matter with the entire family, and, having agreed that it was his civic duty, they were prepared for the reaction from a small but vociferous minority.

Montgomery Ward also came in for criticism. Many complaints were received from irate customers, along with torn up credit cards. Bob Guelich prepared a two-page letter to be used by managers across the nation in answering public criticism of "The Walker Report." Though pointing out that Montgomery Ward as a corporation had no direct connection with the report, the letter stated plainly, "we fully support Mr. Walker's right to fulfill the obligation of his position as a public spirited citizen. Just as we believe that fully informed consumers are our best customers, we believe that fully informed citizens are the nation's best citizens. . . ."

After all, when Dan Walker came to Wards he told Tom Brooker straight out that he had no intention of crawling into an executive shell. Brooker assured him in turn that he firmly believed in executive participation in community affairs. Having bought the Walker package, the company deliberately determined to defend it.

This was by no means the end of Dan Walker's participation in public affairs. He seems to have a built-in supercharger. He managed the successful United States Senate campaign of Adlai E. Stevenson III. Following that, he picked up more headlines by announcing, two years in advance, that he would run for governor of Illinois in 1972 in opposition to both the Republicans and the entrenched organization of his own Democratic party. Until his severance from the company in order to campaign full time he was carrying on his work for Montgomery Ward. This frequently required close collaboration with the man in the next office, Fred Zeni, his classmate at Northwestern and also an indefatigable political worker — for the Republicans.

Walker brought to Montgomery Ward the implementation of several recent trends in corporate activity. Corporations have long recognized their social responsibility to the community in charitable, cultural and educational activities. More recently corporate executives have also become concerned with guttier problems — employment of minorities, public housing, and the environment.

"In another related area," Walker said, "traditionally corporations used to take a flatly negative approach to almost any kind of law that affected the business community, particularly in matters of tax increases and consumer affairs. There's been a marked change in this, and today you'll find corporate executives taking a broader view towards the legislation which may affect their business."

It was Walker and his staff, representing Montgomery Ward, which broke the log jam in Congress over the truth-in-lending bill by positive participation in the hearings and publicly announcing that Montgomery Ward would support the bill. In legislative affairs Walker and his staff have placed less emphasis on taking a legislator out to dinner, more on making available the technical expertise of the retail industry to state and national lawmakers on the merits of pending legislation.

At stockholders meetings Tom Brooker has replied to angry stockholders criticizing this new approach in general, Dan Walker's activities in particular, that to deprive the corporate executive of the right to participate would be to take away from the problem-solution area some of the best brains in the United States, the corporate executive. Walker himself, who came to Montgomery Ward with the professional experience of a naval officer and a trial lawyer, absorbed a great deal of managerial know-how and applied it to his extra-corporate activities. Noting the success of the profit-center concept introduced by Brooker, he organized the Stevenson campaign along the same lines, with political action centers. Thus Tom Brooker, staunch supporter of the Grand Old Party, indirectly made his contribution to the election of the Democratic Senator from Illinois.

In a speech before the National Chain Store Public Relations Conference, Ed Donnell, exhorting his fellow retailers to greater initiative and action, said, "We have the largest number of men and women with managerial responsibilities of any industry—more than one million. This means we have a greater opportunity and greater manpower resources than any other industry to provide leadership. We have the capability to improve the way of life of those people who have not yet been able to share in the material affluence and comforts that our nation has produced in the past quarter century." He went on to say that in Chicago alone more constructive action is coming from business leadership "than from the colleges and universities, the professions or the unions, the youthful activists, or even political and governmental officials."

As a card-carrying do-gooder of long standing, I take Ed's

remarks personally. I can look back on hundreds of meetings of organizations seeking to accomplish some worthwhile purpose in which the other knee-jerk liberals and I just sat around and wrangled. We knew something had to be done, as in that nightmare year when the schools of my hometown were padlocked, but we didn't know how to do it. (We could have used one of those million managers.)

With this background I can fully appreciate the feelings William D. Hunter had when he got involved with a volunteer organization. Bill Hunter had become a national merchandise manager, head of his own profit center, at the age of 26. He participated in various fund drives but without a real sense of participation; Bill prefers running things himself to raising money for other people.

He got his opportunity when he was asked to be president of the Community Industrial Contract Association. CICA serves as a liaison between industry and the sheltered workshops, in which people from retarded children to professionals making a comeback from skid row turn out various products. CICA had been set up to find an outlet for these products. Its board, however, had become so bogged down in talk that it wasn't providing any action. The new president came to the conclusion that the situation was hopeless. There was no business guidance; the board was composed of people whose names looked good on the letterhead but who didn't know how to manage.

So Bill fired the entire board. He got in a new group who were capable of action. He found another businessman with leadership quality to quarterback the team as president, and appointed himself executive vice president to do the work.

Getting all this done was a rathole of time. Bill put out more than a thousand dollars of his own money in transportation alone. But he learned a lot about community activities. For an operation of this kind to be successful the disparate mentalities of the businessman and the social worker must blend.

The businessman must learn that there are factors other than profitability involved. You can close down a store that is losing money, for example, but that isn't the answer in the case of a workshop that is helping a mentally retarded child find self-sufficiency. The social worker, on the other hand, must learn that just because an agency provides a humanitarian service is no excuse for sloppy management. Efficient operation enables it to furnish a far greater service.

Another young manager, Glenn Hoffman, groaned to himself when tapped for the Crusade of Mercy, as the United Fund is called in Chicago. Just another waste of time running around putting the bite on people. His reluctance was overcome by the personal enthusiasm of Ed Donnell — if the president of the company could get excited, it must not be too bad. His next assignment was in increasing the participation of Montgomery Ward employees in purchase of savings bonds. Getting involved, he could see that the low interest rate then in effect was an understandable deterrent. With other business leaders, he convinced the Treasury Department to increase the percentage to a more competitive figure. Ten thousand more Ward employees bought bonds that year.

Next he got involved in the annual auction to provide funds for the Chicago educational TV station. He obtained a larger commitment of merchandise to be auctioned off than ever before. One source of supply was his own company, which just happened at the time to have a slight oversupply of Italian motorcycles.

"I got a big personal kick out of that project," Glenn said. "That's the station that brings my own kids Sesame Street."

The same year he coordinated luncheons hosted by Montgomery Ward for over 100 major corporations for the Crusade of Mercy.

That year, too, Glenn was chairman of the coordinating committee of the Chicago Business Opportunity Fair in which some 300 major Chicago companies participated. Montgomery Ward hosted the Fair; Ed Donnell served as chairman, John

Marchese as president. The Fair makes it possible for minority businesses to demonstrate their wares to the major buyers in the Chicago area. It resulted in over a million dollars' worth of contracts, and meant the difference between success and failure for many minority entrepreneurs.

In Los Angeles after the Watts riots Greg Young volunteered his services to find both products which could be turned out by the people of that deprived area, and markets for them. Out of this grew Minorities Manufacturers Day, sponsored by the Chamber of Commerce with Greg as chairman. He arranged for some 60 small businesses to set up exhibits of their wares, and hundreds of the major buyers in the area to take a look at them.

In the first year more than a million dollars' worth of orders were placed, for everything from candy to dashikis. The candy manufacturer got such a big order that he couldn't fill it; Greg had to arrange financing for him.

The operation so inspired Al Hollingsworth, a former linebacker for the New York Giants, that he took what was left of his football bonus and organized his own company. He manufactures containers for large items—my beanbag chair came in one—and he placed his plant right in the heart of Watts.

"Other people go by and see garbage on the streets and say, 'Oh, how awful,'" he said. "To hell with that. I don't stick my head in the sand—I believe in black capitalism. We've got a good-looking place of business employing 18 people. The whole neighborhood is proud of it. It shows what we can do. But we couldn't have gotten started without Greg Young. He's what's happening."

Another practical method of making the Land of Opportunity more than just a phrase is a program of the Small Business Administration called the Minority Enterprise Small Business Investment Company, or MESBIC. The program exists only on paper; to make it work requires sophisticated implementation and money. Vic Sholis had been involved in a similar type of program on a local scale while at Harvard Graduate

John Marchese, center, president of the 1970 Chicago Business Opportunity Fair which introduced minority businessmen to purchasing agents of major firms.

328

Business School, and it became his baby when he came to Montgomery Ward. (One of his reasons for joining Wards was the assurance that the company had a sincere interest in such projects, and would encourage him to continue working in this area.)

With a group of other young fellows interested in MESBIC, Sholis set out to build an investment company capitalized at $2 million from money raised in the private sector. This money can be levered up through government matching funds and guaranteed bank loans to a potential impact of $40 million. It is a sound business method for capitalizing and advising small entrepreneurs who have more ambition and energy than knowledge of high finance.

Many corporations are interested in helping such a program get started, but are not familiar with the involved precedures. Working lunch hours and evenings, Vic and his associates were able to put the whole thing together and raise the money. Not every trainee, in his first two years with a company, can approach the president and chairman of the executive committee directly and come away with $100,000. Then he got $50,000 from Sears, Roebuck.

All this activity on the part of so many individuals—and hundreds more throughout the country—must certainly further the premise that both industry and the quality of life benefit from corporate involvement. Brooker maintains that the active participation of his people develops their maturity and enables them to gain greater respect from their fellow workers. One day he rattled off the names of a half-dozen executives he has seen grow through the successful completion of their projects. Among them were Curt Ward and Bill Hunter. Not long after, when Robert M. Harrell became company director and vice president of the new southeastern region, Curt was promoted to Harrell's former position as vice president and retail merchandise manager, and Bill took over Curt's sporting goods department. Coincidence?

"It gives them the satisfaction of accomplishment, a glow of confidence," he said. "Wards is a better company because

Helping the Chicago MESBIC venture become the nation's largest gave Vic Sholis both inner satisfaction and recognition by the top brass. Left to right, Benjamin C. Duster, president of the Chicago MESBIC, Leo Schoenhofen, and Vic.

our people have this participation in the community. We're better people and we're a better company. The fact that it's good business to be a good citizen of these communities is more important than even the problems or the pressures."

But the problems are still alleviated whether it's good business or not. In pure voluntarism, accountability can't be reviewed as it can in a well-run business. All of us who work for various agencies or in political campaigns have some motivation or we wouldn't do it. But no matter how great a job we do, we receive no bonus, and no matter how lousy our performance, we don't get fired—there are not enough of us as it is.

"The difference between the voluntary approach and the corporate approach," Tom said, "is that I as a head of a corporation can assign someone to do the job. I may ask him to do

330

it, but he's really assigned and I can appraise the results he gets. All you can do with a volunteer is appeal to him. I can do more than appeal to him. I can say, now we've made a commitment. Either you're going to do it or else I have to do it. Do you want me to do it? He sure as hell doesn't want me to do it, and so he does it. That's the way I tell him, you know, just exactly."

I don't know of anyone who has refused to volunteer for such an assignment, but Ed Donnell made a special point one day of telling me about a young man who had seriously questioned the policy of extra-company activity.

Donnell had inaugurated the custom of having luncheon with a half-dozen different representatives of middle management each month. "Sometimes you get up on this eminence and you really don't know what the younger people in your own company are thinking," he explained. At one of these luncheons he really found out what one of his people was thinking. Though he was a little stunned at first, he realized that he had asked for it, and admired the fellow's gumption for speaking up. He even suggested I look him up.

The chap who questioned the president was A. R. Busch, a buyer who has been with Wards since 1964. Busch was perfectly willing to talk about it; he feared no repercussion. Shortly before the day of the luncheon, he said, he had read a management news bulletin which showed that Ward's increase in sales over the previous eight months had lagged far behind that of Sears, Penney, and Kresge.

"You can see from our performance that we've nailed ourselves right down into the bottom of the barrel," Busch said. "But on the back of this bulletin, instead of some message from our management as to the direction of the company in this regard, we get a long dissertation on the retailer's obligation as a corporate citizen and our involvement with various activities. Now all these things are necessary but what we need today is the same kind of concentration and effort in sales. Look at the work and effort and the dedication of purpose that went behind getting everybody in this company to contribute their fair share. If that same effort and dedication had been put behind going out and getting a 5 per cent sales increase, I think we would have gotten it."

At the luncheon Busch sat quietly for an hour and a half. But that bulletin had made him mad, and finally he brought it up. He did not question the policy in an argumentative way, but it was pretty obvious that Tony Busch felt the company should spend more time improving its sales performance, less on other activities. The president responded in accord to his sincere belief that the company should fulfill its social responsibility.

Busch could hardly tell me that he was dissatisfied with Donnell's answer, but he had certainly not changed his own opinion. He made it clear that he was not opposed to giving— "I give my fair share, I give to my church"—but only to the dilution of the primary purpose of the company, to maximize sales. Although critical, he was also appreciative of the fact

Under Phil Lifschultz's leadership, Ward Employees' Combined Appeal Plan (WE-CAP) raised $360,000 for the 1971 Crusade of Mercy. Left to right, Fred Veach, Miss We-Cap, and Phil.

that the president would accept his question and respond to it. He was doing a good job in his department and he felt secure, but after we'd talked a while he gave a grim little laugh.

"I can see that this is going to haunt me for a long time," he said.

Though some may question the economic wisdom of the effort made by Wards in the area of social responsibility, no one can charge that the leaders of the company ask anyone to do what they have not done themselves over the years, and continue to do. Even if Tom Brooker had never participated in community affairs before, he would have made up for it in his activity in 1970, when he accepted the chairmanship of the Crusade of Mercy campaign.

He immediately began making waves by increasing the goal, in a year of declining profits, to $34 million—$8 million more than the previous year. He set his own personal contribution at 2 per cent of his annual salary, and asked that his fellow corporate executives throughout Chicago pledge 1 per cent. He attended scores of meetings lining up a campaign, broadened the solicitation to large groups previously passed over and made long distance calls all over the country to headquarters of businesses with offices in Chicago.

It is difficult to say no to Tom Brooker because he doesn't hear you. I was sitting in his office one day when a call came in from the chief executive officer of a large company who was obviously trying to get out of taking a leadership role. Tom patiently listened to one excuse after the other, responding to each in the same even tone. But as the conversation went on his lower lip began sticking out, more and more. By the time he had beaten down all the other fellow's arguments and had him where he wanted him it was practically up to his nose.

Brooker had an 18-minute film prepared on the necessity of the Crusade, and took it around with him to show it personally to the leaders of the community. He also proposed to show it to Mayor Daley. When the professionals at the Crusade office heard that they couldn't believe it. It would take the Pope to get more than five minutes of the mayor's time and here

Tom Brooker displays his trophies: a 10-year Ward service pin and a lapel pin from Chicago's Crusade of Mercy, which he headed for two years.

Brooker was, planning to show him a movie. Brooker calmly went about setting up the appointment. The people in the office got up a pool on the number of minutes Brooker would have with the mayor.

Arthur H. Kruse, the executive director, and Robert L. Young, the associate, went with him to City Hall.

"I felt like an idiot," Young said, "trotting over there with this projector. I set it up in the conference room, knowing very well that the mayor would never come in and look at it. But Tom just told the mayor quietly that he had shown it to all the chief executives in Chicago. The mayor was a chief executive just like everybody else, he said, so now if he was free, we'd move into the other room. So we did.

"We were with Mayor Daley 45 minutes. I won the office pool. I had the highest number — 18."

"What Tom Brooker brought to this campaign was a complete reversal in psychology," Kruse said. "He Brookerized us."

After working like a dog on the campaign, and coming even closer to the goal than, he candidly admitted to me, he had expected to, Brooker again broke all precedent by volunteering to head it for the second straight year.

"I've got it pretty well organized now," he told me calmly. "It won't be too difficult." The Crusade of Mercy will never be the same.

Nor will Montgomery Ward. Though Tom Brooker retired as chairman of the board in 1970, he planned to remain as chairman of the executive committee of both Wards and Marcor for another five years. One of his self-assigned projects is the entire neighborhood around Chicago headquarters. On the national scene, he was appointed chairman of the National Business Council for Consumer Affairs by President Nixon in the same executive order which created the council.

Leo Schoenhofen, who succeeded Tom Brooker at Marcor, and Ed Donnell, president of both Montgomery Ward and Marcor, are also individuals whom Thoreau would surely accept as conscientious men, and, therefore, leaders of a corporation with a conscience. An indication of their interest in social responsibility was the formation of the National Affairs Committee. As if corporate executives don't have enough outside activities already, the committee provides a vehicle to come up with more. Brainchild of Dan Walker and approved almost without question by Donnell, it's a kind of hunting license; its members look at national issues — social, environmental, political and economic — and get people involved in them.

At the first meeting of 31 hand-picked, strong-minded people not afraid to rock the boat, the committee got started by hollering out topics to consider. What kind of topics? "Anything that turns you on!"

With that encouragement, the vociferous 31 shouted out some 40 suggestions — alcoholism, air pollution, birth control, violence, welfare, world peace and youth. Name something controversial and it's on the list.

The selection of the chairman, Laurence A. Jones, gave an immediate indication of the new Montgomery Ward. Not too many years ago a black native Chicagoan wouldn't have taken an executive job with the company if it had offered him one. Though nobody in the black community seems to know exactly why, or even if it is justified, Wards has had a bad image among Chicago blacks. But Larry Jones came in as a corporate lawyer, and he is no Uncle Tom.

"I may be a token in that there aren't more of me," he said, "but the beginning of anything has got to start with one. I'm here, I'm doing my job, I'm happy."

As for the National Affairs Committee, it too is a beginning. "Our function," Jones said, "is to provide guidance to this corporation on issues of national affairs. Such issues directly or indirectly affect the interests of large corporations and the people as a whole, which in turn affects large corporations. If people live in poverty they can't buy merchandise. If they get angry because they can't buy merchandise, they burn, they loot. Air pollution costs the company money. All of these things have a cumulative effect. Let's just say that the National Affairs Committee is a sign that management is becoming enlightened."

A century and a half ago the English poet Shelley, in the ode we all read in high school, called on the west wind to scatter his words among mankind and awaken the earth. At that time the wind offered about as much help in this regard as any other medium, but today Shelley would be backing the wrong horse. As management does become enlightened, a new force for making a better world is emerging.

Montgomery Ward is by no means the only corporation with a conscience, but it has definitely established itself as being in the front rank. As a retailer, Wards represents the largest industry in the world, dealing with all the people of America — all sizes and sexes, all colors and faiths. Operating both procurement and merchandising functions, the company moves its people around constantly, from factory to factory, from store to store. Wherever they go, they are encouraged to get involved with the social problems they find, and to apply management-oriented expertise to the solution. In his letter to Marcor stockholders after his first year as chief executive officer, Leo Schoenhofen concluded:

"In public and private sectors our organization continues to be actively involved with governmental and community agencies to improve the quality of life of our neighbors. We intend to continue in our leadership roles for better environmental conditions and more meaningful service to our customers.

"We believe it is our corporate purpose and responsibility to produce social as well as economic dividends."

Index